T0329979

Japanese Technology
and Innovation Management

To Helena, Julia and Osvald

Japanese Technology and Innovation Management

From Know-how to Know-who

Sigvald Harryson

Boston Consulting Group, Zurich
and School of Economics, Gothenburg University, Sweden

Edward Elgar
Cheltenham, UK • Northampton, MA, USA

Published by
Edward Elgar Publishing Limited
8 Lansdown Place
Cheltenham
Glos GL50 2HU
UK

Edward Elgar Publishing, Inc.
6 Market Street
Northampton
Massachusetts 01060
USA

A catalogue record for this book
is available from the British Library

Library of Congress Cataloguing in Publication Data
Harryson, Sigvald, 1966–
    Japanese technology & innovation management: from know-how to
know-who / Sigvald Harryson.
    Includes bibliographical references and index.
    1. Research, Industrial—Japan—Management. 2. Technology—Japan–
–Management. I. Title.
T177.J3H38   1996
338.95207—dc21   97–45498
                                                     CIP

ISBN 978 1 85898 768 2

Printed and bound by CPI Group (UK) Ltd, Croydon, CR0 4YY

Contents

List of Figures

List of Tables

List of Abbreviations

AIST	Agency of Industrial Science and Technology
ATRAC	Adaptive TRansform Acoustic Coding System
BA	Business Area
BU	Business Unit
CAD	Computer Aided Design
CCD	Charge-coupled device
CD	Compact Disc
Cd	Drag Coefficient (measures the wind-resistance of an object)
CEO	Chief Executive Officer
CTIO	Chief Technology and Innovation Officer
CTO	Chief Technology Officer
D&M	Design and Manufacturing
DAT	Digital Audio Tape
DCC	Digital Compact Cassette (Philip's version of DAT)
DRAM	Dynamic Random Access Memory
FLCD	Ferroelectric Liquid Crystal Displays
GM	General Motors
HIFET	Hetero Interface Field Effect Transistor
HP	Hewlett Packard
IPR	Intellectual Property Rights
JIT	Just In Time
JV	Joint Venture
LAN	Local Area Network
LPCVD	Low Pressure Chemical Vapour Deposition (thin film technology)
LSI	Large Scale Integrated Circuits
M&S	Marketing and Sales
MD	MiniDisc (Sometimes MiniDiscman, as the Sony Walkman)
MITI	Ministry of International Trade and Industry
MMIC	Monolithic Microwave Integrated Circuit
MOCVD	Metal Organic Chemical Vapour Deposition (method for growing very thin semiconducting film)
OEM	Original Equipment Manufacturer
P&L	Profit and Loss
R&D	Research and Development
SBU	Strategic Business Unit
TFT	Thin Film Transistor (displays)

TI	Texas Instruments
T&I	Technology and Innovation
VCR	Video Cassette Recorder
VLSI	Very Large Scale Integrated Circuits

Acknowledgements

The key learning of this book is that the innovation process is no longer limited to know-how but depends instead on know-*who*. For companies to maintain speed and respond quickly enough to market shifts, they must change their focus from internal specialization to learning through relationships. Accordingly, the specific responsibility of senior R&D managers and CTOs is to ensure that key staff have a competence profile which goes far beyond being technically sound. Managers at every level must be able to identify who – within and outside their organization – can help them achieve success in their R&D projects.Three in-depth case studies from Canon, Sony and Toyota will demonstrate what learning through relationships means in practice.

Most of the research on which the book is based was conducted between 1991 and 1995, in the preparation of a doctoral dissertation entitled 'Japanese R&D Management: A Holistic Network Approach' (Doctoral Program in International Management, Hochschule St. Gallen, Switzerland; degree awarded 1995). While a visiting researcher at Sophia University in Tokyo in 1992–3, I got the opportunity to make over a hundred interviews with key people in corporate functions and divisions related to R&D and new product development processes at Canon, Sony, and Toyota. I could also return later on to these companies to double-check and update my findings.

I am deeply indebted to all the interviewees who invested large amounts of their valuable time in my empirical efforts. In particular, I would like to mention Dr Makoto Kikuchi and Eiji Toyosaki of Sony and Canon Inc.

Based on his early insights into the importance of Japanese management of Technology and Innovation, Prof. Emil Brauchlin of Hochschule St. Gallen invited me to explore the subject more in depth and accepted me as his doctoral candidate. Needless to say, my gratitude is overwhelming.

Several additional persons provided further support for which I am equally grateful. Prof. Hellmut Schütte of INSEAD met up all around the globe, always honouring his commitment as second director of thesis. Prof. Yasusada Yawata generously invited me as a visiting researcher to Sophia University in Tokyo, where he provided ample support. Profs. Gene Gregory and James Abegglen freely shared their tremendous expertise with me in endless classes, seminars and discussions. They also opened the doors to many of the companies that generously invited me to learn from their impressive managerial techniques. Akihiro Sunaga of the Swedish Embassy provided additional help in this matter.

Among all other friends and colleagues in the world of academia, I would like to express particular gratitude to Prof. Hans Jansson, Dr. Sven-Olof Collin, Dr Jens Laage-Hellman at Uppsala University, and to Prof. Takahiro Fujimoto at Tokyo University.

While I share any credit with all the above persons, I take full responsibility for possible errors.

The initial Ph.D project, was funded by The Swedish Institute, Tore Browaldh's Research Foundation, JDZB and by Dr Marcus Wallenberg's Fund for Studies in International Industrial Management.

Four former colleagues – Nils Bohlin, Jean-Philippe Deschamps, Jane Morris and Tom Sommerlatte – merit special mentioning for their encouraging support to publish both articles and a book.

I am particularly indebted to the Boston Consulting Group for supporting the publication process and thereby making this book possible.

Finally, I dedicate this book to my wife Helena for her unfailing love, understanding and support, and to our daughter Julia for not yet having found out how to press the 'erase all'command.

It would be unfair to leave out my newborn son, Osvald, as he had the courtesy and tact to delay his arrival to this world until this book was completed.

Sigvald Harryson

Preface

This book offers rewarding insights into how to manage in-house transfer of knowledge and skills. Moving from *know-how* to *know-who* is not just a powerful tool to increase innovation capacity, it is the *sine qua non* to manage the continuously increasing complexity of most industries.

In the 1980s and early 1990s , the key to competitiveness lay in short development lead-times with quick response to customer needs. Today, global competition against time has become even more complex. Successful product innovation poses especially tough challenges to those companies which continue to rely solely on internal technology development. Technology and markets change so quickly, product life-cycles have become so short, and R&D projects have become so time-consuming and costly that a focus on in-house development of key technologies no longer yields competitive success. A new set of capabilities is required.

As the millennium approaches, corporate competitiveness increasingly depends on the capability to access and acquire the most current knowledge. More important still is the capability to learn from and make effective use of knowledge, transforming invention into breakthrough innovation. Companies with this capability will create and pre-empt customer needs faster than their competitors and set world-wide standards that others must follow.

While maintaining impressive skills in lead-time reduction, miniaturization or customer satisfaction, Canon, Sony and Toyota now compete on a 'learning through know-who' capability that enables them to cope with the increasing complexity of both technology and product innovation. Indeed, for companies to respond quickly to market shifts, they must redirect their competitive focus from internal specialization to learning through relationships. In this book are unique case studies in impressive detail that demonstrate how this critical capability is created and managed in practice.

Canon, Sony and Toyota have learned to 'borrow' inventiveness from extra corporate sources of technology. This permits them to focus their internal R&D efforts on tailoring results to market needs and on designing efficient production processes to bring new winning products to market.

It is a truism that networking has positive impacts on business results. Nevertheless, there are few companies in which networking takes place even at adequate levels. CTOs and CEOs will be interested to learn that effective internal and external networking at Canon, Sony and Toyota depends on a holistic organizational outlook. Here, the researcher is not required to focus on a single task, as is so often the case in in-house specialized technology development. Instead, Canon and Sony emphasize frequent circulation between research divisions or, in the case of Sony, business units, management that promotes knowledge creation through cross-fertilization of ideas and fields of experience. The value of building, nurturing and leveraging learning relationships is evident to all participants in the seamless innovation process which characterizes these world-class innovators. Holistic performance measurement systems – which most companies will find compelling – further promote this open sharing of resources.

This approach stands in sharp contrast to the more specialized and fragmented approach that is still characteristic of many Western firms. The holistic networking approach of these three companies creates borderless organizations that reward collective action rather than individual performance. Recent examples from Western companies reveal that many management teams remain too focused on optimizing isolated functions and implementing controls to track progress of individual efforts.

The holistic approach of Canon, Sony and Toyota offers an attractive remedy to fragmented approaches to the vital business process of production innovation. When necessary, their multicompetent engineers join forces in a collective pursuit of forceful innovation. New technologies are effectively deployed yet rarely invented in-house. Instead, this unique focus on know-who and global networking allows these truly innovative companies to access and transfer the skills required to win the innovation race.

George Stalk
The Boston Consulting Group, Inc.

1   Preparing the Move from Know-how to Know-who

WHY YET ANOTHER BOOK ON JAPANESE MANAGEMENT

The cost and complexity of R&D efforts today, coupled with accelerating technological change and shrinking product lives, create intractable dilemmas for companies that – like so many in the West – rely on internal technological development to meet their innovation needs. Too many companies today are finding themselves 'stuck' and unable to respond quickly enough to market shifts. Why? Because they have concentrated too much on making their technology more and more specialised, hoping that this will preserve their competitive edge. Unfortunately, this has actually left many R&D staff short of the cross-functional skills they need to make large projects work.

Ultimately, the real challenge they face is not simply advancing technology. Today's senior R&D managers and CTOs operate in a world with four clear features: accelerating change; globalization of markets; customers who are increasingly sophisticated; *and* advancing technology. The challenge is to get the right balance between technology depth and speed of delivery with products (and services) that meet the needs of these sophisticated customers, on an ever wider horizon.

This book therefore argues that the innovation process is no longer limited to know-how but depends instead on know-*who*. For companies to remain competitive and respond rapidly to market shifts, they must change their focus from internal specialization to learning through relationships. The book presents in-depth case studies from three champions of innovation – Canon, Sony and Toyota – to demonstrate what learning through relationships means in practice. Management thinking about improving R&D effectiveness over the last decade has ignored this critical issue, to the detriment of West vs. East competitiveness in several industries. To date, management thinking has given some theoretical advice on two other important principles: the open sharing of ideas, technologies and human resources, and performance measurement systems that reward co-operation and collective achievements. This book is unique in giving concrete examples on how three companies use these principles in practice. In addition, it completes the triangle by adding the 'learning through know-who-principle' and by illustrating how this is linked to the other two.

Accordingly, the book identifies the specific responsibility of senior R&D managers and CTOs to ensure that key staff have a competence profile which goes far beyond being technically sound. More importantly, managers at every level must be able to identify who – within and outside their organization – can help them achieve success in their R&D projects; and they must be able to communicate with, and acquire know-how from, these people across functions within and outside corporate boundaries.

By enabling and empowering project managers and their key-people to work effectively with the identified sources of specific knowledge and expertise, the new Chief Technology and Innovation Officer will ensure his/her company always remains on the competitive technological edge while taking proactive action in identifying and satisfying market needs.

Readers of the book will gain detailed insight into how such capabilities are developed in Canon, Sony and Toyota, and how they as private individuals and corporate citizens can develop the knowledge networks and know-how acquisition skills they need for their own situations. This should be of interest to middle and senior managers of large and medium-sized companies not only in the West but also in Asian countries seeking to emulate Japanese management practices, and to Japanese managers themselves.

Although the R&D productivity gap between Japanese and Western companies is well-known, the fundamental factors that account for it remain little understood. Previous studies of Japanese R&D have tended to focus on intracorporate activities, thus ignoring the relevant extracorporate relationships of Japanese firms. Studies of Japanese technology management, on the other hand, have dealt with extracorporate relationships, but have mostly failed to explore the connection between these relationships and corporate R&D.

This book reveals how Canon, Sony, and Toyota secure this connection through a holistic network approach, not only to R&D, but above all to Technology *and* to Innovation. Hence the title *Japanese Technology and Innovation* [T&I] *Management.* In a highly holistic manner they exploit external sources of technology and commercialize the knowledge so acquired through a synergistic combination of external and internal networking.

'External networking' refers here to the process of linking a firm with extracorporate sources of technology. 'Internal networking' refers to the integration of the research, development, production, and marketing functions that contribute to the innovation process as a whole. The 'synergistic' combination of external and internal networking is a process by which the acquisition of technology from external sources enhances a company's ability to commercialize that technology.

By illustrating how external and internal activities are linked at these champions of innovation, three points will be made that future CEOs and Technology and Innovation Officers should find compelling:

1. Canon, Sony, and Toyota have excelled at product innovation by deliberately eschewing the reliance on internal technology development that is still characteristic of many Western firms.
2. External sourcing of technology does not have to imply a hollowing out of internal R&D capabilities. It can, in contrast, energize and create powerful synergies in a company's T&I management.
3. Western companies wishing to learn from such examples must change not only their R&D practices but their entire organizational outlooks, abandoning certain forms of organizational fragmentation in favour of the more holistic approaches found in Japanese firms.

The rest of this book will outline, in full detail, the holistic network approach to T&I management, and the lessons that this approach offers for a wider audience.

THE INNOVATION PERFORMANCE GAP: CAUSES AND CONSEQUENCES

After Japan's GNP per capita had overtaken most European countries, including Sweden, Norway and Germany by 1986, and the US by 1987 (Wilkinson 1990, 135), the feeling of apprehension with an urge to learn from Japan spread throughout the West. If, in the 1970s, Western managers were anxious about the low cost and high quality of Japanese imports, from the 1980s until the early 1990s they were overwhelmed by the pace at which Japanese companies invented new markets, created new products and improved them, directly challenging the most prestigious industries of Europe and the US. In this era of rapid change in technology, high pace of innovation and short product life-cycles, a company's ability to develop and diffuse successful innovations rapidly became *the* primary source of competitive success.[1]

Although most large companies with world-wide operations recognized that managing innovations was a key strategic capability, Japanese companies were outpacing their Western counterparts in many industries, both in R&D productivity, speed of development, and in the number of products put to market.

From 1980 to 1988, Canon grew by 264% and largely surpassed the previous Western leader, although Canon's R&D budget in reprographics was but a small fraction of Xerox's (Prahalad and Hamel, 1990).

The studies of Fujimoto (1989); Clark and Fujimoto (1991, cf. 1989, 1992) and of Womack *et al.* (1990) demonstrated that Japanese car manufacturers completed a project with one-third the engineering hours and two-thirds the lead time of their American and European competitors. The average development lead-time of a new car model was, still in the early 1990s, 46 months in Japan versus 60 months in Europe and the US. On average, as much as 38% of the parts in a new American car were carried over from previous models, compared to 18% in a Japanese car.

The juxtaposition of individual companies yields even greater differences: even though Toyota is only half the size of GM, in 1990 it was offering an equal number of models. The reason was that Toyota only needed half the time and effort required by GM to develop a new car (Womack *et al.* 1990, 64). To summarize the situation, Stalk and Hout (1990, 121) observe that 'many of today's fast innovators are Japanese . . . The capability of introducing new products four times faster than Western competitors is a pretty astounding advantage. It is an advantage seen again and again'.

Traditional Explanations to the Performance Gap

At the extracorporate level, harder efforts at intra-industry and industry-government consensus building and co-operation are made in Japan compared to the West with an emphasis on commercial applications more than on pure technology development. Antitrust laws and a general lack of trust between countries and companies seem to have prevented equivalent co-operative partnerships in the West.[2]

Links to external scientific information are strong. It appears to be widely accepted that Western universities are more active and dynamic than their Japanese counterparts, but it is often noticed that these Western centres of excellence have their strongest ties with individual Japanese companies. Much of Japan's success is also attributed to the acquisition of foreign technology. When commissioning research by Western companies or establishing licensing agreements, Japanese companies seem to focus on learning to a greater extent than Western ones.[3]

The lead-time advantage of the development process seems to find its primary explanation in earlier and more extensive supplier participation, which is the highest in the world in Japan, often with an average of 85% of production costs located outside the enterprise.[4] Suppliers are said to be highly flexible and co-operative, assume responsibility of much of the product development process, design in particular, of quality control and of JIT delivery.[5] The R&D-relevant linkages in the supplier structure seem to make possible more effective and extensive diffusion of R&D results and technology throughout the supplier pyramid.[6]

At the intracorporate level, self-organizing cross-functional teams with large responsibility for product development are said to act in accordance with visionary strategic directions given by top management. Overlapping development phases in a 'rugby-approach' enhance shared responsibility and cross-divisional co-operation, in contrast to a more individualistic and fragmented 'relay-race-approach' in the West.[7]

The extent of organizational learning seems to be higher through a particularly effective spread of knowledge, which frequently takes place in an environment of creative chaos with little managerial hierarchy and formalism.[8] Shared experiences and values through job rotation are said to facilitate both spread of knowledge and co-operation.[9]

Other explanations are the strong communication links between marketing and production, again through rotation of personnel. Clark and Fujimoto (1991, 167, 203) state that a good part of the Japanese advantage in lead time, productivity and quality is due to superior capability in manufacturing. Equally strong links between R&D and market needs, through mutual awareness of customer feedback and technological possibilities, give rise to terms like 'zero customer feedback time' and 'zero product improvement time'.[10] Parallels to an extensive learning process is drawn by Imai *et al.* (1985).

Accordingly, the management of information and organization of knowledge creation provide a rewarding complement to the traditional approach towards R&D and its management. In effect, Japanese-style knowledge creation is claimed to be a major contributor to successful R&D management (Nonaka, 1988a, 1988b, 1991, 1993).

Traditional cultural explanations are that teamwork is fostered through Japanese group-orientation with a focus on endless improvement, thanks to a particularly high sense of identification with the company for which Japanese employees are said to be obsessed with creating a future.[11]

A well-known trend among many Japanese manufacturers is to go up-market (cf. Prahalad and Hamel 1990, 86), which, according to Porter (1990, 75), is the only way to sustain competitive advantage. A good example of this is when Toyota Motor, a world master of mass production, went up-market by developing the Lexus, a case to be described later in this study.

How deep is our knowledge of all these suggested success factors? What can we learn from them? How might all these perfectly sounding managerial buzzwords actually work in practice? It is common wisdom that domestic competition is the highest in Japan (Porter 1990, 82), but we also notice pronounced tendencies of co-operation (Lamming 1994, 58-61). By what means is the co-existence of competition and co-operation possible?

Towards a Closure of the Gap?

Many lessons have been learnt from Japan already: Hammer and Champy (1993) describe how Ford has improved its supplier management, mainly by learning from Mazda. In the development of the Taurus, Quinn argues that Ford used perhaps the 'most extensive simultaneous design process in industry to date' (1992, 35). Between 1993 and 1995, Chrysler reduced the number of main suppliers from 1,200 to 150, while strengthening their co-operative with the objective to shrink development lead-time to 30 months.[12] Orru (1993) notes an increased use of collectively responsible teams, interchangeability of tasks, reduction of managerial hierarchies and consensus-based decision making in German firms.

Charan (1991) reports on ten Western companies which use networks to form small companies within the large companies, thereby enabling key people to converge faster and increase the degree and speed of intracorporate communication. Helmut Werner,[13] Chief Executive of Mercedes Benz, states that the four new targeted factors of his company are: closer customer-orientation; zero-defect ambition; continuous improvement of production; and delegation of decision making, thereby promoting job-enrichment.

BMW recently closed down their entire central research laboratory and dispatched its 450 researchers directly to the various development divisions within the company.[14] This is one of the most radical efforts demonstrated by a European company to attune R&D activities to market needs.

Professor Heinz Teichmann,[15] Chief Technology Officer of Siemens, reports on plans to reduce hierarchies from five to three levels and to have more market-driven R&D with research and product development activities run in parallel instead of sequentially. Between 1994 and 1996, Siemens increased its number of external R&D co-operation projects by 30 per cent.

Within the Western league, Texas Instruments (TI) is one of the more intelligent users of extracorporate know-how. Alone in Europe, TI has 110 university alliances. Gatekeepers are assigned to each relevant university for effective monitoring of progress and for rapid transfer of new knowledge into the TI organization. All projects and results obtained are logged into the TI intranet for effective diffusion to every employee who might be in need of additional know-how.

Ericsson Radio – which brings in 80 per cent of Ericsson's total profits – has, according to R&D manager Mats Lindoff, stretched the goal for all its researchers to use 30 per cent of all their time to university-collaboration projects in order to secure immediate acces to the latest knowledge.

At Hewlett Packard, each R&D project team is free to establish its own university contacts and is even responsible for establishing partnerships. For corporate-wide coordination, a central university relations manager administers the legal details and has the overall budget responsibility.[16]

Philips is slimming its internal R&D while expanding external partnerships, which currently account for two per cent of the $350 Mio research budget.

Tetra Pak is another know-who expert with more than one hundred university alliances across the globe, and a continuous internal benchmarking process for immediate diffusion of best practice.

Perhaps as a consequence of these lessons, radical improvements among some Western companies have been registered, both in terms of development lead-time and commercial success. It remains however unclear to what extent these improvements are due to increased managerial efficiencies in the West, and how far they are due to the comparative cost advantage that has resulted from the rapid rise of the yen. Although Renault already has adopted some 'Japan-related' success factors, Chairman and CEO Louis Schweitzer still considers Toyota the best benchmarking company.[17] Many other Western companies are still struggling with the implementation of simultaneous engineering, cross-functional teams and technological co-operation in partnerships and alliances (Laage-Hellman, 1997). As will be strongly argued in this book, these success factors can only be implemented in companies with highly flexible and multicompetent engineers. Unfortunately, such engineers are still rare birds in many Western companies.

Today, the only certainty seems to be uncertainty. The recent Japanese bubble economy with a decreasing domestic demand, an increasing exchange rate of the yen and demographic changes with an ageing workforce have had severe impacts on the previously predominant position of Japanese corporations on the world market.[18] Even if Japan's decline, against all likelihood, should be a permanent state of affairs, there remains much to learn from the managerial techniques that helped them reach the top. In any case, neither demographic changes, nor increasing exchange rates, seem related to the management of T&I.

The fact that such large parts of Western companies are learning from Japan calls for a deeper analysis of the managerial mechanisms that have made the achievements possible . This is why Japanese T&I management constitutes a critical object of explorative benchmarking for all those firms, managers and academics in search of managerial mechanisms that enhance the level of R&D results, increase their degree of commercialization and accelerate their time to market.

To illustrate how the entire system works in practice, a short study of Toshiba Computers,[19] will follow. It demonstrates the extensive width and propensity for networking behaviour of T&I management at a Japanese company. It also introduces most of those issues that will be treated more extensively in the remaining chapters.

A BRIEF STUDY OF T&I MANAGEMENT AT TOSHIBA COMPUTERS

The Keiretsu Network

The Toshiba Corporation has 27 factories, one of which is Toshiba Computers in Ome. As a whole, the corporation has ties to some 600 affiliates and subsidiaries, holding a financial stake in about a hundred of them. Fifty-three of these are so-called first-tier suppliers, or core companies of the Toshiba Corporation, which totals close to 70,000 company members (regular employees). Certain development activities have been transferred to its group members, in order to strengthen the links and to keep internal diversification at bay. The group-interaction is very active at the technological level. Important group members receive managers from Toshiba and take part in Toshiba's courses on high-technology.[20]

In addition, there are some 1,300 small businesses with 59,000 employees who supply parts, components and sub-assemblies. A larger intercorporate perspective positions the Toshiba Corporation in the Mitsui Group, one of Japan's six large kinyu shudan, or corporate groups.[21]

Specialized development activities like software development are usually spun off to separate development laboratories that are interlinked to the Toshiba Group.[22] It seems that spinning off activities aims at reducing the level of bureaucratization, which is a problem according to Dr Takayanagi, CTO and Senior Vice Executive of Toshiba Corporation:

> It seems to be an irreversible problem: the more we grow, the more we become bureaucratic and the less we become inventive. Spinning off research activities may be a solution, but it has a drawback too, as evaluation and job rotation of the researchers become more complicated . . . My main concern is to promote creativity and technofusion and the best way of doing this is through rotation of our researchers.

The Global Network of Strategic Alliances

A large network of strategic alliances brings in additional competences to Toshiba. A joint venture with Time-Warner aims at gaining know-how in video software development. In 1992, Toshiba teamed up with IBM and Siemens for work on a second generation 64M-byte chip and later also to work on system large scale integrated circuits (LSI), the next generation of chips that combine MPU, DRAM and other vital components into one chip.[23] By fusing the technologies of the three companies, development time will be shorter, costs curbed and a solid share of the system LSI market in their corporate back pockets.

To secure the accomplishment of a 256-Mbit DRAM, Toshiba joined forces in 1992 with IBM, Motorola and Siemens. For this joint technology development, Toshiba sent 70 researchers to IBM's Microelectronics research centre in New York. As this project was completed in 1995, a revolutionary new chip was launched that was at least 13 per cent smaller and had an access time that was nearly twice as fast as any chip on the market. Manaobu Ohyama, Senior Vice President of Toshiba and group executive of its semiconductor group stated that

> This remarkable breakthrough in advanced research shows what can be achieved by a dedicated alliance of companies that brings leading-edge capabilities to a highly motivated program with clear aims.[24]

The same partners then undertook the ambitious task of moving to 1-Gbit DRAM. In Spring 1997, 60 of the researchers returned to Toshiba to continue the work in their own labs, while the 10 remaining ones are staying to work on the same project at IBM in New York.[25]

Toshiba has also created an alliance with all major semiconductor chip manufacturers in Japan, TI-Japan and Thomson-Italy, to develop advanced microprocessor chips, which should be twice as fast as today's computer 'brain' chips and would sell for half of current prices. The consortium is to be led by Professor Murakami of Kiushu University, who has developed a new type of chip technology that combines memory and logic functions on a single device. The target applications for these chips will be multimedia and networking. The consortium members plan to develop and manufacture chips that outpace those built by Intel.[26]

In 1995, Toshiba joined the General Magic alliance that developed the first online trading system to be used on personal communicators.[27] In November that year, Toshiba also joined forces with 14 Japanese companies to co-operate on integrating document management solutions developed by each company, using a common core technology. They will also exchange technical information, establish study groups, evaluate features required in the document management system in Japan and conduct joint advertising.[28]

For the development of fine ceramics, Toshiba joined a MITI-project formed around this technology with six national research laboratories and 16 Japanese companies. Toshiba also started an intimate technological co-operation with Cummins Engine in the US. From 1984 and onwards, more than 10 Toshiba engineers worked on part-time with four full-time engineers from Cummins' Materials Engineering Department. Today, Toshiba is a leading supplier of structural fine ceramics, producing several key components for, *inter alia*, Cummins. The Material and Components Group of Toshiba now has the mission to enhance and diffuse this technology within the company.[29]

Corporate R&D

At Toshiba Computers, R&D is divided into three levels, beginning upstream with the Research Centre in Kawasaki. Long-term research with a time perspective of ten years from research to commercialization is pursued in this research centre, which is shared with other Toshiba companies. Ten per cent of Toshiba's researchers and engineers are located here or in one of the other five corporate research facilities. The remaining 90% are located in the development divisions of the factories or working with operations management directly on the manufacturing lines.[30]

In an interview with an anonymous senior researcher, it was stated that 'most of the work here is trial-and-error testing of prototypes'. He also emphasized the importance of collaboration with extracorporate actors:

No truly scientific research is being done here. Everything that we do has to have a commercial application. Collaboration with development or production is rare. Instead, it is our own responsibility to take research results via development to production. We often take part in MITI projects as the Fifth Generation Computer Project, or as the present project on magnetic levitation trains . . . We also interact with some foreign universities, mainly by sending engineers to do research there. (Anonymous A, interview)

In Ome, close to Tokyo, a Workstation Laboratory pursues software development and design of product concepts with a time perspective of two to three years. Once a concept is conceived, the Development Division makes hardware development and design. Development is very production-related here, where trial production usually starts as early as six months after the beginning of a new product development project. The workstation lab and the development divisions are located in the same building, neighbouring the actual production site. Also located in the same building are the technical service staff, the production staff and the purchasing staff that manage the external procurement of components.

Intracorporate communication was improved by the development of computer networks started already in the late 1960s at Toshiba. Integration and interconnection have since then been pursued in five steps. Today, a 400 Mbps LAN[31] links all the above divisions and also all branch offices, distributors and many shops, thus enabling electronic direct marketing. Throughout Japan, affiliated and co-operating companies and parts suppliers are connected, as are maintenance companies and headquarters in Tokyo. Overseas facilities in Irvine, USA and Regensburg, Germany are also interconnected via satellite. Domestically, video conferences are said to further enhance intracorporate communication. These sophisticated networks seem to serve as a strategic information tool to top management and facilitate effective spread of information to many company members. As a consequence, CIM has come to stand for Computer Integrated Management,[32] as described by Oka-san, Senior Manager of the Engineering Administration and Factory Information Systems Department:

> Emphasis is put on a close interface between management, development and production, as well as on a close interaction with our affiliates. Partly, we achieve this through CIM, Computer Integrated Management, unifying the entire corporation through an extensive computer network.

The aforementioned affiliated suppliers are usually involved at an early stage of the development process, in which they assume very high responsibility by Western standards.

Interaction between development and production is intense. To begin with, the production line and the development section work very closely together. They have regular meetings once a month, but also meet informally once a week. In the design stage, design engineers frequently consult production engineers. Maeda-san, Senior Manager of the System Computer Development Department, describes the intensity of their interaction:

> Before a new product launch, when a prototype is trial-manufactured, there are usually many breakdowns. In these periods, we work together on a more or less permanent basis. Also, thanks to the physical closeness, we can instantly run down from our development department to the production line if they have a problem. (Maeda, interview)

Market needs and customer feedback are explored in several different ways. Customer feedback on personal computers is received via retailer reports on customer complaints, which are systematically stored and transferred to their source of origin. Files of customers are kept so that questionnaires can be sent to them. In some cases, a new model is sent to customers with an invitation to headquarters, where they take part in focused group discussions, expressing their views and wishes directly to product planning management and to product development engineers. As for mainframe computers, development engineers have meetings with the corporate sales division and service engineers, who maintain close contacts with the customers and also conduct actual interviews with them. In these meetings, customer needs and complaints are discussed. Sometimes, the sales division hires an external market research institute, preferably that of Mitsui and Co., to analyse new trends. Ishiyawa-san, Senior Manager of Purchase Management, assures us in an interview that 'this information is important to us. If for instance the popularity of open systems or UNIX increases, we will immediately have to adjust our product development to these trends'. It can also be added that Toshiba, as a Mitsui Group member, enjoys a large base of quasi-captive customers among members of the same corporate group.[33] Thanks to the high trust and loyalty between group members, customer feedback appears to be faster, more reliable and easier to access.

Flexible project management: at any given time, there is a number of R&D projects within the company, the management of which varies with the size of the project. An exceptionally large project for the development of a new mainframe computer may have a project manager, who gathers a cross-functional team with members from different sections and divisions. Together, these team members will follow the new product through the innovation process, until trial manufacturing of a prototype is satisfactory. More commonly and for smaller projects, e.g. a new personal computer, no such project team is gathered. Instead, the project manager acts as coordinator of the different tasks, shared out by himself, and coordinates interaction between divisions and sections. In both cases, top management proposes a visionary product concept, and assigns the project to a project manager, who translates and disintegrates the vision into smaller and more tangible part-concepts. These part-concepts are shared out among division managers, who again disintegrate them into tasks, which are transferred to appropriate sections and suppliers. Once all the part-tasks are solved and re-integrated, the development department assembles a prototype which is then run in trial manufacturing. The interaction with suppliers is managed at the direct working-level and the development engineers themselves sometimes call on affiliated suppliers for the development of, for instance, production equipment related to semiconductors or displays. Maeda-san puts strong emphasis on what could be labelled 'interactive R&D':

When we have to develop new gate arrays, we usually interact very intimately with the

Toshiba Semiconductor Division. A new colour display is presently being developed jointly with IBM. Establishing external sources of technology is an important part of our R&D management. (Maeda, interview)

Division managers strongly encourage subordinate development engineers to scan patents applied for by other companies and to file new ones. Those who submit patent applications which come to be used in production are rewarded with a percentage of the produced value and radically improve their chances of promotion. A strict overall time deadline is set for the development cycle. Usually, this is kept through high rates of overtime.

Crystallizing Out the Key Factors

Focusing on the factors that seem to have made possible a high R&D productivity in terms of research results, it is stated that no scientific research is being made even in the Research Centre. Instead, scientific technological achievements seem to be ensured through extensive networks of interlinked extracorporate actors, especially Western strategic partners and universities. Moreover, much of the specialized applied research that takes place within Toshiba appears to be either spun-off to separate interlinked units or supported by a MITI project. The example of industry-government co-operation in this case yielded the commercial application of LANs.

The Japanese document management consortium now works on how best to transform document data (based on so-called CALS standards) for effective processing in such LANs. Clearly, the collective efforts in these two projects have the potential to enable optimal leverage of corporate – as well as global – knowledge.

The spin-off mechanism seems to offer an extracorporate solution to the intracorporate problem of increasing bureaucratization. Interlinkages are maintained through bilateral flows of technology.

There are also reasons to believe that support and loyalty within the Mitsui Group, enabling intragroup sharing of competencies and market information, have impacts on Toshiba Computer's research results and its management. In addition, the quasi-captive customer base of the corporate group seems to create a basis for early and reliable market feedback.

At the intracorporate level, the key factors which, according to the author's own observations, have enabled Toshiba to improve R&D in terms of shorter development lead-time[34] and more customer-oriented product innovation are:

- Computer Integrated Management, improving the flow of information with both customers and suppliers, thus enabling more direct feedback of market needs and providing insight in the entire innovation process necessary for top-down-bottom-up management;
- Intensive group activities and quality circles, in which development engineers, production engineers and sometimes also sales engineers jointly

strive for continuous improvement of the innovation and production process;
- Intimate closeness between development and production, improving design for manufacturing;
- Cross-functional and cross-divisional interaction, enabling an increased use of already existing components and a better standardization of new design;
- Use of patents to control performance and to analyse competitors;
- Flexibly powerful and highly interactive project management using strong visions as key coordination mechanism.

Hence, also at the corporate level, networking seems to be a continuously recurring factor that enhances the degree of market feedback and reduces development lead-time by interlinking development activities and production which, again, involves closely interlinked suppliers.

What Remains to be Discovered?

Confronting the key factors with current literature provides extensive support for the emphasis on extracorporate sources of technology. A large number of the studies, outlined in Chapter 2, deal with interfirm networks and industry-government co-operation, but, with very few exceptions, it has not been studied in a systematic way how the activities of these networks are linked to corporate R&D activities.

Moreover, the problematic situation of, and possible solution to, increasing levels of bureaucratization has not been observed.

Many of the intracorporate aspects of our Toshiba description find support in current literature, the most flagrant exception being the use of patents as a factor of inspiration, motivation and evaluation, for which only some indirect support has been found in a report by IVA (1993). However, also at the corporate level, the existing literature is quite fragmented. Key factors like cross-functional teams, visions, spread of knowledge and strong communication occur frequently, but need to be systematzied and located in their situational context, so as to better understand the interrelationships that are vital to innovation processes.

In the context of project management, most literature deals with cross-functional teams as if they always consisted of fully assigned members, whereas our Toshiba description reveals that this is only the case in large projects. Moreover, teams are often described as isolated units, instead of tracing their linkages to, and position in, the corporation as a whole. A holistic network approach is lacking.

To summarize, it is of importance both to Japanese and to Western companies and academics not only to achieve an integrated view of what makes Japanese management of T&I so efficient and effective in terms of isolated factors, but above all to understand how the whole interacting system works before disintegrated parts of it turn into buzzwords that may not be applicable in an isolated context. It may also be of importance to identify possible weaknesses of a so far rather uncriticized system. As Chapter 2 will disclose in greater detail, an endless number of studies has enumerated Japan's success factors. However, we shall also see that most of these sometimes fragmented studies have focused on 'what' questions, omitting the 'why' and, more important still, the 'how.'

There are few detailed descriptions and analyzes of how R&D is organized and managed at the corporate level in Japan.[35] Most literature in the field relates uniquely to the automobile industry. This study will be the first to compare the Japanese champion of this industry, Toyota, with two different champions of innovation: Canon in the office automation industry, and Sony in the consumer electronics industry. Richness in detail will be emphasized in both of these studies.

If we accept the belief that Japanese companies' seemingly unique ability to make groups of disintegrated, but nevertheless interdependent, parts work in concert contributes a major part of their achieved success, it is a natural consequence to adopt a network approach that focuses on structural, organizational and leadership linkages related to R&D processes.

Indeed, this study holds that the total picture is more important than its disintegrated parts and that a holistic network approach to Japanese T&I management will not only increase our understanding of the issue, but also deepen it. Paradoxical as it may seem, a broader perspective needs to be adopted to attain a deeper understanding of how to improve the management of T&I.

A HOLISTIC NETWORK APPROACH TO T&I MANAGEMENT

In Japan, R&D management covers all activities of technological innovation and we do not keep a strong focus on basic research. In fact, there might not be any at all. (Fujimoto, discussion)[36]

The Role of R&D in Japanese T&I Management

Given the topic, one could expect this study to deal with the management of research in Japanese corporate laboratories. On the other hand, we have seen that Toshiba Computers in Ome pursues no research at all and that the applied research activities of the Research Centre in Kawasaki mainly consist of trial and error, which is more of a rule than an exception. This, however, does not mean that Japanese companies neglect the role of research. Quite in contrast, they are usually very interested in scientific research results, but have developed alternative means of acquiring them. In this context, it appears appropriate to add a few comments from an interview with Dr Nakada, who has many years experience in the US where he has conducted his Ph.D:

> As you know, there is no 'R' in Japan. There is a lot of 'D' here, but Japanese companies go overseas to get the 'R' at universities or companies. They never have exchange programs at their own companies, but send company members to business partners in the US. For instance, people are sent from Canon to Hewlett Packard and from NTT to Bell Labs.

Dr Nakada mentions an example of a friend who spent several years at Bell Labs in the US and is now a key person in the development of laser beam printers at Canon. Similar examples are given by several other interviewees.[37]

When NEC decided to develop semiconductor technology into a core competence, it entered into more than one hundred strategic alliances, all aiming at building competencies, or as stated by NEC's director of research: 'From an investment standpoint, it was much quicker and cheaper to use foreign technology. There wasn't a need for us to develop new ideas' (Prahalad and Hamel 1990, 80).

The case of Toshiba Computers has briefly illustrated the situational context of Japanese R&D processes, with 90% of all engineers located in production plants. In addition, we noticed a high degree of interaction with extracorporate fields of action like corporate groups and vertically structured suppliers, MITI and universities, which may reduce the need of intracorporate research. Before stressing the fundamental differences of Japan, the traditional steps along the innovation process will be introduced.

Research, or invention, sometimes initiates the innovation process. Basic research represents original investigation for the advancement of scientific knowledge with no specific commercial objectives, whereas applied research has an expected pay-off in terms of commercial objectives (Mansfield, 1971). One of the great achievements of the nineteenth century was the 'invention of the invention,' which later came to be tantamount to research:

> Before 1880 or so, invention was mysterious; early nineteenth-century books talk incessantly of the 'flash of genius'. The inventor himself was a half romantic, half ridiculous figure, tinkering away in a lonely garret. By 1914, the time World War I broke out, 'invention' had become 'research', a systematic, purposeful activity, which is planned and organized with high predictability both of the results aimed at and likely to be achieved. (Drucker 1985, 34)

A common meaning of invention today is 'the discovery or production of some new or improved process or machine' (*The Collins Dictionary*), i.e., 'a new means for achieving some function not obvious beforehand to someone skilled in the prior art' (Kline and Rosenberg 1986, 292), or simply 'an idea for a novel product or process' (Betz 1987, 6). It was the nineteenth century's 'brightest' inventor, Edison, who converted invention into the discipline of research, but despite successful invention, he had little commercial success and went out of business (Drucker 1985, 12-13). His strong focus on invention prevented innovation from taking place, which is one of the most well-repeated mistakes in the management of R&D.

Innovation aims at the transformation of research findings into practice. It thereby creates 'purposeful, focused change in an entreprise's economic and social potential' (Drucker 1991, 9), and yields competitive advantage (Porter 1990, 74). It occurs when a patentable invention reaches the market, so as to enable its first application.

Deschamps and Nayak (1992, 40) view innovation as 'the introduction of useful change' and Kline and Rosenberg (1986, 275) call it 'the creation and marketing of the new'; thus bringing marketing into the picture. As Joseph Schumpeter (1951) argued long before today's gurus in the field, innovation really is the art of applying inventions and core skills in new combinations by making links across and between skill boundaries. Its effectiveness is not ensured by a specialized task in the R&D organization, but rather through a combination of excellent strategic planning, purchasing, marketing, engineering, and production.

To summarize, research aims at invention, or the solution of a (technical) problem, whereas successful development yields innovation, i.e. production, diffusion and commercially successful use of the invention. If we accept these arguments, it follows that the meaning of R&D management in Japan differs from the traditional one of the West, and that management of T&I is a better term for what actually takes place.

Covering all activities of technological innovation and product development, Japanese T&I management consists of a holistic pursuit of collective invention, innovation and commercialization, interconnected in sophisticated technology networks of coexisting competition and co-operation[38] and also pays high attention to achieving customer satisfaction.[39]

In contrast, the traditional Western literature on R&D management has usually only covered scientific work aiming at invention and its subsequent development, paying little attention to production and none at all to marketing.[40] Below, location of the situational context will further clarify the definition, but also deepen the problem discussion.

Locational Context Inside the Black Box[41]

We know by now that Japanese R&D has a small 'r' and a big 'D'. Its location is not so much in the research labs, but instead in the development departments and above all in the production plants, where most development engineers are. At Toshiba Computers, we have noticed that R&D activities are divided into three levels, the core of which is located in divisional development centres, which in turn are located in the actual production factories, thus housing 90% of Toshiba's engineers.[42] It is, therefore, not surprising that the link between R&D and production is particularly strong in Japan.

By neglecting the importance of the production stage, numerous Western companies have failed to innovate. In a discussion with Professor Gregory, he states that American researchers invented a breakthrough technology of Very Large Scale Integrated circuits(VSLI), but nobody was able to produce them. Meanwhile, they were surpassed by Japanese researchers who reached VLSI technology through incremental improvements of LSI technology, mainly focusing on the production stage.[43]

Strong links between R&D and production thus enhance the prospects of an R&D project resulting in a manufactured product. In order for this product to turn into a commercialized innovation, links to market needs are equally essential. Stalk and Webber (1993) even suggest a dark side of short development lead-time, unless these strong links are kept with customers.

At Toshiba, high priority is given to the relationship between the customer and R&D through the use of retailer reports, customer questionnaires and focused group discussions involving customers, researchers and product planners. Hence, engineers from soft- and hardware development, production and sales, join forces in pursuit of collective innovation.

Ample cross-functional job rotation between divisions such as research, development, production and marketing further broadens the locational context of an R&D management which is based upon a quasi-institutionalized cross-over principle.[44]

Locational Context Outside the Black Box

> Our educational system does not allow for the creativity that is necessary to develop software. However, software is tradable and can easily be sent across borders so we don't need to develop it in Japan. (Dr Mori, Manager of R&D planning at Kobe Steel, interview)

A large number of studies have explored R&D processes, but, with a few exceptions, they have had one single focus on intracorporate activities, and regard the company more or less as an isolated unit in an undefined context.[45] However, it seems imperative to go beyond the internal structure of the firm by including factors outside the black box, so as to meaningfully understand the holistic efficiencies that drive the Japanese T&I process and, above all, to explore how external sources of technology are linked to corporate R&D. The stronger links to external sources of technology, which appear in Chapter 2 and 3, seem to compensate the relatively lesser emphasis on intracorporate research activities.

Contrary to much common wisdom, the initiating step in most innovation processes is not research, but rather an existing invention or analytic design, i.e., the study of new combinations of existing inventions and products (Kline and Rosenberg 1986, 302). Instead of in-house research, it may well be that the innovation process is initiated by technology scanning, in search of a new technology which, if found, usually will be transferred to the firm in question. As a member of the Mitsui Group, Toshiba has access to the extensive technology scanning network of Mitsui and Co., one of the largest trading houses in the world. Chapter 3 will show how this trading house provides access to global know-how.

Intracorporate communication at Toshiba is partly secured by computer and satellite networks. 'No business is an island' (Håkansson and Snehota, 1989) is especially true of Japan, where interaction in different corporate networks plays a considerable role in the innovation process.[46] Consequently, this author believes that structural and organizational mechanisms that encourage interaction with extracorporate actors should be taken into consideration, as these seem to distinguish the modern corporation and enterprise system of Japan from most other industrial economies. As Quinn (1992, 233) argues, it is not surprising that coalitions, similar to those of the Japanese keiretsu structures, are providing a model for improving other countries' competitive strength.

The increasing practice of technology fusion, the fusion of existing technologies into new combinations of hybrid technologies, further intensifies the necessity of networking in Japanese R&D management (Kodama 1991; 1992a).

MITI-organized R&D projects are of great importance and part of the situational context, interconnecting the competencies of sometimes competing companies for the pursuit of precompetetive, long-term and high-risk research.[47]

Based on the above observations and many omitted ones, it seems that the situational context of Japanese T&I management is rather wide and often transcends 'traditional' corporate borders of the Western mind. Main themes are observation, transfer, concentration, combination and coordination of technological competencies, both in terms of actual technology hardware and of human resources.

If we accept the proposition that the locational context of Japanese T&I management is of extensive width, and that R&D projects largely depend on how relevant actors and competencies are interlinked and affected by environmental factors, it follows that a conceptual framework based upon network theories is appropriate for this study, as outlined below.

Conceptualizing Holistic Networks

The combination of actors and resources in holistic networks makes possible activities of tremendous breadth, notwithstanding sharply focused individual efforts. If each individual product development activity can be seen as part of a total technical process, which in turn may be an integral feature of a specific network, it follows that a network perspective will help us more fully to understand corporate technological development processes.[48]

Quinn (1992, 72) proposes that the raison d'être of today's knowledge-intensive company is 'the systematic coordination of knowledge and intellect' in a network of internal and external knowledge bases. Bartlett and Ghoshal (1989, 61) regard the transnational corporate structure as an integrated network of complex communication linkages, work interdependencies and flows of resources, claiming that 'the integrated network configuration is essential for developing transnational innovations'.

A central theme of network theory is that technological development evolves as an interplay among industrial actors with sometimes complementary and sometimes competing resources and activities (Laage-Hellman 1989, 129). Easton's description of the 'industrial network approach' gives a good introduction to its utility in this study:

> It shares with other approaches a belief that the existence of relationships, many of them stable and durable, among firms engaged in economic exchange provides a compelling reason for using inter-organizational relationships as a research perspective. It differs from other approaches mainly in terms of its scope. It is concerned to understand the totality of relationships among firms engaged in production, distribution and the use of goods and services in what might best be described as an industrial system. (Easton 1992, 3)

Relationships, that are central in the industrial network approach, are of major importance in the Japanese T&I management process as well. A general rationale for entering into a relationship is complementarity or communality of objectives.[49] More specifically, this may be the co-development or advancement of a technology, or the access to an information network. This study regards co-operative relationships as vital linkage mechanisms – both between and within firms – that foster innovation.[50]

Coordination[51]

Prahalad and Hamel (1990, 82) argue that management of corporate core competencies is 'the collective learning in the organization, especially how to coordinate diverse production skills and integrate multiple streams of technologies'. That the identification, cultivation and use of core competencies require cross-organizational communication and commitment across divisional boundaries is suggested in the citation below:

> World class research in, for example, lasers or ceramics can take place in corporate laboratories without having an impact on any of the business of the company. The skills that together constitute core competence must coalesce around individuals whose efforts are not so narrowly focused that they cannot recognize the opportunities for blending their functional expertise with those of others in new and interesting ways. (*Ibid.*)

Outspending rivals on R&D is thus not necessarily tantamount to developing a core competence. Rather, it is the coordination of various technological skills and competencies that become core competencies once they are harmonized with production skills and reach the market through incorporation into commercialized end products.

As stated by Buckley and Casson (1988, 32), 'coordination is an appropriate basis upon which to build a concept of co-operation, for it articulates the idea that co-operation is of mutual benefit to the parties directly involved'. Ackoff states that 'the performance of a system depends more on how its parts interact than on how they act independently of each other' (1981, 18). Economists argue that coordination is assured by the invisible hand of the market. Self-directing and managerial coordination in the control of a specific firm has been labelled the 'visible hand'. Network processes constitute a third form of coordination, which often is centred around technological innovation as the continuous interaction between firms offers both the opportunity for innovation and the existence of a known and predictable environment in which it can be realised (Easton, 1992).

Håkansson (1987; 1989; 1990; 1992) considers how companies handle their technological development in relation to external clients and organizations, particularly in terms of collaborative projects, claiming that the question is not how the company manages its technological development *per se*, but 'how it manages to relate its technological development to what is happening inside and between other organizations' (1990, 371), an argument that appears to be highly valid in a Japan-related context. He defines the company as an actor that uses different resources to perform its activities. A company's relationships with other companies constitute links in a network model, which is central to Håkansson's theory and supports the conceptual framework of this study.

All three elements of Håkansson's network model – actors, resources and activities – contain technological dimensions. An R&D manager (actor) will not be able to perform the activity of adequate strategy formulation unless he is aware of the company's resources in terms of technologies, competencies, financial resources and production facilities. Technological dependence occurs between different activities, and technology ties resources together. In line with the essence of holism, the right combination of these resources often yields a whole that is greater than the sum of its parts.

The figure below summarizes the interlinkages of actors, resources and activities that are relevant in this study.

The core element of analysis in this study is knowledge-linkage patterns,[52] i.e., the purposes, types and structural characteristics of those knowledge linkages that relate to innovation projects, located in Japanese corporations, which in turn are linked to surrounding R&D networks.

Three reasons why interlinking relationships are important in the innovation process can be outlined: first, interaction with parties having knowledge in other areas can generate new thinking, as new knowledge often appears in the border zone between established bodies of knowledge (cf. Nonaka, 1991). Second, if a technical invention is mobilized through relationships with extra-corporate parties, its chances of attracting support and turning into an innovation are increased. Third, companies' increased intracorporate specialization in production and R&D urge them to supplement their resources with those of others.[53]

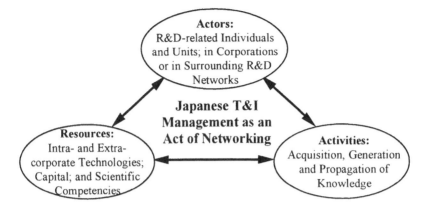

Source: Inspired from Håkansson (1987)

Figure 1.1   Vital Interlinkages in Japanese T&I Management

In summary, network theories support the notion that results of corporate R&D efforts are dependent on how corporate actors manage their activities and resources to combine, coordinate, or integrate them with those of surrounding networks. Consequently, it seems necessary to explore the R&D networks that support Japanese corporations, before a meaningful intracorporate analysis of R&D activities can be made.

Accordingly, the study will be divided into three distinct network foci, at two levels. At the extracorporate level, important actors and resources that surround and support Japanese companies in their innovation processes will be identified. Activities that link these surrounding R&D networks to corporate R&D will be analysed, focusing on their interrelationships and coordination.

Second, at the intracorporate level, actors that participate in the Japanese corporate R&D process will be highlighted to analyze the mechanisms through which their R&D-related activities are interrelated and coordinated.

Finally, the dynamics of these networks will be explored by further intensifying the focus through the analysis of corporate R&D projects. At this third and ultimate level of analysis, the project leader is put at the core of Figure 1.1 to analyze the managerial mechanisms by which he coordinates the previously defined interlinkages of actors, resources and activities.

We know that the Japanese success is pronounced in fields building on the transistor, on integrated circuits and on automobile components. Weaknesses seem to be particularly visible in the chemical and pharmaceutical industries, in which through-put can be totally articulated and where requirements for mutual coordination between employees are low (cf. Hedlund and Nonaka 1991, 31).

In contrast, consumer electronics, office automation equipment and automobile industries all have through-put processes with strong tacit elements and require a high degree of both intra- and interorganizational communication and co-operation, which supports the choice of a network approach to analyse their T&I management.

MAIN OBJECTIVES OF THE STUDY

From the overall research question – what managerial mechanisms enable Japanese companies, in the industries of automobiles, office automation equipment and consumer electronics, to enjoy the shorter development lead-time and higher R&D efficiency that seem to have characterized these industries in the past two decades? – the situational context of the study has been located and an appropriate network approach has been developed with three analytical foci. It is, therefore, time to outline the main objectives that emerge from the overall research problem, before describing by which strategy the objectives have been pursued.

By merging theories on networking, R&D and innovation, three linkages appear to be critical for successful management of T&I (cf. Figure 2.4): (1) gaining and exchanging competencies with subsidiaries and external sources of invention that participate in the innovation process; (2) linking development efforts to market needs; and, finally, (3) managing the link from research, via development, to manufacturing.

However, a theoretical dilemma of technological leadership suggests that the very same linkages that seem to promote product development activities become weaker the more intracorporate technology development advances. Moreover, an organizational dilemma proposes that high productivity, rapid innovation and processing of information thrive in rigid, hierarchic organizations, whereas creativity and progress in technology development seem to require rather flexibly organic and non-hierarchic organizations. These critical dilemmas of innovation are developed in Chapter 2.

This author's main proposition is that the companies in focus of this study have developed managerial networking mechanisms to circumvent the dilemmas, thereby achieving high R&D productivity and short development lead-time. By applying the three network foci to the analysis, the overall research problem can be disintegrated into three different, but strongly interrelated, objectives:

At the highest contextual level, various structural linkages to extracorporate sources of technology reduce the need for intracorporate technology development, thus keeping the dilemma of technological leadership at bay. Moreover, the organic network structure of Japanese corporations appears to interlink creativity and productivity, thereby offering mechanisms for solving the organizational dilemma of innovation. Consequently, the **first** objective is to explore and analyse structural and organizational mechanisms that interlink extracorporate resources, actors and activities with Japanese corporate R&D

activities.

Defining successful T&I management as one that as quickly as possible turns invention into innovation calls for a balanced understanding of market needs, the new product itself, its manufacturing process as well as its marketing and subsequent improvement. Whether developed internally, or acquired through the surrounding R&D networks, strong intracorporate linkages are necessary to allow for fusion of complementary technologies and to turn these inventions into commercialized innovations. Hence, as the **second** objective, the intracorporate level of analysis focuses on organizational mechanisms that encourage analytic design, i.e., fusion of different technologies; interlinkage of market needs; and interlinkage of and transfer to production.

Once the case-study companies have been analyzed at the extra- and the intracorporate levels, the groundwork will have been laid for the **third** and ultimate objective: to study how corporate R&D projects yield innovation through interlinkage and coordination of the previously defined actors, resources and activities.

Delimitations of the Study

In order to deal with complexity in a manageable way, this study will be limited to clearly distinctive links of interaction that contribute to the innovation process of Japanese corporations. At the extracorporate level, MITI interaction and strategic alliances will only be briefly mentioned and the role of national companies like NTT and NHK will be entirely omitted, due to the complexity of the topic.[54]

The intracorporate level of analysis will exclude all corporate functions and divisions that are unrelated to R&D and to the new product development process. Quality control will not be considered.

When finally analyzing the dynamics of three product innovation projects, no analysis will be made of costs or financial outcomes. Management of information flows and linkages from early concepts to commercialized innovations will be in focus.

The case studies will not consider product renewals, but concentrate on R&D processes of three entirely new products.

RESEARCH STRATEGY AND SUMMARIZED CONTENTS OF THE STUDY

The methodology employed in the research project that laid the foundation for this book is described more in detail in Harryson (1995a). Here, a brief note on the research focus and methodology is made, some peculiarities of empirical studies in Japan are highlighted, and the interview process that resulted from it is described.

Epistemological Stance and Research Methodology

As stated by Burrell and Morgan (1979, 7-8), the subjective and the objective dimensions in the analysis of theory are two intellectual traditions that have dominated social science over the last two hundred years. They label the objective extreme 'sociological positivism' and the subjective extreme 'German idealism'. With respect to these perhaps overpolarized extremes, the position of this study is quite opposed to that of sociological positivism, which represents the application of models and methods derived from the natural sciences to the study of organizational behaviour and considers the world to be made up of hard and tangible structures beyond the influence of the individual. In contrast, this author sympathizes to a large extent with the intellectual tradition of German idealism, explained below:

> In essence it is based upon the premise that the ultimate reality of the universe lies in the 'spirit' or 'idea' rather than in the data of sense perception. It is essentially 'nominalist' in its approach to social reality. In contrast to the natural sciences, it stresses the essentially subjective nature of human affairs, denying the utility and relevance of the models and methods of natural science to studies in this realm. (*Ibid.*)

In line with German idealism, an ideographic methodological approach is maintained, believing that obtaining first-hand knowledge of the subject under investigation yields the best exploration and understanding of the subject. It is therefore a natural consequence to embrace some parts of 'The Discovery of Grounded Theory', by Glaser and Strauss (1967), who declare war upon the positivist tradition by claiming that it is the intimate connection with empirical reality that permits the development of a testable, relevant and valid theory.

In order to map out and analyse a complex process like that of Japanese R&D projects, this is 'better accomplished by selecting a few cases and study many aspects than taking out a few aspects and study these for a great number of companies', as stated by Jansson *et al.* (1990, 11), who thus support this author's belief that a qualitative case-study methodology is particularly applicable when conducting network research on organizations. Yin (1984) and Eisenhardt (1989) provided helpful guidelines for the case studies.

Data Gathering in Holistic Networks

An initial literature review of both formal and substantive theories (Harryson, 1992) and some expert discussions suggested a focus on the project team, which was pursued initially (as exemplified in Appendix B). In the course of empirical studies, a need to extend the research perspective beyond the object, *per se*, emerged rapidly. In accordance with the earlier discussion of the locational context of Japanese T&I management, a broader perspective was adopted in order to better understand the flows and origins of information that eventually yield innovation. By limiting the scope to teamwork in a project room, most of those actors, resources and activities that are vital to Japanese T&I management would have been excluded.

Continuously interacting members of one specific project team were hard to find. Instead, most innovation activities appeared to take place at various locations, involving various actors and resources on both sides of the corporate borders. Japanese development projects thus appeared to be more organic and complex than what would be manageable in one team alone.

Much of this complexity is demonstrated in the case studies, but discussion of ties to extracorporate actors and activities were rather taboo when pursuing interviews, as a result of the severe criticism that these ties have evoked in the West. Some interviewees were particularly clear on this point:

> As for our suppliers, I can't give you any information on how or how long we co-operate, under what conditions or on what terms we interact, what kind of work we do together, nor when it begins and ends. These are all confidential issues (anonymous D, at one of the case-study companies).

Instead of closing doors at the case-study companies by asking questions that relate directly to these aspects, they are covered more in general terms and presented separately. In Chapter 3, a description of the interacting networks that surround and support Japanese corporations, as well as the general structure and management of suppliers, will disclose these patterns of interaction and their role in the innovation processes.

The chapter, which is a condensed version of a more extensive paper (Harryson, 1994), builds upon existing literature with complementary data from empirical studies conducted at companies, other than those presented as case studies. Then, Canon, Sony and Toyota will be located in the previously defined surrounding R&D networks. Once this has been done, the exploration of intraorganizational aspects of R&D, focusing on development projects in the respective companies, to a greater extent can trace the knowledge links that are relevant in the process and that are often of extracorporate origin.

Through this cross-fertilization of existing data and empirical studies, the ambitious task of exploring the entire situational context becomes more manageable, thus enabling a deeper and more complete understanding of Japanese management of new product development projects.

Second, by collecting empirical data through a large number of interviews and interviewees, over a long period of time, some 'macrocosmic' information was obtained also at the case-study companies, notwithstanding initial cool reactions.[55]

Access to Japanese companies is relatively limited. A large number of academics and journalists compete for the valuable time of managers and researchers, and the process of getting to them is usually complicated. First, it goes without saying that introductions are of primordial importance. For the interviews, Profs Abegg|en, Gregory and Yawata of Sophia University played essential roles, as did Prof. Fujimoto of Tokyo University. Sunaga-san, Attaché at the Science and Technology Office of the Sweden Embassy, made effective use of the network of connections that he has developed over 25 years of diplomatic duties, to which Japanese companies are rather sensitive. Finally, Mayuzumi-san of SIAR Bossard in Tokyo provided some key interviewees on very short notice. No company was approached without my first being properly introduced at as high a level as possible. The fact of being invited to Japan as a visiting researcher also proved to be clearly advantageous in the eyes of Japanese companies and individuals.

Second, the fact of having and displaying a clearly positive attitude toward Japan and the companies in focus clearly increased the possibilities of access (see Appendix A for an example). This is an additional reason why highly successful companies, regarded as champions of innovation, have been selected. Negative aspects of innovation are considered to the extent that this is possible, but for the purpose of increasing access, the focus of the interviews was on innovation-promoting factors.

Notwithstanding the above measures, it was sometimes very hard to obtain certain information on the companies. One year of effort was for instance not enough to obtain any form of R&D organization chart at one of the case-study companies. At another company, detailed charts were displayed and explained in the course of interviews, but for secrecy reasons it was impossible to obtain copies of them. A third problem is addressed in the following quotation:

> Much of our organizational structure is not tangible, but merely exists in the minds of company members. The organization changes twice a year, but reorganizations do not necessarily affect the locus of our activities (Toyosaki, interview).

In order to circumvent, or at least reduce the impact of these problems, an extensive use of alternative sources was necessary, in addition to those that were offered the 'official way'. Identification and meetings with those who went back to the academic world, either indefinitely or for complementary studies; 'misfits' who had left their companies; sales people working in local stores; and researchers, Japanese or foreign, who took part in scientific meetings, made possible extension or double-checking of information.[56]

Identifying the original location of task force participants or of project members was often difficult due to frequent reorganizations[57] and intensive job rotation, as exemplified by a Canon interviewee:

> It is almost impossible to say where the people of that task force came from because the organization changes too rapidly. Their home divisions or groups may not even exist in a present organization chart (Yasokawa, interview).

As an attempt to circumvent these situations, previous names of functions and divisions have been displayed whenever necessary and possible.

The interview process always started with identification of other contacts who could provide introductions. Before the actual meeting with the targeted interviewee, an initial semi-structured telephone conversation was usually made, introducing the topic to be discussed as well as clarifying his (or very rarely her) past and present activities. Then, usually less than 24 hours before the meeting, a questionnaire was faxed to the interviewee, which specified the desired topic of the interview in more detail. This questionnaire was sometimes extensive, as exemplified in Appendix B, but more often kept brief and as focused as possible (see, for example Appendix C). Sending this fax more than one day in advance proved to have a less good effect, causing the interviewee to plan and discuss possible answers with superiors, which more often than not reduced the outcome of the interview in terms of depth and openness. In some cases, it appeared to be more effective to have open discussions guided by careful diplomacy, rather than by questionnaires.

If possible, interviews were taped. However, this author sometimes also chose not to embarrass the interviewee with a tape recorder, as this would in some cases reduce the level of confidence and openness, thereby biasing or preventing certain statements. In either case, results were carefully transcribed immediately after each interview, thus affecting or indicating further questions to be asked in coming interviews.

Why Canon, Sony and Toyota?

This study focuses on Japanese cases of best practice in the science of managing technology and innovation. Three industries in Japan distinguish themselves through a significantly higher RTA[58] index than the average of all industries: consumer electronics; computers and office automation equipment; and motor vehicles (IVA 1993, 32).

The choice of Canon and Sony[59] is based on their innovative tradition, with a large number of innovative products put to market. Similarities between their core businesses – office automation equipment and consumer electronics – permit a comparative analysis within relatively similar substantive areas (cf. Glaser and Strauss 1967, 33). By introducing a third case, Toyota Motor Corporation, into the picture, differences are maximized instead. The substantive area of an automobile manufacturer thus allows fields of structural and managerial patterns of Japanese T&I to be generalized. One difference is that Toyota, to a greater extent than both Sony and Canon, has a stronger need and tradition of long-term relationships with dedicated suppliers. The size of development projects constitutes another important difference.

Excluding interviewees who remain annonymous, 40 interviews[60] have been conducted at Canon with 14 different persons. First, the new product development organization will be described in general, aiming at the flow of technology and knowledge within the firm. Then, the development and commercialization process of Flat Panel Liquid Displays will be explored as an action network (Cf. Jansson *et al.*, 1990).

Also in the case of Sony, general issues on R&D management and organization were explored initially. Later, these interviews were followed by a typifying study, focusing on the development of a recent innovation, the 'Mini Discman'. A broad spectrum of company members were interviewed, ranking from junior sales staff, marketing managers, researchers, project leaders and research directors to Chairman Akio Morita. Twenty-four interviews were conducted with 13 different interviewees.

Due to a shortage of time and a relatively low accessibility, only four persons were interviewed at Toyota, at the end of the one-year period in Japan. That an adequate amount of information still could be gathered, was to some extent possible thanks to the author's increased experience with empirical research in Japan, but above all, thanks to the support of Professor Fujimoto at Tokyo University.[61] Moreover, another four interviews were made at Toyota during a second research period, in late 1994.

Apart from the above case studies, data collection has been done at many other Japanese companies, the most important of which are Hitachi, Mitsubishi Research Institute, Mitsui and Co., NEC, NHK, Nippon Steel, Nissan Motor, NKK, NTT, Onex, TDK Corporation, Toshiba, Sharp, Toray and Tsukuba Research Consortium. The research was in most of these cases only of exploratory nature and not aiming at any in-depth studies. Rather, the goal was to gain broader sight and experience of Japanese T&I management. At an early stage, some interviews were also pursued at Western consulting companies, located in Tokyo: The Boston Consulting Group, Gemini Consulting, McKinsey and Co. and Siar Bossard K.K. The multicultural frame of reference of these companies enabled them to distinguish sharply Japan's managerial peculiarities which provided a valuable introduction to further research.

In addition, various expert interviews and discussions were made with university professors, i.e. Fujimoto, Hirasawa, Kodama and Nanao at Tokyo University, Nannichi, Odagiri and Teramoto at the University of Tsukuba, Nishizawa at Tohoku University, Kusunoki and Nonaka at Hitotsubashi University and Yamanouchi at Yokohama National University.

Thanks to meetings organized by associations of researchers to which this author belonged: Swedish Researchers in Japan, STAG (British association of researchers) and NEST (Network of European Scientists and Technologists in Japan), interviews with researchers at both governmental and corporate research laboratories were possible, focusing on interaction between governmental- and corporate research.

In all, approximately 150 interviews were conducted but, most important of all, a one-year invitation as a visiting researcher to Sophia University in Tokyo made possible a large number of classes, seminars and endless discussions with professors Abegglen, Gregory and Yawata for which this author is extremely grateful.

Summarized Contents of the Study

There are few guidelines on how to evaluate theory-building research using case studies. The ultimate goal, to arrive at clearly defined propositions on how the vital interlinkages of R&D processes are managed in three innovative Japanese companies, is however clear. In order to facilitate reading and hopefully also the understanding of the book, the outline is rather sequential compared to the actual research process.

In Chapter 2, traditional regional differences between Japan and the West will be outlined, so as to develop a clearer picture of Japanese T&I management and its possible peculiarities.

Second, an exploration of theories on R&D management and innovation will highlight the activities that are considered to be most important, and the dilemmas that arise in this context.

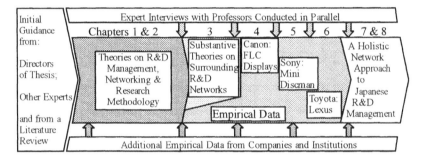

Figure 1.2   Building Blocks of the Study

In the third chapter, the locational context of technology management outside the black box will be explored. External sources of invention that surround and support Japanese companies will be located in surrounding R&D networks. Finally, the three companies will be positioned in these networks and their technology linkages to corporate R&D activities will be outlined.

Chapters 4, 5 and 6 will be entirely devoted to empirical confrontation, presented in the form of three in-depth case studies. In a 'microcosmic' perspective, organization and management of R&D and innovation at the corporate level will be explored, with a focus on how the linkages identified in Chapter 2 are organized and managed. Finally, when a detailed view of the organizational context is outlined, the description of three specific R&D projects will explore the dynamics of the previously defined networks.

In Chapter 7, similarities and differences between the cases will be examined in a cross-case analysis, following the theoretical framework outlined in Chapter 2.

Finally, Chapter 8 will summarize how the case-study companies arrive at circumventing the dilemmas of innovation, and what we can learn from this. It will be proposed that there are few cases in which it makes competitive sense for large companies to pursue invention in-house. In most cases it is faster and more efficient to develop the necessary know-who skills to acquire externally generated inventions as well as the know-how required to transform these inventions into commercialized innovations.

NOTES

1. Bartlett and Ghoshal (1989, 63); Nevens *et al.* (1990); Stalk *et al.* (1992); Wheelwright and Clark (1992, 70).
2. Aoki (1988, 246); De Woot (1990, 39, 45, 144); Evan and Olk (1990, 40); Gerybadze (1993); Hagedoorn and Schakenraad (1994); Hollomon (1982, 617-618); Kenney and Florida (1993, 70); Nester (1990, 293).
3. De Woot (1990, 154); Giersch (1992, 58); Leontiades (1991, 49); Murakami and Nishiwaki (1991, 44); Nester (1990, 290); Sigurdson and Anderson (1991, 247); Tselichtchev (1994); Vogel (1979, 23).
4. Clark and Fujimoto (1989, 49); De Woot (1990, 101); Karlsson (1989, 33); Takeuchi and Nonaka (1986, 140, 144).
5. Kennard (1991, 186); Nichiguchi (1994); Smothers (1990, 523); Walker (1991, 279).
6. Cf. Hedlund and Nonaka (1991, 13); McKelvey (1993, 209); Turnbull *et al.* (1992, 165); Whitley (1990, 53); Waldenberger (1992, 276); Quinn (1992, 49-50); Teramoto *et al.* (1993, 65).
7. Smothers (1990, 523); Takeuchi and Nonaka (1986, 137-41); Walker (1991, 279).
8. In the aforementioned literature review, this is above all claimed by Nonaka (1991, 96-104), but also by Ealey and Soderberg (1990, 8) and Hedlund and Nonaka (1991, 34).
9. Karlsson (1989, 37); Nonaka (1991, 98-102).
10. Adler, Riggs and Wheelwright (1989, 9); Aoki (1988, 243, 246); Schütte (1991, 266); Smothers (1990, 526).
11. Adler (1991, 47); Gregory (1985b); Karlsson (1989, 36); Kennard (1991, 187); Kobayashi (1990, 269); McKelvey (1993, 202); Nonaka (1991, 97); Saha (1992, 5); Schütte (1991, 268).
12. Kindel (1994); Lindsay (1994) and various *Company news* reports.
13. Keynote lecture held on May 30, 1994, at the 24th International Management Symposium (ISC) at the University of St. Gallen.
14. According to discussions (04.04.97) with Mr Wagenstaller and Ms. Welitz, Manager and Deputy Manager of the OD-unit at BMW in Munich.
15. Presentation at a workshop of the European Institute of Japanese Studies on: 'Corporate Technology Strategies in Japan', August 17-19, 1994.
16. According to interviews conducted by a research assistant, Reine Wasner, with Corporate communications manager K. Dahlgren of HP.
17. Discussion at the ISC (01.06.94).
18. The changing situation of Japan is well captured by Arthur (1993) in the *New Scientist's* special issue on Japan, 2 October 1993.
19. The description of Toshiba Computers is based on a half-day visit to the premises in Ome, a rather official company presentation and personal interviews with the Chief Technology Officer (overall R&D manager) and with four engineers, one of whom is anonymous.
20. A detailed discussion of Toshiba's increased emphasis on group-wide management is made by Teramoto *et al.* (1993, 66-77).
21. For a detailed discussion on some of Toshiba's 1,900 interorganizational connections, see Fruin (1992).
22. In 1990, Toshiba had 30 software-related spun-off subsidiaries and close links to another 40 non-Toshiba spin-offs (Kenney and Florida 1993, 80).
23. *Computerworld*, (June 1994, p. 40); *Japan Industrial Journal*, (23.10.96, p. 1.); *Semiconductor Industry and Business Survey* (22.4.96)
24. Quoted in Business Wire, June 6, 1995

25. *Electronic Buyer's News* (26.5.97); *The Financial Times* (20.10.95).
26. Nikkei Weekly (23.10.96).
27. Stated in Reuters News Service (August 29, 1995.)
28. Stated in Business Wire (November 13, 1995).
29. Laage-Hellman (1997) provides an extremely detailed description of this technology development.
30. Stated by Dr Takayanagi, CTO of Toshiba, at a workshop of the European Institute of Japanese Studies on: 'Corporate Technology Strategies in Japan', August 17-19, 1994.
31. It convenes to add that in the Fifth Generation Computer Project, organized by MITI, Toshiba was assigned the task of developing Local Area Networks and related general-purpose parallel computers. Source: Tatsuno (1990, 170).
32. Instead of Computer Integrated Manufacturing, the traditional meaning of CIM.
33. *Kinyu shudan*, or *kinyu keiretsu*, is sometimes referred to as financial, or horizontal group. During a visit to Mitsui Busan, the trading company of the Mitsui Group, the author noticed that all mainframe computers and nearly all lap-top computers were from Toshiba.
34. Indexing total development lead-time at 100 in 1987, Toshiba was down at 52 in 1990. In the same period of time, stocks were reduced to 42% of those in 1987 (Maeda, interview).
35. Sigurdson and Anderson (1991, 140-62) unfortunately only devote one chapter to corporate R&D in their otherwise detailed description of science and technology in Japan.
36. Takahiro Fujimoto, Professor at Tokyo University, Faculty of Economics. See also Womack *et al*. (1990, 137)
37. Nishisawa; Sunaga; Mayuzumi; Nannichi, interviews. See also Murakami and Nishiwaki (1991).
38. See, for example, Fransman's (1990) description of how the Japanese government (MITI) aided the computer industry, while maintaining strong competition between the participating firms.
39. See, for example, Fujimoto (1989, 143) and Schütte (1991, 266).
40. The 'traditional' definition of R&D – as proposed by the American National Science Foundation – includes basic and applied research and design and development of prototypes and processes, but excludes quality control, product testing and marketing activities (Mansfield 1971, 39; cf. Betz 1987, 50; Wheelwright and Clark 1992, 74).
41. The term refers to its use by economists, who have long treated technological phenomena as events transpiring inside a 'black box' (Rosenberg 1982, vii).
42. Similarly, of NEC's 5,000 technicians who are directly or indirectly involved in R&D, 90% work directly in the factories Ballon (1992, 73-4); cf. Aoki (1988, 237); Gregory (1985b, 29-30).
43. See also Betz (1987, 53) and Kenney and Florida (1993, 66-9) for similar discussions.
44. See, for example, Abegglen and Stalk (1985); Tatsuno (1990); Whitley (1990; 1992).
45. Håkansson (1987, 87) raises this criticism against previous research regarding R&D processes with a too narrow focus. Instead, he claims that collaboration in networks is an essential factor in corporate technical development, for which a broader network perspective is necessary (1989, 35).
46. See, for examples, Fruin (1992); Gregory (1985a); Imai (1989a); Imai and Baba (1991); Perrow (1993).
47. Fransman (1990); McKelvey (1993, 216); Orru (1993, 186); Whitley (1990, 56, 67).
48. See De Meyer (1992); Håkansson (1987; 1989); Laage-Hellman (1989); Laage-Hellman and Nonaka (1994); Rappa and Debackere (1989) for similar discussions. Krackhardt and Hanson (1993) stress the importance of informal networks at the intracorporate level.
49. Cf. 'mutuality', as stated by Ford *et al*. (1986).
50. See also Håkansson and Henders (1992); Imai and Baba (1991).
51. For a detailed review on the concept of coordination, see Larsson (1990).
52. Cf. Jansson *et al*. (1990); and Schön (1982).
53. In his development of a new approach to technology forecasting, Gerybadze (1994) proposes that actors in corporations or in intercorporate networks establish patterns of specialization and complementarity, thus forming competitive differentiation.
54. NHK, Japan's national television company, has played an important role in, *inter alia*, Sony's development of the Betamax technology. Similarly, Canon's development of laser printers was

initiated through joint research with NHK. It was Canon's successful acquisition and application of laser-beam technology that prompted NTT, Japan's national telecommunication company, to invite Canon as a co-developer of ultra-high-speed facsimile equipment (Isobe; Nishisawa; Nosuo, interviews).

55. By completing formal company interviews with less formal ones, *inter alia*, over a few beers or at cocktail parties, additional data could be gathered.

56. The wish of some interviewees to remain anonymous has been fully respected. That they are coded by A, B, C and so forth, simply serves the purpose of enabling a control by Directors of Thesis.

57. In the course of empirical studies at Canon Inc., beginning in October 1992 and ending in July 1993, the author was confronted with three reorganizations and four different organization charts.

58. The Revealed Technology Advantage Index indicates a country's relative share of patents in the different industrial sectors (IVA 1993, 30).

59. A large number of statements support the belief that Canon and Sony may be among the world's fastest innovators. At Sony, this seems to be particularly true for the portable audio products line. See, for example, Deschamps and Nayak (1992; 1995); Parsons (1991, 12); and Schlender (1992, 22). Itami (1987, 102) states that new product development is Sony's core competence.

60. Phone interviews (indicated in parentheses), represent approximately 20% of the total number.

61. By assisting Professor Fujimoto in the preparation of a Harvard Business School case study on Toyota Lexus, the author greatly benefited from a vast pool of data that Professor Fujimoto and a group of his Japanese students had gathered through numerous on-site interviews. Hence, it was possible to focus entirely on the organization and management of R&D in the process of own interviews. Data relating to the Lexus case was thus not gathered directly by the author.

2   Identifying the Dilemmas of Innovation

> Due to our different cultural backgrounds, we are better at working with tangible hardware, especially in production, whereas Western researchers are better at software and making inventions. To make up for our weakness, we need to maintain close links to Western friends. (Kikuchi, interview)

With even the largest and technically strongest firms finding themselves unable to control their technical destinies in significant techno-market domains, many firms turn to external sourcing strategies.[1] Some of the factors contributing to this trend include:

1.   the growth in cross-technology and field interdisciplinarity,
2.   the globalization of technology and proliferation of sources, and
3.   the necessity for rapid commercialization.

A yet undiscovered, but critical rationale for outsourcing specialized R&D is that two fundamental dilemmas of innovation limit seriously the efficacy of internal technological development:

- The dilemma of technological leadership is that successful pursuit of such tends to focus firms on intracorporate activities. This decreases their sensitivity and responsiveness to external technological and market factors that ought to guide product development. Moreover, the rigidity of typical technology problem-solving processes impedes cross-departmental collaboration and technology fusion, which are vital enablers for radical innovation.
- The organizational dilemma of innovation is that the creative development of inventive technologies appears to require a small and organic organizational structure, whereas rapid innovation, in contrast, calls for large and stable organizations. Companies trying to achieve both creative invention and rapid innovation are most likely to be caught in this dilemma.

In this chapter, the purposeful circumvention of these two dilemmas is offered as a theoretical rationale to the short lead-times and the high R&D efficiency of the case-study companies.

An initial comparative analysis will shed some light on traditional[2] regional differences in the management of R&D and product innovation. The next section examines whether existing universal R&D theories support the linkages which appear to be vital in the management of Technology and Innovation in Japan and provide critical input to the development of the dilemmas of innovation. The dilemmas also complete a theoretical framework for Japanese T&I management that will guide the case analysis in Chapter 7.

CRYSTALLIZING THE PICTURE OF JAPANESE T&I MANAGEMENT

The Japanese are rather seeking to gain knowledge and new competence; in addition, they are trying to create a meaningful pattern composed of a multitude of alliances. American companies, in contrast, rather concentrate on fast and immediate results, look primarily for new outlets for their core skills, and show a strong tendency for unbundling rather than bundling capabilities. (Brauchlin 1988, 203)

In the 'japanization' of Rover through the partnership with Honda, Walker (1991) registers a radically increased use of suppliers who, with earlier involvement, greater responsibility and stronger links to manufacturing operations, take on broader responsibility for the vehicles, and stronger interlinkages at the corporate level through cross-functional teamwork. In this sub-chapter, a systematic picture and rationale of these traditional differences is developed.

For the purpose of clarity, comparative studies usually call for generalizations which may or may not correspond to reality. By mainly limiting the comparative perspective to the automobile industry, too broad generalizations are kept at bay.

Differences in Lead-time and R&D Productivity

Lead-time is a measure of how quickly a company can move from concept to market. In his DBA thesis, Fujimoto (1989) concludes that the Japanese volume producers in general enjoy significantly shorter lead-time and engineering hours than their Western counterparts. Unlike engineering hours, lead-time is not merely the sum of the individual activities' lead-times, but depends both on the length of the individual activities and the extent to which work is done in parallel. Most automobile companies around the world follow the four major stages of development (Clark and Fujimoto 1991, 98): concept generation; product planning; product engineering; and process engineering, the creation processes and the critical linkages of which are vital for overall performance. It is the management of these linkages that differs between the companies, mainly in terms of a firm's ability to build channels of communication and attitudes toward co-operation. In Figure 2.1, regional differences in automobile development lead-time are displayed.[3]

US Average in Months

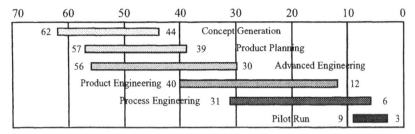

European Average

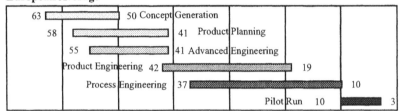

Japanese Average

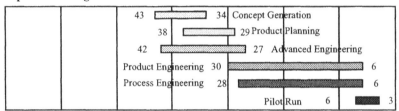

Source: Clark and Fujimoto (1991, 78)

Figure 2.1 Average Project Schedules

To begin with, Japanese companies seem to have radically shorter concept generation and product planning stages than their Western counterparts, but the degree of overlap between these two stages is similar among the regions. Much to the contrary, there is a higher degree of overlap between product and process engineering in Japan than in the West.[4] In American and European companies, process engineering is started respectively nine and five months later than product engineering, whereas Japanese companies begin and end product and process engineering at about the same time.

Recent data suggest that the Japanese lead-time advantage vis-à-vis the US has been eliminated, but that the gap in engineering lead-time remains, i.e., between the beginning of product engineering and the beginning of sales (Fujimoto, 1994a). Hence, US makers have radically shortened concept generation and product planning, but are still behind in speed of product and process engineering. Meanwhile, Japanese manufacturers have made concept and planning lead-time longer, due to a conversion towards luxury-oriented models.

Development productivity indicates the level of resources required to take the project from concept to commercial production. It includes engineering hours, prototype materials and equipment and services used for the project. To develop a $14,000 compact car, Europe's volume producers and high-end specialists would both need 3.0, those in the USA 3.2 and those in Japan 1.7 million engineering hours.[5] In manufacturing productivity, Vogel (1979) identified even greater differences.[6]

The more recent data of Fujimoto (1994a, 20) suggest that the European average of development productivity remains unchanged while the US average has approached that of the Japanese, which reflects a preference for 'leaner' US models and a tendency of 'over-specialized' Japanese models.

Another parameter that may be related to R&D productivity is the number of patents, where Japanese companies rank significantly higher than their Western counterparts in a large number of industries (IVA 1993, 32). The relative advantage seems to be particularly high in three industries: electronic consumer goods; computers and office machinery; and motor vehicles.

Linkages to Extracorporate Actors and Activities

Mansfield (1988) notes that both the lead-time advantage and the cost advantage of Japanese companies, compared to American ones, are significantly greater in projects where innovation is based on external, as opposed to internal, technology. To summarize his extensive study, it seems that Japanese companies are particularly effective and rapid users of external technology.

Stronger academic interlinkages seem to be assured in several ways: by scanning relevant scientific and engineering information in journals; by having researchers actively participate in scientific conferences; by maintaining university ties with professors; and by attending universities overseas.[7] Furthermore, there is an increasing tendency to build new laboratories on foreign university campuses.[8] More than one-third of the corporate funded chairs at the MIT are funded by Japanese companies (Roussel *et al.* 1991, 128).

Strategic alliances for the acquisition of new competence seem to be more frequent among Japanese firms. They focus on learning to a greater extent than Western firms when commissioning research by Western companies or establishing licensing agreements.[9] The Japanese patent law system appears to aim more at sharing technology than protecting it (Spero, 1990).

The cost-effectiveness of the Japanese R&D system is claimed to be higher than that of other countries much thanks to more effective interaction between private industries and government institutes.[10]

Nakatani (1990, 158) argues convincingly that the combination of horizontal and vertical keiretsu networks in Japan provides member firms with 'positive stimuli and incentives to more aggressively undertake innovative activities than might otherwise be the case'. It is certainly true that cross-industrial boundaries are stronger through keiretsu linkages and interpersonal relationships.[11] Kodama (1991; 1992a; 1992b) indicates a shift in the Japanese innovation pattern towards an increasing use of technology fusion, which is largely facilitated through the aforementioned linkages. He notes, for example, that NSG, NEC, SEI and NTT were main actors in a joint effort to develop optical communication technology (1991, 120). The first three companies belong to the same corporate group, the Sumitomo group, and NTT is the most important customer of these companies.

The relatively stronger linkages to suppliers appear to constitute the perhaps most important isolated rationale of Japan's development lead-time advantage.[12] Japanese automobile suppliers do four times more engineering work for a typical project than US suppliers and two times more than European suppliers. Thanks to the highest supplier participation in the world, an average of 85% of production costs are often located outside the enterprise.

Moreover, it is argued that the organizational structure of subcontractors displays a reduction of transaction costs equal or superior to vertically-integrated in-house production arrangements, notwithstanding a low number of employees. With 58,000 employees, BMW is a rather small automobile manufacturer by German standards. Still, Mazda and its mere 28,000 workers posted nearly 30% higher sales figures than BMW in 1988.[13]

On average, Japanese 'lean' producers only deal directly with 300 to 350 suppliers, whereas most Western counterparts, as of 1990, had to deal directly with an average of 1,000 to 1,500 suppliers.[14] Information flows are denser through frequent interaction and some sharing of personnel. Far greater responsibility for detailed design and engineering is given to key suppliers in Japan.[15] Lamming (1993) stresses that the main difference in terms of Japanese and Western vertical integration is that the Japanese system maintains a dynamic tension between customers and suppliers, notwithstanding strong elements of co-operation.

Suppliers' proprietary parts are standard products sold to the assembler through a catalogue, where the supplier assures the whole development process from concept to manufacturing.

When developmental work is shared between assembler and supplier, the result is black box parts.[16] The contribution of the assembler is then restricted to cost/performance requirements, exterior shapes, interface details and other basic design information based on the total vehicle planning and layout.

Detail controlled parts is a third system in which most of the component engineering work, including parts drawing, is done in-house. Only process engineering and production is taken care of by the suppliers, selected through inquiries and bids.

As depicted in Figure 2.2, an average Japanese project relies more heavily on black box parts, the average US project on detail-controlled parts and European projects somewhere in the middle.[17]

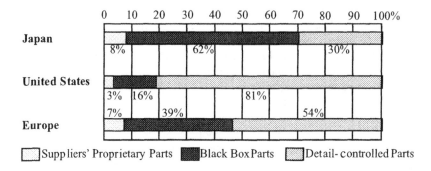

Source: Clark and Fujimoto (1991, 145)

Figure 2.2   Types of Parts Produced by Suppliers

The percentage of newly designed parts in an average vehicle project is 82% in Japan, 71% in Europe and 62% in the US. It is claimed that Japanese auto makers can rely on supplier engineering without jeopardizing their edge in conformance quality and lead-time thanks to the higher supplier engineering capabilities and tighter assembler–supplier coordination. Consequently, Japanese assemblers can devote more of their engineering resources to new component designs. The situation in the US is quite the opposite. As engineering work mainly has been done within the assemblers, the use of common parts has been the only way of limiting scope.[18]

In summary, Japanese companies seem to enjoy a multitude of linkages to extracorporate actors through complex industrial networks. Boundaries are set through demands for communication and interaction, rather than through ownership and company names. Studies made so far mainly deal with competitiveness in general terms. A few of them mention extracorporate actors in the context of R&D and new product development, but no study has, to this author's knowledge, systematically traced the linkages to extracorporate actors in these surrounding networks, or examined through what mechanisms they are related to corporate R&D activities.

This author believes that these networks are vital both to development lead-time and to R&D productivity, as a consequence of which a more detailed analysis will follow in the exploration of surrounding R&D networks in Chapter 3.

Linkages to external sources of invention will not generate innovation on their own. Regardless of whether an invention is acquired or internally developed, interlinkages at the corporate level seem necessary to mobilize it through research, development and production. Also, unless market needs are carefully considered, commercialization may not succeed. The lack of communication seems to prevent these interlinkages from being activated in many Western firms,[19] which, according to Rosenberg and Servo (1991), frequently suffer from three different communication gaps: one between the idea generator and those who can mobilize the resources that are necessary to realize the idea; a second when top management fails to communicate a clear mission of the corporate activities to subordinates; and finally, the physical separation and differences in jargon between actors in research, development, marketing, manufacturing and administration constitute a third communication gap.[20]

Beginning with market needs, let us turn to the task of exploring possible differences in the management of intracorporate linkages.

Interlinking Market Needs

In the comparative automobile studies, Japanese designers, production engineers and project leaders alike seem to pay strong attention to meeting customer needs.[21] In contrast, this link is said to be rather weak within Western manufacturers.

Bartlett and Ghoshal (1989) describe how Matsushita employs an internal market mechanism to ensure that research activities correspond to market needs. A further exploration of how this mechanism is managed appears to be necessary.

Experimental commercialization as a means to accelerate technological improvements is said to be frequently used among Japanese companies (Itami 1987). This activity allows feedback links both from production and from the market to be activated at an earlier stage of the innovation process.

The existing literature indicates a few mechanisms to interlink market needs and R&D, but a deeper and more systematic understanding of how they are managed is necessary.

Interlinking Production

The degree of integration of manufacturing seems to be another important reason for lead-time differences in the automobile industry. In the Japanese automobile industry, this integration is frequently achieved by putting prototype production at the centre of the development process, where it can both verify design and reveal problems to be solved before commercial production. Design, product and process engineers all seem to gather in the so-called war room,[22] instead of throwing blueprints over the wall that often appears to separate design from production in Western companies (Clark and Fujimoto 1991, 208-14).

Production suppliers are involved at an earlier stage of the innovation process to build prototype parts and knowledge-sharing communication between prototype engineering and production is more intense.[23]

European high-end producers have a more 'perfectionist' approach. To them, a high-quality prototype is one that entirely conforms to drawings and that captures the design intent so that highly-skilled test engineers can discern how well the design performs. The resulting engineering prototype is a 'master model' to be copied by the production model, as opposed to the Japanese 'early problem detector'.

Information moves less quickly between design engineering and the prototype unit in US firms, which also suffer from a lack of scheduling discipline at prototype parts suppliers and in engineering drawing release. They usually have a practice of subjecting design change orders to a series of formal approvals before allowing them to reach the prototype shop floor (Clark and Fujimoto 1991, 177).

As depicted in Figure 2.1, the Japanese product- and process engineering phases are more overlapped than those of Western manufacturers. Above all, this seems to be made possible through collocation of product and process engineers.[24] Kenney and Florida (1993, 61) note that, in a historical perspective, Japanese R&D engineers

> were not distinctly separated into the artificial categories of science and engineering favoured by Western industry. In effect, no rigid caste system emerged to separate the R&D laboratory from the factory.

Pilot runs ensure the link between the prototype and its production line. The usual characteristics among Japanese projects are relatively short pilot runs with compressed pilot run periods, often carried out on commercial production assembly lines.

US and European firms tend to locate pilot production in a separate facility which lengthens the problem-solving cycle and complicates knowledge transfer to commercial production. Figure 2.3 depicts three different production startup approaches:

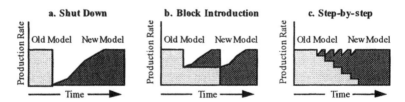

Source: Clark and Fujimoto (1991, 193)

Figure 2.3   Production Startup Approaches

For the production startup of a new model, US and European manufacturers favour the shut-down model (a), which is a relatively simple approach avoiding mixed-model production but risking some production loss. Japanese manufacturers practise a more incremental block introduction (b), or step-by-step introduction (c), which allows a smooth transition and no production losses, but require continuous adjustments in material handling, work assignments and scheduling. This approach is possible as problem-solving on the Japanese shop floor involves experienced supervisors, line workers, technicians and engineers, all of whom are needed and included also in real time production, thus merging process development and volume production during ramp-up. Their so called 'war-time approach' contrasts sharply with that common in Western companies, employing isolated ramp-up teams assigned on a temporary basis. Similarly, Japanese companies have a more incremental 'kaizen-approach' to innovation, as opposed to a Western 'breakthrough-approach'.[25]

Design constitutes a link between product concept and detailed engineering. Regional differences are such that US design departments tend to reflect a higher degree of differentiation between engineers and designers.[26]

In Europe, a tradition of Bauhaus philosophy (form follows function) promoted closer relationships between design and engineering. As a result, European engineers and designers work more closely together.

In Japan, design is a fully integrated function, treated like any other engineering department.

Intraorganizational Link-building

Departmentalization is amplified by a strong education-related hierarchy in Western automobile industries, where specialization by process step, e.g., basic design, drafting, testing, and analysis) is common. This kind of specialization is not common in Japan, where engineers and technicians, regardless of education level, begin with drafting and gradually shift to piece-part and sub-assembly design. Consequently, errors in detailed drawings can be detected earlier, thanks to the broader knowledge base of the cross-trained engineers. Moreover, Japanese organizational structures are said to be simpler and flatter.[27]

Perhaps as a consequence of having cross-trained engineers in flatter organizations, the capacity for sharing and mobilizing resources quickly within the corporation seems to be higher in Japan. Prahalad and Hamel (1990) argue that, in comparison to many Western companies, Canon, NEC and Honda have had a lesser stock of people and technologies that constitute core competencies,[28] but could move them much more quickly from one strategic business unit (SBU) to another.

Project Leadership

American project managers seem to devote considerable effort to coordinating large numbers of engineers, most of whom have narrow assignments. It is also claimed that they – in contrast to the Japanese approach – frequently pay insufficient attention to the complementarity of skills among the project members (Roussel *et al.* 1991, 170).

Project managers of European firms are typically regarded as neutral coordinators, being low in rank and having little informal power. They work on someone else's product plan instead of being in charge of it, and spend more time doing paperwork.

Contrarily, Japanese project managers usually rank as high as division managers and exercise strong informal leadership. They coordinate entire projects including production and marketing and have, if necessary, direct influence on working engineers. Through their strong power and status, they can mobilize all the resources necessary to design and develop a car and defend the project against interference from top management.[29]

It seems that very challenging targets either are induced by top management, or emerge within the team. They usually seem to begin as overall visions that involve contradictions in terms of opposing views or technological limitations, which make them hard to reach.[30] The initial visions are often equivocal and gradually disintegrated into more tangible tasks and goals.[31] The Lexus case in Chapter 6 will illustrate how visions are used in practice.

Cross-functional teams with full-time members have been described by a large number of authors,[32] and seem to constitute a very direct way of interlinking functions and divisions beyond the scope of the automobile industry as well.[33] The teams are said to be quite self-organizing, autonomous and assure overlapping development phases in a rugby-approach[34] where engineers follow the project across its overlapping phases, thus assuring that generated knowledge is incorporated into the project until it turns into a manufactured product. A tradition of frequent interaction between divisions and, perhaps more important still, across corporate borders are factors that seem to promote parallel development in Japanese R&D projects.[35]

Sharing of information through open communication is well reported.[36] It may partly lay the ground for the greater degree of overlap in R&D projects. It is usually argued that information-sharing activities take place in an environment of creative chaos with little managerial hierarchies and formalism.[37]

In contrast to supposedly flat organizations with little hierarchy, some authors describe Japanese organizations as 'archetypes of hierarchically layered functional organizations' (Deschamps and Nayak 1992, 49). The paradoxical coexistence of hierarchy and its opposite, 'heterarchy' (Hedlund, 1986), is an issue to which more attention will be devoted later on in this chapter.

Crystallizing a Preliminary Model

Figure 2.4 below summarizes the main differences which provide a preliminary model of Japanese T&I management.

It appears that the most critical organizational and managerial differences between Japan and the West relate to interlinkages and their coordination both within and between corporations, in particular between the activities of marketing, research, design, product engineering, prototype production and process engineering. Job rotation seems to be vital in assuring these interlinkages.[38] In the industries that are relevant to this study, rotation seems to be most common between marketing and sales functions, R&D and production.[39] The perhaps most cited company in this context is Honda.[40] Still, little detail is provided on how this job rotation is managed.

Figure 2.4   A Preliminary Model of Japanese T&I Management

The project leader is said to be the key coordinator of most actors, activities and resources, but it is difficult to find any description of organizational mechanisms that serve the purpose of coordinating R&D activities.[41]

Empirical studies at Canon, Sony and Toyota aim to fill these gaps but, before that, a brief review of theories on R&D and innovation will provide support for the previously identified linkages.

UNIVERSAL THEORIES ON R&D AND INNOVATION

Many Western authors, identified and more thoroughly discussed in a previously conducted literature digest (Harryson 1992), agree that innovation is a corporation-wide task, heavily dependent upon cross-departmental communication and smooth co-operation.[42] Frequent personal interaction in combination with a strong corporate vision is usually proposed as the best solution.[43]

These factors all seem to be derived from (or at least successfully applied in) Japanese practices, but no model has yet been conceptualized that encompasses the vital linkages of Japanese T&I management.

Interlinking Extracorporate Sources of Technology

In the development of the theoretical perspective in Chapter 1, we find ample support for the use of extracorporate sources of technology in the management of R&D. Accordingly, Mansfield (1971) argues that corporate technological change, i.e., innovation, is influenced *inter alia* by the kind of interdependence among industries: supply factors; the way in which scientific and technological activities of relevant governmental actors is performed; and the amount and character of R&D carried out in domestic and overseas universities.

We may consequently regard boundary-spanning as an important part of R&D management for the scanning and possible acquisition of new technology and technological capabilities, an argument supported by many authors[44] and an important building block of our model for Japanese T&I management.[45]

Interlinking R&D and Market Needs

Innovation can be generated in different ways: market pull signifies that new ideas in markets for services and goods seek new technology; technology push is when new ideas in technology seek applications. Addressing the question whether it is market needs or technological advances that initiate innovation, Freeman (1982) concludes that any theory on innovation must take both factors into account, with which Von Hippel (1982) agrees. Later, he proposes (1988) a customer-driven paradigm of innovation, in which he regards innovation as at least as much a product of co-operative linkages between inventors and users of technologies as of corporate R&D laboratories. Similarly, Quinn (1992, 170) argues for the use of 'knowledge-building feedback loops', which bring detailed customer information back to the core of corporate activities.

A large number of authors agree that strong links between market needs and technological opportunities are necessary for innovation,[46] which in most cases is market-derived.[47] A challenging key to innovation seems to be the capability to combine information flows deriving both from science and from the market.

Interlinking R&D and Production

With arguments, similar to those above, that different forms of feedback constitute an inherent part of the innovation process, Kline and Rosenberg (1986) propose a chain-linked model of innovation. Their model covers the interlinkage of production, a factor that also is argued for in some publications in the field.[48] However, this link from research back to the innovation process is often considered as problematic and rare. It thus appears to be particularly important to explore how this link is maintained in the case-study companies.

Technology Fusion as a Key Capability in T&I Management

According to Kline and Rosenberg (1986, 292), input from science 'is not usually the initiating step', but may be called on along the central chain of innovation. As they see it, a more common initiator of the central chain of innovation is 'analytic design', which:

> consists of analysis of various arrangements of existing components or of modifications

of designs already within the state of the art to accomplish new tasks or to accomplish old tasks more effectively or at lower cost. (*Ibid.*, 292)

In similar terms, Rosenberg (1982) stated a few years earlier that invention rarely functions in isolation, but rather depends on complementary technologies and their availability. Betz (1987, 7) defines systems innovations quite similarly: 'Systems innovations create a new functionality by assembling parts in new ways'. That innovation is increasingly based upon combination has also been noticed by Klein *et al.* (1991). As shall be demonstrated through the case studies, the capability to organize for analytic design, or technology fusion, is critical for successful T&I management.[49]

Kline and Rosenberg (1986, 295-305) hold that far more rapid and reliable innovations are possible when the underlying knowledge allows accurate predictions. In the process of reviewing relevant literature, a frequently recurring point is, in effect, that the management of R&D processes to a large extent consists of uncertainty reduction. Hence, it seems that the willingness to take risks and the possibility of reducing them often decides whether, or at what speed, a company is going to innovate.

Managing Uncertainty Reduction

There are three types of uncertainty in R&D (Itami 1987): discovery does not always result from technology development efforts; markets do not always accept products from new technologies; and newly developed technologies can become obsolete.

Several ways of uncertainty reduction are proposed in theory. The use of parallel R&D efforts is one of them, but this of course requires more resources and perhaps also more time.[50]

Although R&D can provide information on technical information and market research can provide information on the need of an invention, Mansfield (1971, 74) argues that 'there are many areas of uncertainty which can be resolved only by *actual production and marketing of the invention*', which also may bring the advantage of being first on the market, thus pre-empting market share. Clearly, Mansfield was a forerunner in delineating the experimental commercialization, mentioned earlier on, which seems to reduce uncertainty in technology development by providing valuable feedback links at a stage where adjustments still can be made more easily (Itami, 1987).

This establishment of co-operative links to extracorporate actors is another way of reducing uncertainty, as this spreads risks and costs over several firms.[51] Key linkages are depicted in Figure 2.5.

In summary, this section has provided theoretical support to those linkages that appear to be strong in successful Japanese T&I management: gaining and exchanging competencies with extracorporate sources of invention that participate in the innovation process; linking development efforts to market needs; and, finally, managing the link from research, via development, to manufacturing. The link from research back to the corporate development process of analytic design, however, seems to be particularly complicated. In the remaining sections of this chapter, the interrelatedness of research and development and the pros and cons of their interlinkage will be examined.

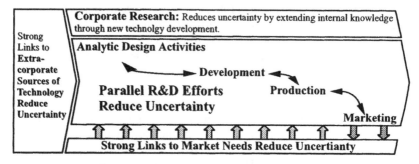

Figure 2.5   Managing R&D to Reduce Uncertainty

Experience has shown that when uncertainty is high in technologically complex products, the Schumpeterian forerunner usually experiences numerous difficulties to iron out, whereas the rapid imitator, who stands back and learns from the mistakes of the pioneer, may experience great commercial success. Technological leaders actually run the risk of merely delineating a new market to be captured by a technology-follower with stronger marketing and production capabilities.[52] Hence, as an epilogue of this section, the following question may be raised.

IS TECHNOLOGICAL LEADERSHIP A COMPETITIVE WEAPON?

> From the point of view of the individual large firm, it is often wise to leave the pioneering to others and to stick to less far-reaching research and development. Whether this is wise from the point of view of society is a different and more difficult question. (Mansfield 1971, 68)

Addressing the issue of whether technological leadership is vital to commercial success, Prahalad and Hamel (1990, 87) may be inclined to hesitate. In effect, they state that 'by sheer weight of investment, a company might be able to beat its rivals to blue-sky technologies yet still lose the race to build core competence leadership'. Similarly, Kline *et al.* (1991, 5) note that 'there are plenty of companies with world class skills in particular areas but poor records in innovation'. Kline and Rosenberg (1986, 288) even state that 'the notion that innovation is initiated by research is wrong most of the time'. Today's widespread expertise and speed of information make it much more difficult for a company to build competitive advantage solely on the basis of a unique technology. 'Patent issues notwithstanding, other firms can either duplicate a technology or find alternative means to achieve similar results' (Clark and Fujimoto 1991, 4). In 1995 – a decade after most US-based (technologically leading) semiconductor companies gave up on DRAM production – Hitachi and Toshiba flooded the market with 64-Mbit DRAMS, both co-designed with American partners, TI and IBM. Although US automobile manufacturers have spent more on R&D, their Japanese counterparts have brought more patented innovations to market (Womack *et al.* 1990, 133).

These statements suggest that technological leaders are not necessarily the fastest and most competitive companies in the innovation race.

In most cases, technology is a kind of knowledge. In a world of instant transmission of knowledge, a superior technological edge, *per se*, will not guarantee success, as it hardly matters whether the discovery occurs in Cambridge, England, or Cambridge, Massachusetts; it is equally available in Tokyo, Silicon Valley or Cologne.[53] Hence, due to the intractability of nature and the constant introduction and mitigation of new competing knowledge, it seems clear that inputs and outputs are not well correlated in the process of innovation. Intracorporate technological leadership is no longer a *sine qua non* for superior intracorporate knowledge creation, nor for innovation.

If we accept the idea that the central issue of competition is not invention, but innovation, then basic research may lose some importance in the competition between nations or firms, whereas the development of marketable products and usable processes provides the stronger competitive weapon. Consequently, speed and effectiveness in acquiring and applying knowledge to products and processes play major strategic roles in a company's T&I management. Successful innovation seems to rest on co-operative networks rather than on individual technological leadership, which on its own may even impede radical innovation, an argument that will be theoretically motivated below in the development of two dilemmas of innovation.

THE DILEMMA OF TECHNOLOGICAL LEADERSHIP

> By watching the master and emulating his effort in the presence of his example, the apprentice learns unconciously, picks up the rules of the art, including those which are not explicitly known to the master himself. These hidden rules can be assimilated only by a person who surrenders himself uncritically to the imitation of another. (Polyani 1948, 53)

Rather than being confined to a research laboratory or to a few firms, Mansfield (1971, 82) regards innovation as a learning process that takes place among a considerable number of users and producers. The improvements that emerge from this learning process may be almost as important as the new idea itself. Accordingly, Badaracco (1991, 109) argues that 'in order for two organizations to learn, create, or strengthen specialized capabilities, personnel from each must work closely together'. He further states that, at bottom, managing knowledge links is a process of learning, creating, sharing, and controlling knowledge. Allen (1977, 43) adds that 'the best way to transfer technical information is to move a human carrier'.

It seems to be widely accepted that innovation is based more upon personal interaction, emulation and joint learning among a variety of actors, than upon the upstream technology development process. In fact, it seems that technology development, or the invention of new technologies, is in a symbiotic relationship with product development and sometimes impedes it.[54] Kusunoki (1992) suggests that there is a mechanism embedded in the problem-solving process of a technological leader, which paradoxically impedes radical innovation. Let us turn to the task of exploring this mechanism.

Product development can be seen as an activity that transforms technological knowledge into a product with a concrete form by selecting, applying and integrating technological knowledge, which derives from technology development. Conversely, the process of product development may cause a need to develop a new technology. Hence, the two processes are interdependent, as depicted in Figure 2.6 (cf. Kusunoki 1992, 65).

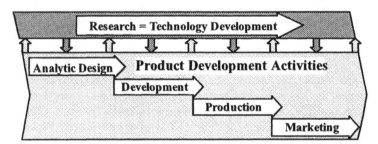

Figure 2.6   Technology and Product Development as Interdependent Processes

Both product development and technology development can be described as a series of problem-solving cycles (cf. Von Hippel, 1982), but display considerable differences, which will be outlined below.

Problem-solving in Technology Development

As illustrated in Figure 2.7, problem-solving in technology development is normally started by defining a general problem. The goal is then to give specific solutions in terms of technologies to this general problem. As the distance normally is great between the general problem and the still unknown final solution, the problem-solving has to be done step-by-step, by repeatedly redefining or identifying more specified sub-problems. The result is a hierarchically progressing problem-solving process which requires more steps the more complex the technological problem (Kusunoki 1992, 67). The know-how deployed in this process has normally been generated in previous and perhaps similar problem-solving. To aim for a radical, new, solution means destroying, or at least neglecting, part of the accumulated technological knowledge. This ultimately requires the researchers involved to unlearn old knowledge, which tends to be more difficult the more specialized and advanced the researchers.

Moreover, as problem-solving in technology is so much based on individual, specialized, knowledge, it is generally insensitive to external influences such as competitive activites or changes in customer needs (cf. Kline and Rosenberg 1986, 300). Accordingly, the further the process advances, the more it becomes irreversible and closed to the factors that ought to guide it.

Problem-solving in Product Development

Product development also calls for a disintegration of the main-problem into sub-problems at the initial stage. A main difference is, however, that the solutions to these sub-problems are more easily integrated so as to present a final end, or solution, to the main-problem, which also has the advantage of being *tangible*. Hence, it becomes much easier to secure a clear correspondence between the general problem, i.e., the product concept, and the final solution, which is a product. In contrast, solutions become inevitably *intangible* in the case of technology development.

An additional advantage of the product development process is that it has a clearly defined completion-point. Once the initial product concept has been disintegrated to a level at which technological knowledge is available to secure problem-solving, the resulting individual solutions can be integrated into a tangible product. As indicated in Figure 2.7, problem-solving in technology development typically generates yet more problems to solve, without a clear turning-phase for integration to begin. This is why the problem-solving process tends to be more time-consuming and irreversible, the more technology-oriented it is.

Synchronizing Product and Technology Development

The synchronization of product and technology development is necessary for realizing product innovation as it allows developed technologies to be incorporated into products. A dilemma of this synchronization is that the more progress a firm makes in problem-solving of technology development, the more this process becomes dominant in realizing the synchronization. Consequently, the problem-solving in product development becomes subordinate to the increasing technological knowledge. The reasons for this technology dominance are twofold:

First, the more a firm progresses in its pursuit of technological leadership, the more it tends to focus on its intracorporate activities. Consequently, external factors, which normally should indicate future directions of the technological development, are neglected and the process becomes more and more self-driven.

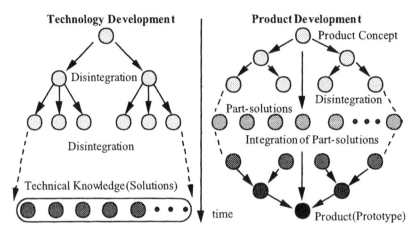

Source: Author's own arrangement of Kusunoki (1992)

Figure 2.7   Technology vs. Product Development

Second, changing the direction of technological development becomes increasingly difficult, the greater the amount of accumulated technological knowledge. 'Through inertia of ideas, dollars, or people, the force of prior commitments may keep the project from changing paths when it should' (Kline and Rosenberg 1986, 298). To the technological leader, it thus appears to be more rational to adjust the problem-solving in product development so as to make the most effective use of the accumulated technological knowledge. In these situations, product development becomes entirely technology-driven and may not even result in innovation.

Moreover, the pursuit of invention and technological leadership requires a very stable and deeply-rooted architecture or architectural stability in its technology problem-solving process.[55] Hence, when a new product development process is initiated, the existing architecture of problem-solving in technology development is transplanted into the process of product development. Consequently, even if a new product concept needs unique and independent disintegration into sub-problems, the stable architecture of technology disintegration is imposed, thus preventing unique and new combinations of technological knowledge. This is why the internal development of deep, specialized technologies also impedes intracorporate linkages of cross-departmental collaboration and technology fusion, which are vital enablers for innovation. The dilemma is depicted in Figure 2.8.

The dilemma implies that new innovative ideas are isolated from the fixed ideas that characterize individuals working for many years on a narrowly specialized field. 'For such individuals it is always easy to find many reasons why an innovative idea won't work', thus developing the Not Invented Here syndrome in the organization (Kline and Rosenberg 1986, 300).

Hence, the problem-solving process of technology development is disconnected from external linkages, the more it progresses towards technological leadership. Similarly, intracorporate linkages to development, production and to market needs decrease with the progress in technology development. Moreover, intracorporate networking and analytic design linkages – that are necessary to fuse existing technologies into new combinations – become weaker.

Strength of Linkages that Enable Innovation

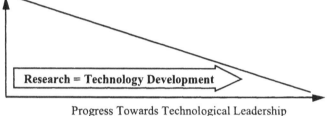

Progress Towards Technological Leadership

Figure 2.8   The Dilemma of Technological Leadership

Unless these vital linkages are established and maintained, the technological leader may lose the very same market that he was first to delineate to rapid technology-followers, who are more open to external influence on their technology development, and better equipped with internal linkages. Both external and internal linkages are also necessary to reduce a second dilemma, related to the organizational needs of innovation.

THE ORGANIZATIONAL DILEMMA OF INNOVATION

The first study to analyse how organizational structures and management systems affect innovation was probably that of Burns and Stalker (1961), who found that a mechanistic management system was appropriate to firms operating in stable conditions, i.e., to incremental innovation. In contrast, an organic system appeared to be more appropriate in an environment of (technological) change. This organic system lacked a clearly defined hierarchy and individual tasks were continuously redefined through interaction with other participants (cf. Bonora and Revang, 1993). Mansfield argues that the independent inventor is more willing to undertake research projects that corporate R&D is not imaginative enough to pursue. In research, the optimal size may thus be fairly small. In contrast, the optimal size of development efforts, ending with production, tends to be larger. The dilemma is further supported by Mansfield's argument that 'when the size of R and D expenditures is held constant, increases in size of firm are associated with decreases in inventive output' (1971, 137-8). Similar findings are discussed both in previous (Mansfield 1968, 43) and more recent publications (Mansfield *et al.* 1977, 85). In this context, Kline and Rosenberg (1986) agree that radical change, or invention, tends to occur in an unbureaucratic, chaotic environment.

It seems to be widely accepted that radical innovations require flexible organizations that are relatively flat in hierarchical levels, informal, and collegial with cosmopolitan researchers who have numerous contacts outside the firm.[56] It is also widely argued that these heterarchical, i.e., non-hierarchical, organizations stimulate the generation and acquisition of new knowledge.[57]

Conversely, rapid processing of an invention towards innovation may call for institutionalized routines in a rather bureaucratic organization with clear hierarchies. Above all, it seems that large, hierarchic and departmentalized organizations are desirable for the production-stage.[58]

Hence, the ideal organization for creative invention seems to be the opposite of the one that yields rapid innovation. Put differently, the organizational needs change from one extreme to another when we move from the upstream stage of the innovation process to the downstream production stage. This is why there is 'a symbiotic relationship between big and small' in innovation processes (Hamel and Prahalad 1994, 271). Figure 2.9 depicts the paradoxical needs of radical innovation.

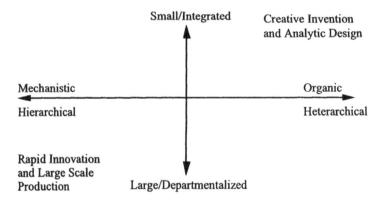

Figure 2.9   The Paradoxical Organizational Needs of Radical Innovation

THE PARADOXICAL NEEDS OF RADICAL INNOVATION

Magnitude of product innovation can be framed along two dimensions: the change of product function and the scope of innovation. The first dimension represents the impact of an innovation on the product's function. The latter indicates the scope, or the extent, to which an innovation covers the functions of the product, i.e., whether it only covers a few elements of a complex product, or if it covers all major elements. Radical and incremental innovation are the counter points along these two dimensions, whereby radical innovation involves both great change of product function and large scope of innovation (Betz, 1987).

In order to achieve a great change in product function, a firm would have to restrain from integrating small, incremental improvements in technology into the product and, instead, set the small improvements aside until their number is great enough to cause an important differential. This, however, causes the dilemma of impeding early market feedback during the development process. This feedback, through experimental commercialization, appeared to be an important way of reducing uncertainty in the previous section.

As for the large scope of impact, a firm would need to coordinate and integrate several different units of technological knowledge into the problem-solving process in product development (through analytic design activities). The aforementioned architectural stability however seems to hamper the integration of highly specialized and closed technology development projects. Consequently, unique and new combinations of technological knowledge seem to be more difficult to obtain in organizations that focus on technological leadership (cf. Kusunoki 1992, 75).

The dilemma of technological leadership also suggests that the product development of a technological leader is subordinate to, and thus synchronized with, its technology development, rather than the opposite. Consequently, external factors, like competitive threats, customer needs and new technologies are neglected and the development process becomes increasingly self-driving, focusing more on the development of a 'great technology' than on innovation.

Radical innovation may call for initial inspiration, which, for example, can be achieved through market linkages or interaction with extracorporate fields of action, as outlined earlier. However, we have also seen that a deep focus on technology development requires specialization, which often causes isolation from the very same linkages, and that this isolation may both cause the NIH syndrome and hamper the possibilities of technology fusion. The organizational dilemma further suggests that creative invention thrives in a small, organic laboratory, wheras rapid production may call for institutionalized routines in a large, bureaucratic organization.

As we have seen earlier, interlinkages at two different levels are of vital im-

portance to T&I management. In the Figure 2.10, it seems imperative to examine how Japanese companies (1) interlink extracorporate sources of
technology and (2) manage to interlink technology- and the product-
development processes. Are there possibilities to circumvent the dilemmas?
How can a company be large, technology-oriented *and* innovative? Paradoxical as it may seem, the coexistence of heterarchy and hierarchy is possibly required to take an R&D project from corporate research to production and
marketing.

The theoretical framework, which will provide a guideline for the case studies and the subsequent cross-case analysis, is based on the following criteria:

1. Linkages to extracorporate sources of technology: which actors are rele-
    vant and how are they interlinked to corporate R&D activities?
2. Interlinking technology and product development:
    How can companies organize for analytic design, i.e., what mechanisms
    allow for fusion of existing resources?
    How are market needs linked to technology and product development
    processes?
    How is the interlinkage of and transfer to production managed?
3. Project management: how are the above linkages established and coordi-
    nated in R&D projects?

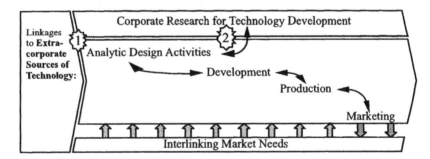

Figure 2.10 Vital Interlinkages of R&D Projects

This author's hypothesis is that the propensity to networking of Japanese companies, both at the extra- and the intra corporate level, provides mechanisms to
circumvent the dilemmas of innovation. By exploring three R&D projects in
Japanese companies from three different industries, empirical foundation will
be provided to this hypothesis.

To begin with, the following chapter will explore the surrounding R&D networks of the case-study companies. Although Quinn (1992, 72-5) argues for
an increased use of a disaggregated network of technology suppliers, the dangers that he emphasizes are numerous: loss of skills; loss of control of potential
suppliers; overdependence on a supplier who may become unreliable; loss of

accidental innovations stemming from random interaction of people with different skills; and conflicts between the buyers' and the suppliers' priorities. Clearly, Quinn's potential dangers presuppose a one-way transfer of skills, a lack of trust and common goals, and no direct interaction between supplier and assembler.

The following chapter will show a rather different use of suppliers by outlining a unique form of disaggregation. Instead of letting internal bureaucracies extinguish a company's inventive fires, the 'starburst organizations' of Canon, Sony or Toyota split off units to focus around its core competencies. This organizational growth arrangement provides the case-study companies with an effective mechanism to circumvent the organizational dilemma of innovation. In addition, their unique capability to acquire inventiveness from extracorporate sources of technology has enabled them to focus their internal efforts on what it takes to innovate, instead of being caught in the dilemma of technological leadership.

The remainder of the book outlines how they do it in practice and what we can learn from this.

NOTES

1. See, for example, Bleeke and Ernst (1993); Lamming (1994); Pisano (1991); Radnor (1991); Speir (1989); Turner (1992); Welch and Nayak (1992); Yoshino and Rangan (1995).
2. As nothing endures but change, some of these differences are certainly in the process of changing, as indicated in Chapter 1.
3. The thesis of Fujimoto (1989) and the subsequent book with Clark are based on data gathered between 1985 and 1988 in the 20 largest car producers: three in the US, eight in Japan and nine in Western Europe (Clark and Fujimoto 1991, 369). Fujimoto's (1989) data has also found its way into the study of Womack *et al.* (1990), in particular into chapter five on R&D activities.
4. Cf. Clark and Fujimoto (1991; 1992, 138-40); Jones (1990, 6); Parsons (1991, 18).
5. Tyrni (1994, 44) agrees that Japanese firms enjoy both higher R&D productivity and shorter development lead-time.
6. Neither Fiat, Renault, nor Volkswagen was able to produce 20 cars per man-year of labour in 1976, whereas Nissan produced 42 cars and Toyota 49 cars per man-year (Vogel 1979, 12).
7. Aoki (1988, 239); De Woot (1990, 154); Giersch (1992, 58); Hedlund and Nonaka (1991, 10-18); Leontiades (1991, 49); Nester (1990, 290); Sigurdson and Anderson (1991, 244).
8. Kenney and Florida (1993, 60); Westney (1990; 1992).
9. This statement is supported by Brauchlin (1988); De Woot (1990, 154); Hamel (1991, 96-9); Gerybadze (1993, 138-139); Lewis (1990, 49); Nester (1990, 290); Samuels (1994, 24-6); Schütte (1989; 1991, 266, 269); Yoshino and Rangan (1995). It exemplifies what Badaracco (1991) characterizes as knowledge links, as opposed to product links in strategic alliances.
10. See, for example, Aoki (1988, 246); De Woot (1990); Evan and Olk (1990, 40); Nester (1990, 293); Watanabe *et al.* (1991).
11. See, for example, Ballon (1992, 151); Hagedoorn and Schakenraad (1990, 21); Imai (1989a; 1989b; 1990); Kenney and Florida (1993, 70-75); Laage-Hellman and Nonaka (1994, 98-104); Samuels (1994, 22-3); Tselichtchev (1994).
12. Clark and Fujimoto (1989, 49); De Woot (1990, 101); Florida and Kenney (1991, 381-98); Karlsson (1989, 33); Laage-Hellman and Nonaka (1994); Peck and Goto (1982, 639); Porter (1990, 80-81); Radnor (1991); Takeuchi and Nonaka (1986, 140, 144) to mention a few.
13. Orru (1993, 179-81); cf. Aoki (1988).
14. In 1987, GM had 6,000 employees in its parts purchasing operations while Toyota had only

337 (Womack *et al.* 1990, 156).

15. See, for example, Howard (1990, 94-6); Jones (1990, 7); Nichiguchi (1994); Sheard (1992b, 19); Clark and Fujimoto (1991, 140).

16. See Fujimoto (1994b) for a detailed discussion on black box parts and their origin.

17. Clark and Fujimoto (1991, 140-42); Fujimoto (1989, 675-6). 1993 data show that US manufacturers have increased their average of black box parts from 16% to 30% (Fujimoto 1994a, 17).

18. Clark and Fujimoto (1991, 148-51); Womack *et al.* (1990, 146-8).

19. Brockhoff (1990, 28, 107-8); De Meyer (1991, 51); Freudenberg (1988, 120); Yamanouchi (1987, 150).

20. Similarly, Senge (1990, 210-11, 231) notes that Western managers often lack a language for expressing and examining how problems and strategies are interrelated across divisions and functions, and that they also lack an integrated view or a holistic perspective of the corporation (cf. Nonaka and Kenney 1991, 69).

21. Clark and Fujimoto (1990, 110; 1991, 258-9); Fujimoto (1989, 638, 831); Song and Parry (1992); Womack *et al.* (1990, 130). Beyond the scope of automobile manufacturing, Brauchlin and Wehrli (1991) note a lack of knowledge about market needs among engineers in European SMEs.

22. 'War room' is the term used in Japan for the large room in which the most involved engineers are gathered with their chief engineer to plan and execute a development project (Fujimoto, discussion).

23. Clark and Fujimoto (1991, 181); Womack *et al.* (1990, 117).

24. See Clark and Fujimoto (1991, 221). In this context, Aoki (1988, 215) notes that CEOs of typical American auto firms are six or seven management layers above the typical plant manager, whereas plant managers in Japanese auto plants are typically appointed to the board of directors. The figure for the US has probably decreased to three or four in recent years.

25. Clark and Fujimoto (1991, 206); Imai (1986, 23-41).

26. Cf. third communication gap of Rosenfield and Servo (1991, 31).

27. See, for example, Brauchlin (1988, 203); Clark and Fujimoto (1988, 9-10; 1991, 103); Ealey and Soderberg (1990, 8); (Kenney and Florida 1993, 61).

28. Itami (1987, 90-91) was first in arguing that Japanese companies pay particularly strong attention to core competencies and their diffusion through diversification. See Timlon (1994 and 1997) for a complete review of the concept of core competence.

29. Cf. Clark and Fujimoto (1991, 104, 267); Jones (1990, 6-7); Womack *et al.* (1990, 109-13). Similar observations are made by Nonaka and Kenney (1991, 78) in electronics-oriented consumer goods companies.

30. Itami (1987, 92); Nonaka (1988a, 15; 1988b, 66-67).

31. Bartlett and Ghoshal (1989, 204); Clark and Fujimoto (1990, 110, 118); Schütte (1991, 266). See Kusunoki (1992, 69-70) and Nonaka (1988a, 10) for examples of disintegration.

32. The earliest extensive description of cross-functional teams was made by (Imai *et al.*, 1985), who opened a track to a large number of authors, e.g., Bartlett and Ghoshal (1989, 125); Fruin (1991, 6); Fujimoto (1991, 33); Kenney and Florida (1993); Laage-Hellman and Nonaka (1994, 109).

33. The practice of cross-functional activities is said to have started at Toyota in 1962 (Imai 1986, 134).

34. Kenney and Florida (1993, 61); Parsons (1991, 16); Smothers (1990, 523); Takeuchi and Nonaka (1986, 137-41); Walker (1991, 279).

35. Cf. Aoki (1988, 216); Hamel (1991, 96-99); Imai *et al.* (1985, 543); Takahashi (1994, 51); Takeuchi and Nonaka (1986); Nonaka (1990, 28-32); Schütte (1991, 267).

36. Hatvany and Pucik (1982, 528-9); Ealey and Soderberg (1990); Kenney and Florida (1993, 43); Kobayashi (1990, 270); Nonaka (1993, 19).

37. This is often claimed by Nonaka (1988b, 61-2; 1990, 28-33; 1991, 96-104; 1993, 24), but also by Ealey and Soderberg (1990, 8); Hedlund and Nonaka (1991, 34); Itami (1987, 92); Nonaka and Yamanouchi (1989, 306-9).

38. Hatvany and Pucik (1982, 526-27); Hedlund and Nonaka (1991, 10-18); Karlsson (1989, 37); Lu (1987, 33-4); Nonaka (1991, 98-102); Prahalad and Hamel (1990, 91).

39. Adler, Riggs and Wheelwright (1989, 9); Aoki (1988, 243, 246); Clark and Fujimoto (1990,

110); Kusunoki and Numagami (1993); Smothers (1990, 526).

40. Clark and Fujimoto (1991, 205); Ealey and Soderberg (1990, 3-6); Womack *et al.* (1990, 129-30); cf. Quinn (1992, 206).

41. Shibata (1984, 45) reports that, in the early 1970s, the Hitachi Research Institute was founded to do the strategic R&D planning for the entire Hitachi Group, and that a Systems Engineering Division was created to coordinate interrelated activities of various business divisions. He unfortunately neither reveals how these different units work, nor gives examples of other companies. In addition, we need more recent studies in this field.

42. Allen (1970; 1977); De Meyer (1991, 51-6); Freudenberg (1988, 120); Pearson (1991, 20, 23); Pilditch (1991, 316); Rosenfeld and Servo (1991); Rosenbloom (1978); Schneiderman (1991, 55); Tushman (1982, 349-62). The need for collaboration between the frequently too separated functions of technological development, product design, production and marketing is argued for in a rather unconventional, but highly interesting way by Beer (1985, 113)

43. Adler, McDonald and MacDonald (1992, 28); De Meyer (1991, 56); Freudenberg (1988, 153-4); Peters (1991); Senge (1990, 234).

44. Cf. Allen (1977, 126-81); Bartlett and Ghoshal (1989, 89-90); Betz (1987, 196); De Meyer (1991, 51); Doz and Prahalad (1989, 136-9).

45. For a detailed discussion of the role of boundary spanners, see Niederkofler (1989, 100-106; 225-6).

46. Fujimoto *et al.* (1991, 7); Laage-Hellman (1993, 322-32); Mansfield *et al.* (1977, 32-40).

47. Cooper and Kleinschmidt (1991, 128); Erickson *et al.* (1990, 78).

48. Cf. Cooper and Kleinschmidt (1991, 128); Erickson *et al.* (1990, 78); Laage-Hellman (1993, 318-22); Wheelwright and Clark (1992, 74); Quinn and Mueller (1982, 60-83).

49. Kodama's (1991; 1992a; 1992b) main thesis, related to a Japan-specific context, is precisely that the Japan-specific interindustry relationships allow for more effective technology fusion, i.e., new arrangements of complementary technologies.

50. See, for example, Mansfield (1971, 60); Pearson (1991, 18-27). Lee, Fisher and Yau (1986, 36) actually state that it is 'dangerous – and expensive – to embark on a new stage before the project is ready'. Cf, Kline and Rosenberg (1986, 295).

51. Badaracco (1991, 66-69); Contractor and Lorange (1988, 11); Lamming (1993); Speir (1989).

52. See, for example, Betz (1987, 113-21); IVA (1993, 14); Kline and Rosenberg (1986, 301).

53. Cf. Badaracco (1991, 9, 34); Meyer and Utterback (1993); Ohmae (1985, 8); Peck (1990, 236).

54. See, for example, Mansfield (1968, 168); Leonard-Barton (1992, 111).

55. Kline *et al.* (1991, 7) and Kusunoki (1992, 75) argue in this direction. In similar terms, Leonard-Barton (1992, 111-25) argues that innovation requires core capabilities, but that these have a down side, called *core rigidities*, that paradoxically inhibit innovation.

56. Cf. Betz (1987, 55); Brockhoff (1990, 83); Peck (1990, 244); Quinn (1985); Schneiderman (1991, 54-7). Hayes and Schmenner (1982, 456-7) make a similar distinction between product- vs. process-focused organizations. Shibata (1984) argues that a high degree of bureaucratization tends to reduce the possibility of complex innovation.

57. Hedlund (1986); Nonaka (1988a, 1993).

58. Research by Kline and Rosenberg (1986, 300) and by Mansfield (1968, 84-102) support this statement.

3   Surrounding R&D Networks

In an era of total digitalization and fusion of previously unrelated industries like optics, mechanics and electronics – yielding 'digital optomechatronics' – the most profound advantages seem to go to companies that have access to a large variety of technologies in different industries, that maintain close links to universities, component- and equipment-developers, and that can afford large, long-term investments in R&D.[1] In accordance with the theoretical perspective and framework, this chapter will examine those surrounding R&D networks that link extracorporate sources of technology to corporate R&D activities in Japan.

A BRIEF INTRODUCTION TO JAPANESE CORPORATE NETWORKS

Japan's *keiretsu* have in the last few years constituted a topic of vivid debate. Consequently, there is much literature, as far as keiretsu in general are concerned. The debate has, however, mainly focused on free-trade issues and whether keiretsu close the Japanese market or not,[2] and few authors have treated the aspects of research and new product development extensively within the context of keiretsu networks. Therefore, this chapter will not rely entirely on previous research, but to some extent be based also on interviews.

Introducing Definitions

Literally, keiretsu means 'series or being linked' (Japan-US Business Council (1992, 2). In order to boost production to meet military demand in the wartime economy, companies set vigorously about the task of using subcontracting companies. Accordingly, the word came into being to describe 'the arrangement under which a parent company uses subcontracting of small and medium-sized companies' (Okumura 1991, 2).

Metaphorically, the word keiretsu has a second meaning, which symbolizes an informal network of relationships with trading relations that are non-exclusive but nevertheless preferential in varying degrees (Gerlach, 1992b). Half of these Japanese corporate groups are direct products of the break-up of the zaibatsu and the other half seem to be an emulative response to the first half. Therefore, the historical links of Japan's *zaibatsu* will be retraced below.

Brief Historical Background

Ordered to enter Japan and to open the country to Western trade, Commodore Perry's black ships and their modern weaponry presented, in 1853, a major shock to Japan's so far rather closed society. This shock, which was the catalyst for the rapid transformation of Japan into an industrial nation, brought about the overthrow of the ruling Tokugawa Shogun, and the installation of the Meiji Emperor in 1868.[3] An urge to catch up with the West arose and technology was given the highest national priority as trade and diplomatic missions were dispatched to study foreign industries.[4] The driving vision that captured the new realities of the Meiji period was *wakon yosai* – 'Japanese spirit, Western technology'.

In the Meiji era (1868-1912), the government came to develop and control strategic industries: mining, ship-building, transportation, communication and weaponry. Later, in the Taisho era (1912-26), these industries were placed in private hands: a few favoured families who were allowed to purchase key industries at extremely low prices. These family-owned corporate enterprises became known as *zaibatsu,* which literally means financial group, or clique. The evolution and concentration of Japanese industry into the four great zaibatsu: Mitsui, Mitsubishi, Sumitomo and Yasuda, affirmed 'the pronounced Japanese social tendency to group formation' (MAP 1991, 6). Thanks to strong co-operative links between the affiliated companies and their trading company and main bank, which came to constitute the core of each zaibatsu, commercial and financial managerial skills were assured centrally. Hence, manufacturing companies could concentrate their resources on innovation.[5]

Kinyu Shudan, or Financial Corporate Groups

In the aftermath of World War II, the occupying US authorities broke up the zaibatsu, accusing them for having been among the instigators of the war. As an example, the Mitsui group was split up into some 180 different companies (Skully 1981, 11). As the occupation ended in 1952, previously dismantled zaibatsu were however reorganized. Subsequent horizontal linkages between the former zaibatsu affiliates created the enterprise groups: today's 'horizontal' keiretsu. As many of the groups maintain the hierarchical, top-down control, in which each member-company has a well defined position in the ranking, the term 'horizontal' keiretsu may, however, be misleading.[6] In Japanese, they are called *kinyu shudan, kinyu keiretsu,* or *kinyu grûptan,* meaning 'financial group', which indicates the central position of a main-bank in each kinyu-keiretsu (Gerlach 1992a, 4). We know of at least six traditional features that characterize them:[7]

1. Mutual stock ownership or cross-shareholding.
2. Presidents' councils (shacho-kai): Each of the six[8] major groups has

presidents' councils, or shacho-kai, gathering the presidents or chairmen of the member companies regularly.
3.   Main-bank relationships: at the core of each of the six major enterprise groups is a major city bank.
4.   Sogo shosha: a general trading companiy is also at the core of each group.
5.   Personnel transfers: according to Japan's Fair Trade Commission (1992, 4-10), 49.5% of all companies belonging to one of the major groups had, in 1989, executives who were dispatched from their main bank, and the ratio of companies with executives who were dispatched from the sogo shosha of the same group averaged 10.25%.
6.   Fusion of resources: member companies usually join forces in undertakings which require large initial investments and R&D spending like, for example, information technology and space communications.

The extent of kinyu shudan

Taking the first section of the Tokyo Stock Exchange in 1990 as an example, 577 firms[9] out of 986 listed (58.5%) had identifiable affiliations with one of the big six. These companies accounted for 76% of total sales for all first-section firms (Gerlach 1992b, 88). The quantity of inter-firm ties does not seem to be declining, but possibly becoming more flexible and less exclusive.

Kigyo Keiretsu, or Vertically Interlinked Suppliers

> Our parts and components manufacturers, organized in vertical kigyo keiretsu, are a main key to Japan's successful automotive and consumer electronics industries. Thanks to their long-term relationships, suppliers, assemblers and consumers all enjoy the benefits of scale economies. (Vice MITI Minister Hatakeyama, interview)

In order to achieve economies of scale, scope and speed, large Japanese manufacturers seem to act like mere coordinators of the innovation process, in which large parts of the development-, design-, manufacturing- and sometimes even the research-activities are often performed by affiliated suppliers, and very little is done by the manufacturers themselves. Large Japanese companies, capitalized at over $700,000, only represent one per cent of all companies in Japan. The remaining part, small to medium-size companies – 'chuo-sho kigyo' – make up more than 99% of Japanese industry. In 1980 the US counted 570,000 SMEs, compared to 1,100,000 in Japan. Hence, a large company sits on the top, dealing directly with a limited number of first-tier suppliers who make major components and subassemblies. These first-tier suppliers manage relations with a more numerous second-tier of rather specialized manufacturers, who in turn subcontract increasingly narrow tasks to a third, fourth, etc., tier.[10]

The extent of kigyo keiretsu

This varies between industries, corporate groups and companies. Almost all large Japanese companies have their own kigyo keiretsu, in terms of vertically structured suppliers. As an example from the automobile industry as a whole, there are 11 vehicle manufacturers in Japan and approximately 1,400 large parts suppliers, out of which 500 are first-tier suppliers, which supply approximately 85% of the parts needed by the motor manufacturers (Turnbull *et al.* 1992, 163).

Interlinking Kinyu Shudan and Kigyo Keiretsu

In order to better clarify the structure of Japan's most common corporate networks, Figure 3.1 depicts how kinyu shudan and kigyo keiretsu are interconnected.

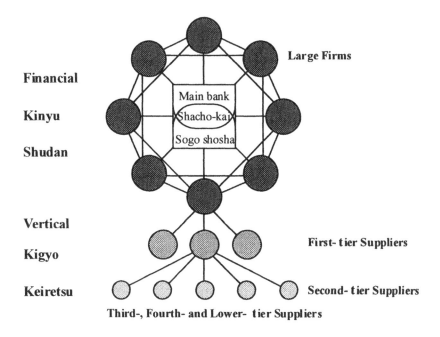

Figure 3.1   The Interlinkage of Kinyu Shudan and Kigyo Keiretsu

Now that the structure has been described and depicted, interorganizational linkages with implications for T&I management are to be scrutinized in both kinds of corporate networks.[11] The case-study companies will then be positioned in these networks, thereby identifying possible keiretsu linkages to their corporate R&D activities.

R&D LINKAGES IN KINYU SHUDAN

Many authors claim that the corporate structure constitutes the ultimate force in Japanese industry (e.g., Fruin, 1992; Sakai, 1990). In this section, key features of the kinyu keiretsu structure and their effects on R&D and innovation will be more thoroughly developed.

Coordination of Co-operation

> Of all keiretsu functions and activities, it is in the shachô-kai that we can really see 'where the rubber meets the road', where political activity, finance, research, technology transfers, market strategies and personnel exchanges are coordinated. (MAP 1991, 14)

The *shacho-kai,* or group presidents' meeting, is seen as the most straightforward means of classifying group affiliations in Japan.[12] In an interview with Dr Nakada, he states that these meetings fill important functions:

> The presidents talk about how they can co-operate, generally in terms of mutual interests, loans and technology co-operations. The meetings also went on during the occupation, although they were prohibited.

According to much literature,[13] the shacho-kai discussions focus on the general economic and financial situation, promising businesses, the state of R&D and future possible mutual interests and co-operations. New technologies, new products and R&D seem to be subject to discussion, and plans on joint R&D may be initiated. One of many examples is that, at a shacho-kai of the Sanwa group, fifty member firms decided to form an inter-industrial committee, 'the Sanwa Bio Kenkyu-Kai', to engage in joint R&D and information exchange in the biotechnology field (Dodwell 1990, 113).

Conflicting literature claims that meetings of company presidents are more like social gatherings and that neither business decision-making nor strategic planning for these groups is conducted there.[14]

A straightforward and unequivocal answer to what is being discussed and decided at the shacho-kai is all but impossible to obtain. It seems to be widely recognized among most experts on Japan[15] that these meetings are not unimportant for the coordination of corporate activities and that they lay the groundwork for later decisions, which also facilitates implementation.

The phenomenon of building up consensus through both formal and informal discussions, before formal deliberation takes place – *nemawashi* in Japanese – is deeply rooted in the decision-making process of the Japanese management style and not unique to kinyu keiretsu at all.[16] However, as the shacho-kai enables keiretsu-wide nemawashi, it may eventually lay the groundwork for group-wide R&D co-operation, as we have seen above.

Concentrating Resources on R&D

A long-term orientation has become conventional wisdom about Japanese management. Increasing policy and academic interest is focusing on this per-ceived difference in managerial orientation as a key contributor to Japan's cor-porate competitive success (Sheard 1992c, 1). Whereas 73% of all Japanese companies' top-ten shareholders remained stable during two-year intervals in the early 1970s, this number had increased to about 87% by the mid-1980s (Gerlach 1992b, 96). The difference in corporate control between the US and Japan is depicted in Figure 3.2.

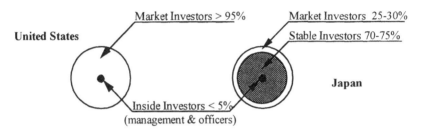

Source: Gerlach (1992c, 55) (rearranged)

Figure 3.2 Investor Composition in Large US and Japanese Companies

Stable, long-term-oriented shareholders, who agree not to sell the shares to third parties unsympathetic to incumbent management, are more interested in long-term growth than in short-term profits. Instead of letting individual inves-tors play a central role in corporate governance, more discretionary power is given to managers who can concentrate on innovation, even if this sometimes hampers short-term profits.[17] That shareholders have virtually no role in man-agement is also illustrated by the fact that annual shareholders' meetings usu-ally last but a few minutes.[18]

Another consequence of having either friendly or powerless shareholders is that transactions in corporate assets through mergers and acquisitions are rare in Japan and that hostile take-overs are all but impossible,[19] which enables greater R&D spending, as will be further discussed below.

In a country-specific survey[20] on corporate R&D spending, five countries – France, Germany, Japan, the US and the UK – have more than ten companies on the list of the world's 200 biggest spenders on R&D (Kenward 1992, 66-9). Table 3.1 juxtaposes corporate R&D spending and dividends as a percentage of total turnover.

Undeniably, British companies pay greater attention to dividends than to R&D spending according to Kenward's numbers. His explanation of Britain's position is that too much R&D spending attracts hostile takeovers: 'Comp-anies with a large R&D portfolio are, so the argument goes, vulnerable to attack by those with a shorter-term view' (*ibid.*).

Table 3.1   R&D Spending and Dividends

Country	R&D £bn Sales	R&D to Sales	Dividends
Germany	10.3	6.8%	1.0%
Japan	13.3	5.5%	0.6%
US	14.2	5.1%	2.0%
France	4.0	3.8%	0.9%

Source: Own arrangement of data from Kenward (1992, 69)

To the extent that this argument reflects reality, the Japanese corporate structure allows for greater corporate R&D spending than what is possible in many Western countries.

Innovation Through Effective Allocation of Resources

As reliable sources of business contacts and information, the main banks appear often also to decide whether a project is going to be pursued or not.[21] It seems that the intertwined nexus of information and capital flows that characterizes corporate groups is one underlying factor that enables member firms to take on higher levels of debt financing than Western counterparts, which in turn allows for higher spending on innovative activities.

Innovation through sharing of risks
It is argued that the formation of kinyu shudan stabilizes corporate performance through a risk-sharing mechanism (Nakatani 1984; 1990). In times of financial or managerial difficulties, main banks provide necessary assistance 'at a far greater cost and risk' (*ibid.* 1990, 154) than expected in the West.[22] In exchange, the non-financial firms attempt to keep high and stable outstanding debts against their member banks, giving them stable flows of interest payments.

The risk-sharing structure has provided efficient mechanisms of inter-corporate (financial) assistance for coping with external shocks like the oil price increases of the 1970s and the present rapid rise in the value of the yen.[23] Much thanks to the mutual assistance, main banks are relatively willing to commit to risky projects, which frequently helps manufacturers to overcome innovation-based uncertainties, and thus benefits innovation.

Innovation through low-cost capital
As mentioned earlier, large Japanese companies have found a way to keep their shareholders at bay. 'In effect each keiretsu creates a private equity market around a main bank' (Nakatani 1992, 27). Group formation thus allows indi-

vidual firms to insulate themselves from the imperatives of market forces, particularly of the capital markets, which tend to demand higher rates of return and in a shorter period.[24] Accordingly, a new product project that produces a negative income stream in its initial phase but is expected to yield profits later is, compared to many Western countries, more easily accepted. In this respect, kinyu shudan members have a comparative advantage within innovation and R&D, as most such activities require a long period of time before the return on investment turns positive.

In addition, 'the policy of the Japanese government is, and long has been, to hold interest rates to industry at as low a level as prudent monetary policy management allows' (Abegglen and Stalk 1985, 178). So, thanks both to corporate and national governance, Japanese firms seem to enjoy the access to low-cost capital,[25] which may allow more resources to flow towards T&I activities.

On the other hand, as most monetary resources are tied up in the rigid networks of kinyu shudan and their main banks, there is hardly no venture capital avaliable for new start ups in Japan (Tatsuno, 1990).

Technology Scanning and Transfer of Competence

> Any participant in office automation, robotics, and consumer electronics must develop a supersensitive control-tower function to constantly scan and monitor externally available technologies and at the same time concentrate on fewer, critical internal R&D projects. (Ohmae 1985, 14)

The *sogo shosha*'s scanning and channelling of technology is of critical importance to each member-company's T&I management. Thanks to information system networks, spanning all important industrial areas of the globe, relevant data is gathered and employed at all major trading companies.[26] Hence, member companies can more rapidly make strategic responses to innovative foreign thinking.

In discussions with Professor Gregory, he suggests that the sogo shosha take second place, after the CIA, when it comes to information gathering and effective channelling of it to the right end-users. The technology-scanning role will now be described in more detail, through a short study of Mitsui and Co., based on interviews with Kamoshita, manager of the Corporate Communications Division at Mitsui, as well as on a visit to the Mitsui headquarters in Tokyo.

Founded in 1876, Mitsui and Co. employs some 11,000 people in more than 200 cities world-wide. It is the world's largest trading company in terms of employees, but Mitsubishi's trading company had in 1992 a larger turnover than Mitsui's $120 billion. The entire Mitsui Group has a total of 519 domestic subsidiaries and affiliates, as well as 425 overseas. The Mitsui Inter-Business was established in 1978 to gather and distribute information on R&D activities in close relation with Mitsui and Co.'s information network. At the network's hub is the computerized communications centre in Tokyo. This is linked by satellite to subcentres in London, New York, Sydney and Bahrain. They, in turn, are linked to offices in over 200 cities, 57 in Japan and 164 in 87 countries overseas. Each day an average of 100,000 messages traffic this network.

For reasons of secrecy and constant accessibility, the company has its own telephone lines. Their technology divisions in Tokyo, Osaka, London, Paris, Düsseldorf, Milan, New York, San Francisco and Singapore focus on technology scanning:

> At home in both the research laboratory and the marketplace, our scientists, engineers and technicians have a keen eye for the commercial potential of innovations in most technological fields . . . Our specialists track the progress of R&D projects throughout the world, looking for the breakthroughs that can be translated into improved or new products and services . . . We negotiate licensing agreements and patent-rights transfers. We also coordinate inter-industry projects. (Kamoshita, interview)

Kamoshita-san strongly emphasizes that the policy in these matters is 'to buy only the key-technology, even if the product is good. Then we'll assemble this product in China, where labour costs are still low, or here in Japan, to acquire competence within the technology'.

Relationships[27] are an important factor underlying Mitsui's success in obtaining information from key persons, both at private companies and at official institutions:

> Key to our success in monitoring the frontiers of technology have been the many relationships we have forged with leading corporations, universities, laboratories and other research pioneers. We are, for instance, sole agent in Japan for the Southwest Research Institute, an independent centre in the United States specializing in aerospace, automotive engineering, engine design, bioengineering and chemistry. (*ibid.*)

The relationships are often personal, obtained through the dispatch of Mitsui members. 'Out of the 150-200 male[28] members who are employed in Japan every year, 60 are dispatched to foreign companies, e.g. General Electric, NBC or AT&T, after three to five years of domestic experience'. Kamoshita was for instance sent to Hughes, a satellite manufacturer in the US. When he came back to Japan he was requested by his company to work three years for a Japanese satellite venture, JCSAT, in which Mitsui has a 20% stake (and is therefore definitely a member company).

Mitsui and Co. also has manufacturing and development agreements with technologically leading companies like McDonnell Douglas in the aerospace business and with Bell Helicopter Textron. In reply to the question of why foreign companies are willing to receive Mitsui members, Kamoshita-san points out that Mitsui has a buyer's position to these companies. 'Besides, they don't pay us anything as we remain on Mitsui's payroll'. Many Mitsui members are also sent to foreign universities and among the Japanese new entrants, the number of Japanese US graduates has increased from three in 1982, to ten in 1992.

Kamoshita-san keeps around 4,000 business cards, all classified in different priority groups. He maintains particularly close relationships with MITI officials:

> Usually, we communicate over the phone, but every now and then we get together over a drink. The exchange of information is on a give and take basis. The kind of information that I can give is highly interesting for them. The same thing goes for me, as MITI's sources of information are different from mine.

Keiretsu-wide (Dif)fusion of Technologies and Competencies

A variety of joint activities are conducted within the networks of kinyu keiretsu. These include joint R&D projects, pooling of technological expertise and sharing of acquired technology.[29] In the 1980s, the most particular expansion has been in the so-called C&C (Computers and Communications) industries. In 1981, Mitsubishi was first on stage to form the Mitsubishi C&C *Kenkyû-Kai,* a study team bringing together 40 Mitsubishi companies to develop technologies related to high-level data transmission (Gerlach 1992a; 1992b). In a traditional pattern, the other groups followed suit and Mitsui and Co. started similar projects in 1982 together with 39 Mitsui companies. In 1983, ten more firms were added, this time, however, including several large firms that maintain close connections with the Mitsui group but do not participate in its presidents' council, e.g., Sony, Ito Yokado, and Tokyo Broadcasting System.

Moreover, customer relationships also appear to be shaped by keiretsu linkages.[30] On the visit to Mitsui and Co. headquarters, clear signs of intra-keiretsu loyalty in purchases were noticed: all their mainframe computers and most laptop computers were from Toshiba, a Mitsui group member.[31] Thanks to an intra-keiretsu outlet of a new product, an invention reaches the market faster and more reliable customer feedback is possible. In addition, the fact of having an initial market share to count on increases the chances of survival of the product. Consequently, the member company can allow itself to increase investments at an earlier stage in order to achieve high-growth in the 'winner's competitive cycle', typical of the *kaisha,* i.e., the Japanese company (Abegglen and Stalk 1985, 42-3).

R&D LINKAGES IN THE KIGYO KEIRETSU STRUCTURE

> As I see it, loose vertical integration in kigyo keiretsu is the main factor explaining the relative competitiveness of Japanese industry, because our system allows for coexistence of *both* long-term relationships *and* competition. (Miyamoto, interview)

The comparative analysis in Chapter 2 suggested that the Japanese lead-time advantage to a large extent stems from earlier and more intensive supplier interaction. Let us, therefore, turn to the task of examining R&D-relevant linkages in the kigyo keiretsu structure.

Coordination of Competition and Co-operation

Just as the kinyu shudan are coordinated in shacho-kai, kigyo keiretsu have their *kyoryoku-kai,* where management of the assembling company discusses future trends and business plans with its first-tier suppliers. Hence, a kigyo keiretsu member is not only well informed of the business strategy and long-term management plan of his partners, but also has the opportunity to exchange useful information and opinions with the parent firm as well as with competitors. Moreover, technical subcommittees of the kyoryoku-kai help diffuse new technologies as well as best practice in manufacturing and management.[32]

Gregory (1985a, 45-6) states that the heavy capital commitment in terms of R&D spending, observed at Mitsubishi Electric and Matsushita among others, can only be made 'by widely diversified and vertically integrated manufacturers able to assure rapid diffusion of new technology once it has become operational'. Vertical integration, in this case from semiconductors to end-products, thus enables a faster return on investment in applied integrated circuit research.

Notwithstanding early and intense co-operation, suppliers do not escape competitive pressures. In a case where the assembler relies on a single subcontractor for the supply of a particular component, he will still maintain a long-term relation with other suppliers, thus enabling the double-checking of costs and the threat of a potential shift, but also keep them updated through continuous diffusion of technology.[33]

This intra-kigyo keiretsu competition through long-run evaluation and 'promotion' or 'demotion' in the subcontracting hierarchy has an accelerating effect on the assembling company's innovation process, as do also the cooperative transfer of technologies and competencies. Suppliers will make every effort to stay competitive at their level of the vertical keiretsu. First-tier suppliers that fail to meet their responsibilities risk to be demoted to a lower tier. At the same time, newcomers who would like to become group members make all possible efforts to upgrade capabilities and competitiveness so as to surpass existing suppliers in the group.[34] At Toshiba Corporation, it was noticed that the ten best suppliers of the month are announced on displays together with the ten worst suppliers. These rankings seem to be based on delivery-time and quality.

Interlinking Actors and Activities

In the rather paternalistic employment system of Japan, smaller subsidiary firms provide a convenient means of placing employees for their post-retirement employment, while simultaneously strengthening the social bonds between the firms.[35] Staff members from the Big Six are dispatched to member firms, where they serve as executives or presidents. The transfer of 'redundant' company members to suppliers was particularly common in the mid-1990s' wake of the burst bubble.[36] By sometimes serving concurrently at both the main firm and at the member firm, good communication and coordination are secured. As of March 1991, a total of 4,774 executives[37] at companies listed on stock exchanges were sent from key companies of the Big Six. Totalling 2,070 in Japan, the listed companies receive an average of more than two executives from the Big Six at any given time (Fujigane, 1991). In this respect, the economic value of kigyo keiretsu is very high as customers provide their suppliers with sophisticated management, which enables a higher efficiency throughout the supplier pyramid.

Exchange of engineers
Several interviews (Guy, Mayuzumi, Shill) indicate an extensive kigyo keiretsu personnel rotation of development engineers. In a development department of NEC, a Sumitomo member with a total of 3,500 engineers, as many as 700 of these would at any given time belong to and come from NEC's own vertical supplier keiretsu and not be actual NEC employees. The system also implied that NEC could send some of its own company members to work within supplying companies, if there should be a need to learn from them.

As the kigyo keiretsu structure actually enables such a close and integrated co-operation with a seemingly open exchange of engineers, it most probably has a mutually positive effect on the efficiency of new product development, above all in terms of development lead-time.[38]

When Mazda developed the Miata, the whole project group was collocated in one of Mazda's so called 'war rooms'. As much as 50% of the group consisted of 'guest engineers',[39] dispatched from key suppliers. This radical and even for Japan unusual approach enabled Mazda to complete the entire project within 2.5 years (Fujimoto, discussion).

Design-in versus Black Box Design
Nissan is worried about giving away too much of their competence and knowledge base to the suppliers. Above all, they find that too much responsibility is given to the suppliers in terms of design, as their own engineers no longer even draw the groupings. Instead, they merely send specifications to their parts suppliers, who then themselves make the drawings and the prototypes. Mitsuhiko Yamashita, manager of vehicle design at Nissan, therefore clearly sees a problem in supplier design-in. Only 20% are blueprint parts, i.e. designed at Nissan. The other 80% of Nissan's parts are entirely designed by suppliers:

> When we only provide specifications to what become black box designed parts, we have no knowledge at all about how the part is designed and are unable to make modifications afterwards. So, we should definitely try to make more of the drawings ourselves. (Yamashita, interview)

Even parts designed within Nissan may not be designed by its own engineers, as it is very common that supplier engineers join Nissan at the early design stage, in order to enable concurrent engineering. Sometimes, Nissan engineers are sent to some suppliers but in such a case, the purpose is education rather than concurrent engineering, as 'they have the expertise knowledge which we don't have' (*ibid.*).

Innovation Despite Specialization

Parent companies usually serve as the primary source of technological upgrading of their own affiliates, both in terms of engineering expertise and other forms of technical support and in lending or selling production facilities at nominal prices.[40] Also, parent companies provide equity capital to supplying firms by taking shareholding positions. When the position exceeds a certain percentage, the firm will be an affiliated first-tier supplier.

However, many of those first-tier suppliers that are affiliated to a Japanese corporation were not acquired, but rather spun-off from the mother company (cf. Quinn 1992, 147-8: 'starburst' organizations). As labour is a fixed cost due to lifetime employment, companies must grow through this mechanism and decentralize in order to keep internal growth at bay. Japan's relatively low degree of industrial diversification is thus compensated for by spinning off subsidiaries in new related industries as legally separate, but strongly interlinked companies.[41] At large companies like Hitachi, Sony and Canon, it is virtually impossible to specialize in one activity, given the imperative system of job rotation. Only at a small spun-off company, or laboratory, can researchers devote their lives to one and the same field, with a long-term view. 'People are forced to be generalists at big Japanese corporations' (Gregory, discussion).

Examples of this tendency have been noticed at several large Japanese corporations. Tsutomu Sugiyama, assistant general manager of Corporate Communications at Sony Corporation, states that the establishment of relationships with small high-tech research-labs or manufacturers, and the spinning-off of research labs, is a way for Sony to allow for free spirit in research:

> Sony Corporation has become so large and budget conscious that innovation today is less free. Less digression is allowed among our engineers and R&D departments because of the increased bureaucracy. However, Sony still has a much freer spirit than regular Japanese companies.

The Sony Kihara Research Centre (SKRC) is a joint venture formed in 1988 between Sony and Dr Kihara, a talented scientist who previously worked for the Sony Research Centre. The number of researchers is kept as low as 30. Few members and lack of bureaucracy foster an invention-promoting atmosphere:

> SKRC can invent and innovate more freely. Dr Kihara might just as well have opened his own lab, but we wanted to make a JV with him as an experiment instead. SKRC does not necessarily work for Sony, but we are in first place when it comes to using their inventions. (*Ibid.*)

The official form may be that of a joint venture, but given the powerful position of Sony, it could also be argued that SKRC is a dedicated subordinate supplier of inventions to Sony. Seen in that perspective, SKRC is a member of Sony's kigyo keiretsu.

'Democratic management' in the allocation of capital prevents individual divisions from growing faster than others (Abegglen and Stalk 1985, 179-80). Again, spinning off a subsidiary offers a convenient means of allowing promising businesses to grow. Fanuc, which is now the world leader in numerical control equipment, was a division of Fujitsu until 1972. Then, internal competition for financial resources became too great and management spun off the division, but holds 43% of the stock (*ibid.*; cf. Kodama 1991, 117). The tendency to spin off specialized activities is particularly noticeable in the software industry. All major Japanese electronics firms have spun off the majority of their software development to small interlinked labs (Kenney and Florida 1993, 77-81). Dr Takayanagi, CTO and Senior Vice Executive of Toshiba Corporation states that this is because

> large Japanese companies are too bureaucratic and have too rigid salary systems. Such a culture cannot satisfy young creative and ambitious engineers that are required for software development.

Interlinking Complementary Competencies

Sloughing off more of the work on small subcontractors is a means of adding flexibility into the production system (Lincoln, 1992). Time pressure leading to excessive rates of overtime extends throughout the network of kigyo keiretsu members (Nonaka, 1990). A shock absorber system within assembler-supplier relationships which reduces the impacts of a rapid change in market-demand has obvious advantages. It is, however, widely debated whether shocks are absorbed uniquely by subcontractors, or also by the assemblers. Most studies claim that only core assembly firms in Japan are granted flexible shock absorption.[42]

As in the case of shacho-kai, it is difficult to acquire the 'true' picture of whether suppliers are exploited or not. A certainty is, however, that being on top of a kigyo keiretsu yields impressive economies of scale, scope and speed, but also that only by ensuring the suppliers' survival can the situation of intense supplier competition be maintained. A summary of the situation is provided by Dr Abegglen, who stated in a discussion that 'in Japan you squeeze your suppliers so hard that they can't eat, but not so hard that they can't breathe'.

In manufacturing, large companies often operate as large-volume manufacturing sites and small ones as organizations skilled at making products efficiently in small lots. Considering these complementing competencies and the fact that keiretsu relationships are aiding in the division of labour between large and small businesses, kigyo keiretsu provide effective networks for efficient use and fusion of technology.[43]

Using value-added production per employee as a measure of productivity, large companies with 1,000 employees or more are found to be two to three times more productive than their smaller counterparts (Kodama, 1992b). This difference in productivity is however mainly due to the expensive manufacturing equipment of large corporations. In contrast, small businesses raise productivity through technological advances which are *not* embodied in manufacturing equipment, and this suggests that small businesses can more effectively absorb technological progress thanks to their greater flexibility, both in spirit and in manufacturing equipment.

It thus seems that kigyo keiretsu interlinkages can bring flexible creativity and large scale production capability together, thereby circumventing the organizational dilemma of innovation (cf. Figure 2.9).

Acceleration of Innovation

Interlinkages based on mutual trust result in important time saving, as quality control and JIT delivery are assured by the suppliers and technical secrets can be kept within the 'family'. Fewer test units of a product need to be done before commercial manufacturing can begin. A US company like IBM, which has much more in-house production with close controls, usually makes 100 to 150 test units and runs them through a large number of tests before commercial production can begin. In contrast, NEC, Fujitsu or Toshiba make as few as five or six trial units of a corresponding product because most of the necessary checks are already taken care of by subordinate suppliers (Sakai, 1990).

Interlinking market needs

A survey conducted by the Medium and Small Firm Centre of the Industrial Bank of Japan[44] indicates that the leading source of ideas for new technologies among Japanese firms is technology users. While nearly half of the firms, 47%, cited users as sources, only 37% cited the second leading source, firms' own research laboratories. As we have seen in Chapter 2, a co-operative relationship, in which innovators are able to get users of technology to provide key information, promotes innovation.

The advantages of bringing the users of technology on board early are dual: for the user, it allows an opportunity to develop familiarity with important new products and processes; for the innovator, it can facilitate input in the design process, making products more user-friendly and helping to get the 'bugs' out early.

Eliminating paperwork

When a larger manufacturer subcontracts a complex part or instrument, the subcontractor normally receives a large quantity of documents, giving all necessary specifications to develop and to produce the part. It goes without saying that the more extensive the paperwork, the slower the pace of development. But 'in a long-term relationship, innovation becomes simpler and mutual understanding develops' (Kojima (1992, 55-7). Thanks to the high degree of mutual trust, time-consuming contractual agreements are usually not necessary either, which further decreases the transaction cost and speeds up innovation.

A synthesized impression is that a close vertical keiretsu network, connecting manufacturer, assembler and sometimes also the customer, increases R&D productivity in terms of more market-related results, higher quality and shorter development lead-time.[45]

KEIRETSU INTERLINKAGES OF CANON, SONY AND TOYOTA

Canon's Macrocosmic Position

The source of technology depends on our stage of development . . . When doing basic research or material development, we would mainly go to universities, national or overseas. Then, when we have reached the production phase, we will rather get production engineering expertise from our suppliers. (Kawashima, interview)

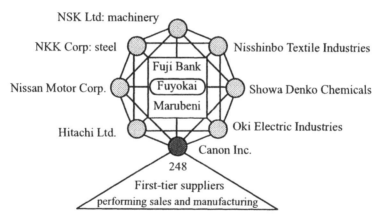

Source: Based on data from Dodwell (1992/93, 12-51) and from interviews.

Figure 3.3 Some of Canon's Keiretsu Interlinkages

Canon is a full member of the Fuyo Group, which was established in 1966. It consists of 29 large companies (some of which are depicted in Figure 3.3) centred around the Fuji Bank and their trading company Marubeni. The president of Canon is a member of the Fuyo-kai, which is the shacho-kai of the Fuyo Group. There is also a Fuyo Group R&D co-operation council, in which Canon participates. Canon frequently appears in joint research reports, published by Fuyo Group companies, and takes part in various information sharing activities. Toyosaki, manager of public information, states that 'our President at Canon Inc. is at the same level as the President of Marubeni. They meet on a regular basis'. Below, some of Canon's keiretsu interlinkages are depicted.

Canon's Kigyo Keiretsu

> Canon's system of managing subsidiaries is similar to the policy of the Tokugawa government, which established secure hegemony over the warlords, who were granted autonomy in their territory. I am 'shogun' [Head of the Tokugawa regime] and the subsidiaries' presidents are the 'daimyo' [warlords]. (Chairman Kaku)[46]

Canon's kigyo keiretsu consists of 248 first-tier suppliers and sales-subsidiaries, which are owned by Canon to at least 50%. Fort-five of Canon's numerous second-tier suppliers are owned to 20-50% (Toyosaki, interview). They can either have been purchased by, or spun off from Canon, which seems to have enabled flexible growth of intrapreneurial ventures. In order to make room for laser printers, Canon's most important plant in Toride[47] transferred its production of calculators, word processors and typewriters to what became spun-off affiliates. On average, 80% of all parts and components are manufactured by subsidiaries (Emura, interview).

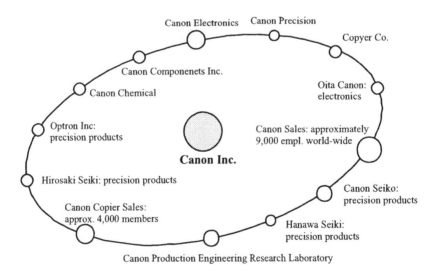

Source: Based on data from Dodwell (1992/93, 259-61) and interviews.

Figure 3.4   Canon's own Macrocosm of Spun-off Units

First-tier suppliers can be requested to produce at the same price or less than the competitors and we can send staff to their product development department whenever we want to . . . If a second-tier supplier has an interesting technology, we may purchase it. (Toyosaki, interview)

The original president, who normally also was the owner, steps aside and Canon secures the presidency and usually also key managerial functions. Strong co-operative relationships, however, seem to be possible also without shareholding. In recent years, Canon has avoided taking financial stakes in the suppliers if possible. 'It gives us too much responsibility if they go bankrupt' (Tanaka, interview).

Spun-off specialized units
These usually assume a supporting role in Canon's T&I processes. Engineers from the specialized units frequently join development projects of Canon's different development divisions. Figure 3.4 depicts the most important spun-off members of the Canon Group in a size that gives an approximate reflection of their number of employees.

Sony's Macrocosmic Position

Sony is not a member of any Shacho-kai, but has quite strong ties with the Mitsui Bank, and takes part in at least one Mitsui joint R&D project on computers and communications technologies.[48] The Sakura Bank (formerly the Mitsui Taiyo Kobe Bank) is not only a major source of financing, but also Sony's fifth largest shareholder. Its director, Kenichi Kamiya, is also one of Sony's directors, which strengthens the indirect relationship to the Mitsui Group. Financing of overseas operations is usually secured by the Bank of Tokyo, the Chairman of which concurrently serves as one of Sony's directors.[49] Apart from this, Sony puts a greater emphasis on global intercorporate relationships than domestic ones. Supplier- and main-bank linkages are depicted in Figure 3.5.

Sony's Kigyo Keiretsu

You know, we cannot make everything ourselves so, naturally, we have to depend upon many suppliers. To enhance co-operation, we organize them into supplier councils, with frequent meetings. They are true partners in our business. (Chairman Morita, interview)

As of September 30, 1992, the Sony Group consisted of Sony Corporation, 16 affiliated companies and 703 consolidated subsidiaries (Sony 1992b, 3). They have either been acquired by Sony or, as in most cases, spun off as separate but affiliated companies. Some of these affiliates and subsidiaries are first-tier suppliers of manufacturing capacity and/or R&D services in Sony's kigyo keiretsu. Others are pure sales and marketing units, domestically and overseas. First-tier suppliers are said to enjoy a very open exchange of information.[50]

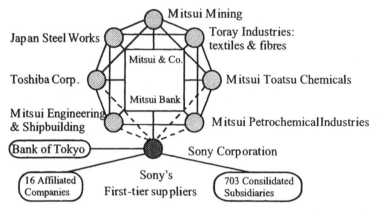

Source: Own interpretation of data from Sony and Dodwell (1992/93, 247)

Figure 3.5   Sony's Main-bank Relationships and First-tier Suppliers

For the supply of simple and cheap standardized components, Sony has a large number of suppliers that not are affiliated subsidiaries. But when it comes to key parts that must meet the specific needs of Sony, 'we usually propose to buy equity of the technologically advanced supplier after some time of co-operation' (Gérard, interview). Suppliers that become subsidiaries, usually enjoy a strong increase in productivity, thanks to Sony's investments in machines and tools.[51] Sony engineers, possessing great expertise within production, are commonly dispatched to these new 'family members', to upgrade their skills and enable them to meet Sony's requirements of quality and costs more adequately. Aiwa (owned to 50% by Sony) has a somewhat peculiar position, being both an affiliated subsidiary and a competitor of Sony.

> Competition between Sony and Aiwa is very fierce. As Aiwa is smaller and perhaps more flexible, they are sometimes able to innovate better and faster than we can at Sony, because we are growing too big and bureaucratic. When this happens, our engineers feel shame and do everything to improve. (Gérard, interview)

Spun-off Domestic R&D-related Units

Apart from the aforementioned Sony Kihara Research Center, Sony has a number of spun-off mini labs, where researchers can enjoy a greater freedom to specialize in one specific field:

Sony Engineering Corporation, located across the HQ building, employs an army of designers and artists who give the distinctive Sony look to the casing of all products, including their buttons and even the cardboard packaging. It is therefore involved in most development projects.

SALA Science Art Laboratory is a 185m^2 office, filled with the most recent different Western and Japanese computer systems. This computer laboratory, which is open 365 days a year, 24 hours a day, attracts young computer experts from the whole Tokyo-area. Any interested expert, aged between 18 and 25, may apply for a one year membership to do his or her own research and experiments here. By working jointly with Sony engineers, the goal is to learn from each other. Research results may be published in joint papers and possible copyrights do not necessarily belong to Sony alone.

The Sony Computer Science Laboratory is run jointly by Dr Doi, who is one of Sony's directors, and by Dr Tokoro, who also works as a university professor. To Japan, this laboratory is unique in many aspects of its management philosophy, as well as in its compensation system and working conditions. President Doi's aim is to 'provide an ideal research environment where upper-echelon scientists from around the world can work with enthusiasm to achieve breakthroughs of universal value' (Eda, interview). Research work is less restrained by commercial needs. Its mission is to seek innovative new technologies in areas like distributed operating systems, programming languages, system architecture and user interfaces. Each researcher is expected to set his or her own goals within the basic research themes. Individual initiatives and creative abilities are respected and rewarded.

Everyone at the lab is strongly encouraged to attend international meetings at any suitable occasions and to exchange information with the entire world. Salary depends on performance and has nothing to do with the promotion-by-age system. In an effort to make each member of this lab equal, signs indicating titles and seniority have been eliminated.

The most important spin-offs are depicted below, in a size that represents the number of employees.

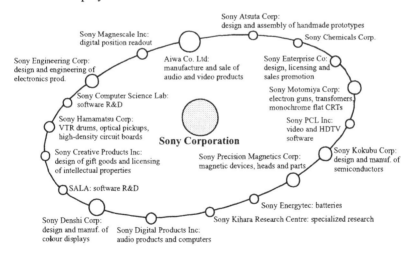

Source: Own interpretation of data from Sony and Dodwell (1992/93, 247)

Figure 3.6 Sony's R&D-related Domestic Macrocosm

Toyota's Macrocosmic Position

Toyota Motor is a full member of the Mitsui Group. The president, Shoichiro Toyoda, is a member of *Nimokukai,* the shacho-kai of the Mitsui Group. Toyota Motor and Toshiba Corporation, a Mitsui member, jointly established a company for computer system development with IBM Japan. Toyota also has five overseas joint ventures with Mitsui and Co.[52]

In the early 1980s, a series of developments in suspension systems, like electronic height control and braking control systems, required rapid progress in electronics technology. In 1985, almost half of Toyota's vehicles were equipped with electronic fuel injection systems and the need for electronic systems used in engines, transmissions and chassis was continuously intensified. Hence, Toyota found it necessary to increase its competence within electronics. In addition to hiring more electronics engineers, the company set up in-house training courses in electronics, held by experienced electronics engineers from Toshiba who joined Toyota's mechanical engineers uniquely for this purpose, for a limited period of time.

There are other important players in the Mitsui Group than Toshiba, some of which appear in Figure 3.7.

Toyota Motor's Kigyo Keiretsu

Toyota suppliers are organized in two different associations. The Kyohokai, founded in 1943, gathers 234 manufacturers of auto parts and components and the Eihokai, founded in 1983, consists of 77 manufacturers of moulds, gauges, jigs, etc. and contractors for plant facilities. In a pyramidal structure, second- and third-tier suppliers support the first-tier suppliers. In all,[53] some 36,000 to 47,000 suppliers and subcontractors are related to this pyramid.

First-tier suppliers frequently come to a large conference room, called the International Design-in Room. Continuous interaction is facilitated through geographical proximity. Most important suppliers are located within a 50 kilometre radius of Toyota City, to the north of Nagoya.

Mohri-san, project general manager of the technical administration division, believes that intimate interaction with suppliers has a clear advantage in the fact that Toyota City is in an isolated area,[54] with most suppliers gathered around. In addition to monthly official gatherings, there are daily meetings between Toyota managers or engineers and supplier presidents or engineers, focusing on issues around their collective technology and component development. The main advantages that Mohri-san sees are that

> we trust them, they trust us and are a great support both in the development and in the production phase thanks to their flexible and co-operative attitude.[55] They interact both with the Head Office Technical Centre and with Higashi-Fuji Technical Centre.

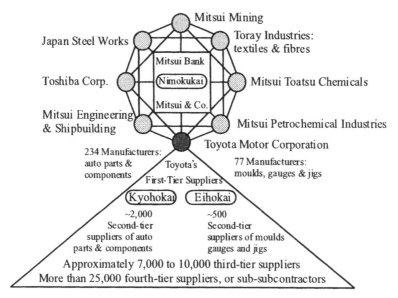

Source: Own arrangement of data provided by TMC and Sunaga, interviews; Dodwell (1992/93, 12-51) and Fruin (1991, 272).

Figure 3.7 Some of Toyota Motor's Keiretsu Interlinkages

The practice of 'design-in', means that suppliers are invited to Toyota Motor, where they develop and design parts and components. This close co-operation starts at an early stage of development and lasts throughout the production-face, but it is not always done at Toyota's premises. So called 'black box designed' parts are entirely designed and developed within the suppliers' premises. The contributions of Toyota engineers are in these cases rather limited. All they usually do is present a 'request for design and development of parts'. The same request is usually given to several suppliers who thus have to compete on speed of development and quality, but usually not on price. In the end, the order is given to the supplier that has developed the best prototype in the shortest period of time. Once an order is given Toyota's production engineers will help the supplier to decrease costs, in accordance with demanding cost-reduction schedules. Knowledge-sharing seems to be intense, and technical assistance from Toyota is frequent.

Takeshi Miyamoto, Director of MITI's Research Institute, supports the aforementioned impression that supplier competition is the most important contributor to Toyota's high speed of new product development:

> When Toyota needs a part, several suppliers will have to compete for the contract and the best one will be selected. Thanks to this competition, all suppliers are eager to increase their level of quality, technology and speed of development in order to get a larger chunk of Toyota's orders. (Miyamoto, interview)

That automobile manufacturing is prone to integration and combination of a wide range of technological fields can easily be seen in the case of Toyota Motor, which enjoys support from several complex networks of small and large companies. The historical origin of these networks date back to 1937, when Toyoda Automatic Loom decided to launch Toyota as a separate company instead of producing automotive vehicles in-house.[56] At the same time, departments that specialized in particular products or functions such as electrical components or steel were spun off as non-consolidated subsidiaries, e.g., Nippondenso and Aichi Steel (Cusumano, 1989).

Today, the Toyota Group includes three automobile manufacturers: Toyota Motor, Daihatsu Motor, Hino Motor and a large number of spun-off principal subsidiaries.[57] Some group companies are active in unrelated areas like insurance, prefabricated housing and real estate development, which makes the composition of the group look similar to that of a kinyu shudan.[58]

Figure 3.8 depicts the most important members of the Toyota Group in a size that gives an approximate reflection of their number of employees.

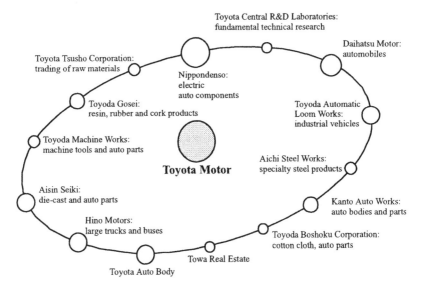

Source: Own arrangement of data provided by TMC

Figure 3.8   Toyota Motor's Macrocosm of Principal Subsidiaries

Personal ties are particularly strong with 19 core members,[59] only one of which does not have a director coming from Toyota Motor. At one-third of the core members, more than 30% of all directors are from the parent company. Approximately 60% of the core subsidiaries generate more than half their sales from transactions with Toyota.[60]

Co-operation across the group is seamless: in the development of an O_2 sensor for a three-way catalyst, the engineering staff at the head office technical centre engaged in close co-operation both with the spun-off Toyota Central R&D laboratory and with Nippondenso (Toyota, 1988).

Effects on R&D of the Keiretsu Interlinkages

Compared to the relative importance of keiretsu networks in the Japanese economy, the data on the case-study companies are brief in length, omitting many topics and details. By adding data from the previous sections of this chapter, some additional effects of keiretsu linkages on R&D and innovation at Canon, Sony and Toyota can be suggested:

Risk-sharing: Most authors argue that both kinyu and kigyo keiretsu partly reflect the motive of sharing risks, and to the extent that this corresponds to reality, links to a kinyu shudan and its main bank make possible a greater number of risky R&D projects, other things being equal.

Long-term innovation: Horizontal affiliations facilitate long-term R&D projects through mutual shareholding and intra-keiretsu financing, which insulate member companies from the pressure of capital markets and from myopic shareholders.

Higher R&D investments through access to low-cost capital: This is possible without fearing the risk of hostile takeovers thanks to the stable owner structure.

Scale economies in R&D: These are achieved through efficient pooling together of many kinyu shudan members' capacities in large R&D joint projects, in which they enjoy the sharing of technological know-how.

Project members operate in diverse fields of business and have different core competencies, which enables cross-industrial technology fusion that may result in inventive combinations of new key technologies. The collecting of information on technological developments within their diverse specialities, a prerequisite for technology fusion, is enabled at low cost through networking both within corporate groups and among vertically-affiliated suppliers.

An advantage of Canon and Toyota over Sony is the access to extensive information networks through the sogo shosha, which scan the globe in search of new technologies and competencies, thus assuring global gatekeeping.

Effective diffusion of R&D results: Through exchange of engineers and through informal discussions between presidents in shacho-kai (with the exception of Sony) and other forums of interaction, R&D results seem to be effectively spread throughout a kinyu shudan. Each group member company can then easily dissipate the new knowledge through its own kigyo keiretsu by exchanging engineers with its suppliers and by having executives or presidents serving concurrently at both the main firm and at the supplier.

Access to users: The leading source of ideas for new technologies in many industries can provide important information to the supplier throughout the development process. Similarly, corporate group members can enjoy links to early and reliable customer feedback.

Co-operation between suppliers and customers also rationalizes business behaviour and yields minimized cost of transaction and increased speed of development. Less paperwork is necessary in a long-term relationship and suppliers usually wish to maintain a good position in the kigyo keiretsu hierarchy, by developing higher-quality products and components faster, in the fierce supplier competition.

Hence, the Japan-specific coexistence of both competition and long-term co-operation appears to promote rapid innovation of increasingly high-quality products, notwithstanding lower prices.

Furthermore, an assembler can focus on a reduced number of first-tier suppliers, who in turn will manage integration and exchange with lower-level tiers. This makes possible a more effective management of subcontracting.

Increased secrecy in the management of new technologies: To be kept from external parties, this is enabled through the widespread mutual trust within both kinyu and kigyo keiretsu. Trustful relationships also enable suppliers to assume entire responsibility of quality control, which reduces the assembler's need for costly and time-consuming test runs before starting commercial manufacturing.

The possible negative effects of the keiretsu linkages

When purchasing policy is affected by intragroup loyalty, group members may be restricted in their choice of components or machinery. In this context, Sony's 'semi-outsider' position may provide an advantage.

The practice of dispatching directors from the bigger to the smaller in the supplier pyramid certainly promotes good communication, but may be cumbersome for the receiving party, who perhaps wants to promote somebody from within the company instead in order to motivate and assure the competence of company members.

Too much use of design-in and of black-box design decreases the assembler's knowledge about its own components. It seems that Canon and Sony have a lesser degree of design-in than Toyota, but all companies seem to enjoy a very open exchange of information with their first-tier suppliers.

Finally, the intensive regimentation of corporate groups and their kigyo keiretsu may reduce inventional efforts towards path-breaking technologies. This can, however, be compensated by spinning off specialized units.

Apart from the keiretsu networks, many additional sources of technology and innovation feed into the case study companies' T&I management. Governmental R&D networks, overseas labs and alliances with universities and other companies provide important knowledge links that will be traced in the following sections of this chapter.

GOVERNMENTAL R&D NETWORKS

Our primary goal within MITI is to increase collaboration between government, or rather government labs, universities and industries. The main way in which we can promote this triadic co-operation is simply to secure their budget. (Hatakeyama, Vice Minister of International Affairs at MITI, interview)

Access to Resources

An anonymous researcher (B), who is spending his fourth year in one of Sharp's R&D labs, is mainly building and developing production devices. The basic physics are already known from a British university, so no scientific research has to be done. 'Instead we work with the practical application of this science, by initially getting inspiration from a British device'. A MITI project is going on in a related area. Three researchers from B's lab are participating in this MITI project. There is no joint lab for the MITI project. Instead, all research is being pursued separately within the companies. 'For us it is more a question of funding our research than doing research together with other companies'.

As pointed out in interviews with Mr. Bergman,[61] the main benefit of co-operative research organized by MITI is the individual development of competencies. The actual cost of information and competencies is very low for each company, as MITI usually sponsors part of the project and the rest of the funding is shared among all participants. 'I would actually find it difficult to imagine a company that cannot afford to participate'. Several other interviews[62] support the argument that the main advantage of MITI resides in highly leveraged R&D spending and the internal development of competencies, with a lesser emphasis on the actual results of the project.

Coordination and Interlinkage of R&D Activities

It is widely argued that national institutes and universities in Japan sponsor or conduct R&D activities that are too basic, too long-term, too risky and too costly for private Japanese companies. The role of MITI, therefore, seems to be significant within R&D, particularly in organizing co-operative projects that interlink the R&D activities of various actors, and in coordinating the R&D activities of independent companies.[63] Transfer of top officials to private companies seems to be the most frequently used mechanism to secure the link between private industry and MITI. The procedure of MITI can to be divided into three steps:

1. Penetration and identification of future prospects and selection of strategic areas;
2. Formulation and publication of visions;
3. Provision of policy measures in order to induce industries to increase

their R&D intensity in accordance with the direction indicated in the vision.

MITI also encourages the sharing of knowledge and of patents in order to diffuse technology (McKelvey, 1993). Since 1961, MITI's industrial research associations have encouraged both fusion and diffusion of technologies and the creation of inter-company engineering infrastructure. In the past three decades, there have been over 75 such associations formed (Kodama, 1992a).

Another interlinking mechanism is provided by the 'interindustry technology fusion index', showing the research spending by different industries, but in similar fields and thereby indicating the potential for synergies in R&D (Tatsuno, 1990).

The perhaps most famous coordination mechanism of MITI is its issuing of 'visions of the future', which started in the early 1970s, in an effort by the Japanese government to encourage private industry to become more creative and visionary. The mixed management approach in this technology forecasting process provides valuable insights not only to how MITI's networks are managed, but also how Japanese companies and the Japanese system are managed as a whole.

MITI's Information and Research Office (IRO) appears to be involved in the vision-making process. Much like the technology scanning office of a sogo shosha, the IRO has 120 Tokyo-based members who are supported by a larger number of expatriated agents, charged with world-wide technology-scanning. The vision is not merely the result of MITI bureaucrats' brainstorming, but rather a consensus between the diverse members of an Industrial Structure Council and a great number of study committees, involving leading professors, researchers, journalists and corporate leaders.[64] Hence, intelligent judgement of the power of judgement of others seems to constitute a greater competence than personal visions and initiative.

We will now take a brief look at the MITI linkages of Canon, Sony and Toyota.

Canon's MITI Interaction

The most important MITI projects of Canon were probably those related to the famous VLSI project, in which Canon was requested to develop a mirror projection aligner and also a stepper machine, in 1977 and 1978. Canon received both monetary resources (50% of total development costs) and development support from MITI's joint laboratories (Sigurdson, 1986). Apart from these projects, it seems that Canon has few links to MITI's activities.

Sony's MITI Interaction

When Sony Research Centre decided to join some MITI projects on Superstructure devices and Photo Hole Burning processes, both aiming at the achievement of very high density memory, we were granted 30 million yen a year during a five year period. The main reason for joining was not financial at all, because this sum was of little importance to us. Instead, the possibility to establish co-operative relationships with researchers in other companies that also participated in these projects was very useful to our research activities and made us keep abreast of state-of-the-art developments in these fields. (Kikuchi, interview)

After 26 years of R&D within MITI, Dr Kikuchi joined Sony as the Director of the Research Centre. He was given a clear objective by Chairman Morita and President Iwama to establish good relationships with MITI. Consequently, Dr Kikuchi arranged the involvement in two projects, related to compound semiconductors.[65] Sony could send two persons to MITI's monthly meetings, reporting on all recent research activities (Kikuchi, interview).

The development of a hot-electron transistor (HET) was done through participation in MITI's next-generation industrial basic technology program, which started in 1981. As a result, two-atom layer super lattice thin film technology was achieved, which radically improved Sony's MOCVD technology and enabled the launch of the world's first BS tuner.[66]

Presently, approximately ten Sony researchers are working on MITI-financed projects.[67] Two Sony researchers, who are working on research projects in a MITI laboratory in Tsukuba, come to Sony's Research Centre on a monthly basis to meet with their colleagues and report on research results (Le Bellégo, interview). For the development of the next generation CCD,[68] Sony Research Centre conducts joint research with the National Laboratory for High Energy Physics (SONY, 1992a).

In 1995, Sony joined a 6-billion-yen MITI consortium to develop multimedia technology. The six other members in this collective attempt to catch up with the US in this field are NEC, Matsushita, ASCII Corp., Fujitsu, Toshiba and Hitachi.[69]

Dr Kikuchi is the member of a *kyo kai,* which is a study group consisting of 25 opinion leaders from MITI, universities and companies. The main function of this kyo kai is to gear financial support to applying researchers,[70] who present their prospective projects. The benefit for participating companies is that research projects are discussed and their results are distributed. 'It's a hidden way of supporting research in Japan' (Kikuchi, interview).

Toyota's MITI Interaction

Traditionally, Toyota has been very closely linked to MITI. One of Toyota's board members has been transferred from MITI.[71] Noda, who is working in the industrial affairs division at the Tokyo office, is in close interaction with MITI. Among his large field of activities, one is to scan MITI policies:

Usually, we meet two or three times per week, sometimes on my own but more often in larger groups, including my boss . . . MITI policy is not my main activity, however. For more intense interaction, we have a special technology section acting both as observer and partner of MITI's technology policy and forecasting. (Noda, interview)

The above-mentioned technology section is located in the Tokyo engineering division, a separate building close to MITI. The only activity of its some 30 'contact officers' is exchange of information with MITI, not only regarding possible R&D co-operations in key technologies, but also on issues like environment, safety regulations and foreign trade restrictions. Toyota has joined MITI-sponsored research councils and organizations within the field of mobile communication and pursues R&D of related hardware. MITI's CALS-project is one example which focuses on the development of new power-generation technology with more than 80 leading Japanese companies.[72]

ADDITIONAL LINKAGES TO EXTERNAL SOURCES OF TECHNOLOGY

Interlinking Domestic and Foreign Universities

Takeshi Miyamoto, Director of MITI's Research Institute, finds that domestic university-industry links are too poor in terms of co-operative research, which he attributes to the low level of Japan's academic centres of excellence:

> The best students go to the corporate research labs instead of staying in the under-equipped universities. (Miyamoto, interview)

Still, it seems as if university-industry interaction is rather strong within certain technologies. A visiting researcher at the robotics department of AIST's mechanical engineering department in Tsukuba states that 'Kobe Steel pays for all the equipment of the lab, and communication floats very freely between engineers of Kobe Steel and the Chief Professor of the lab' (Bayrleithner, interview). Similarly, Dr Mozjetckov at the Department of Nuclear Engineering of Tokyo University, received all his funds for expensive equipment from Hitachi, which had open access to all results. A large number of researchers have reported similar interlinkages.[73]

Overseas R&D Facilities and Strategic Linkages

Instead of merely gathering information on and emulating foreign inventions, Japanese companies are said to pay increasing attention to more upstream activities of foreign research.[74] A French study (PLAN 1994, 160) reports 280 'expatriated' Japanese research laboratories employing some 5,000 researchers, of which 45% are located in the US and 35% in Europe. It is, however, our impression that these numbers are too low.[75] According to the same report, close to 80,000 Japanese researchers went overseas for shorter periods of time in 1991.

Canon's Additional Sources of Technology

University interaction

As the development of steppers[76] moves toward shorter wave technology, we need new scientific knowledge. This is the easy part, because scientific knowledge is available everywhere: Chalmers, MIT and Tokyo University all make it at our disposal. The difficult part is to transform their scientific knowledge into practice (Toyosaki, interview).

Canon fosters close linkages to both domestic and foreign universities. When a research project in the Canon Research Centre was discontinued, the seven researchers involved were asked to move to more product-oriented development. Two of the researchers accepted, but five of them resigned and found research positions in laboratories of three universities[77] in the Tokyo area.[78] At the same time, Endo, R&D manager of Canon, donated the related research equipment, worth about one million US dollars, to one of these laboratories and dispatched two additional researchers to the university team, but these stayed on the payroll of Canon's Research Centre, thus retaining with the obligation of generating patent applications.[79] The other five researchers who had left Canon enjoyed the freedom of no longer being forced to generate these applications, which caused strong jealousy among their previous colleagues at Canon.

Canon usually offers an average of five researchers the opportunity of conducting scientific studies overseas. Those who are selected may freely choose institutions, as long as they are technology-oriented (Bergquist, interview).

To take an example, Canon signed an agreement in 1992 with Chulallongkorn University in Thailand to establish an Imaging Technology Research Laboratory. Canon offers a support of approximately $2 million and has the right of free exchange of researchers and engineers between Canon and the University.

Domestically, a much higher number of researchers is sent to universities for a year of research in fields that are closely related to Canon's activities. Those who are in universities not too far from Tokyo usually come to Canon once a week, thus maintaining a strong knowledge-link between university activities and Canon's own activities.[80] Moreover, Canon maintains contracts of co-operation with approximately twenty Japanese professors, who come to Canon for scientific discussions and receive Canon researchers in their own laboratories (Kanbe; Bergquist, interviews).

Overseas R&D facilities

'We can invite foreign minds to Japan, but as they usually get Japanese habits and ways of thinking if they are here, we prefer to keep them overseas' (Emura, interview).

Canon has established five R&D facilities overseas in, respectively, the UK, France, Australia and the US:[81]

- Canon Research Centre Europe Ltd was established in 1988 in the Surrey Research Park of the UK;
- Canon Research Centre France SA was established in 1990 in Rennes;
- Canon Information Systems Research Australia Ltd was established in 1990 in Sydney;
- Canon Research Centre America Inc. was established in the Stanford Industrial Park California in 1990, as was
- Canon Information Systems Inc. in Costa Mesa, California.

Top management functions are performed by Japanese, but most of the researchers are locals. Altogether, some 200 researchers are employed in the five centres, the core activity of which is software development (Kozato, interview).

Commenting on Canon's activities in Silicon Valley, Dr Mitarai, then Senior Managing Director of Canon's global R&D, states that 'there, we are tapping an entrepreneurial spirit that is hard to find in Japan'. Similarly, it was 'the availability of experienced researchers and experts' that caused the establishment of the Research Centre in the UK.[82]

Robert Burmeister,[83] director of the US-Japan Technology Centre at Stanford University, argues that Canon's strategy of having decentralized R&D labs in the West aims at enjoying 'the very informal and non-hierarchical' atmosphere that these labs seem to offer.

Kozato-san,[84] Manager of Overseas R&D Promotion Department, holds that the overseas R&D laboratories partly aim at avoiding the increasing bureaucratization of R&D at Canon in Japan.

Canon's strategic alliances
Canon made the biggest single investment[85] in Apple Computer founder Steven Job's NeXT venture, and supplies laptops as OEM both to Apple and to Hewlett Packard.[86] Canon is also sending engineers to Powerhouse – a regrouping of NeXT's design team – in Silicon Valley.

Technical agreements are signed with Siemens on facsimile interfaces and with Eastman-Kodak[87] on leading-edge medical equipment and with General Electric. 'We have mutually rewarding exchanges with these companies' (Emura, interview). A joint venture was established with Olivetti of Italy in 1987 to develop and produce business machines, extended in 1992 to develop and sell bubble jet printers and optical card systems as well.

In 1989, a joint venture was set up with Plasma Physics Corporation in New York to develop solar batteries. A similar joint venture was set up in 1990 with Energy Conversion Devices, based in Michigan.

In 1991, TI, Canon and HP set up a joint venture for production of 4 and 16 DRAM semiconductors in Singapore.

Canon also plans to establish a joint venture subsidiary with the Japan Key Technology Centre – a MITI-sponsored R&D organization – to work on the development of 3-D image technology.[88]

In an alliance with Kodak, Live Picture, HP and Microsoft, Canon will develop a new file format for easier handling of high-resolution images on a computer and across the Internet.[89]

Sony's Additional Sources of Technology

University interaction

> There are some cases in which our efforts in technology development of for instance integrated circuits, gives new contributions to fundamental science. As sciences of this kind require very expensive instruments, at least 50% of all state-of-the-art research is being conducted within private companies. We do this research within Sony because product development in these areas calls for a close integration of the actual technology development. University interaction is of course mutually beneficial in these areas. Anyway, Japanese university labs lack the resources to do this kind of research on their own. (Kikuchi, interview)

Semiconductor-related electronic technology has become so scientific that Sony has a hard time evaluating its research results. Hence, crystals grown by Sony's advanced manufacturing technology are being evaluated by, e.g., the Tanigawa Laboratory of Tsukuba University and by Technische Universität Berlin. 'There are several ways to involve university research in our R&D at Sony: The first way is very informal. I simply invite old friends at Tokyo university and some other universities'. Usually, only one or two professors attend at the same time, which enables intimate and open-minded discussions. First, Dr Kikuchi spends half a day showing them Sony's results and problems. Then, they have 'very creative discussions' for the rest of the day.

The second and more formal way also involves colleagues at other companies like Fujitsu, Nippon Electric and Hitachi. Including some leading professors, they are at most 25 researchers meeting on a weekly or sometimes monthly basis. Sometimes, these local conferences are held in Sony's Research Centre, sometimes in the Sony HQ building and sometimes at the other companies.

The third and most formal way is when MITI or AIST organize conferences around their research projects. These conferences include a large number of competing companies in addition to the professors. Therefore, 'even if we meet to share information around specific research areas, it often happens that we don't disclose a new finding of strategic importance. At least, we will keep this information to ourselves for three or six months and perhaps patent it'. Each time that Sony makes a breakthrough, they carefully judge its strategic impact before disclosing it or not. This is an important task of the R&D manager:

> Of course, other members do the same, but sharing strategic information is not the purpose anyway. Rather, the purpose of joining a government-organized project is to keep

channels of general information open. This gives us a basis for fundamental understanding of the research problem. (Kikuchi, interview)

The Sendai Technology Centre

This provides another example of close university interaction. Its research on magnetic tapes and magnetic head materials enjoys the benefits of close co-operation with the Tohoku University. The transfer of research results into production is immediate, as the Sendai Technology Centre in effect is one of Sony's affiliated production plants.[90]

Foreign universities

University interaction at an international level with mutual understanding and communication is very important. The personal relationship, in itself, is actually more important than the institution to which the person belongs . . . The more people you know, the better it is. (Morita, interview)

After a few years within Sony Corporation in Japan, some members are offered the possibility to go overseas for studies. A development engineer within the audio group went for example to ESSEC in France, where he took an MBA. Afterwards, he joined Sony France instead of returning directly to Japan (Eda, interview). On a yearly basis, between 20 and 30 engineers are sent overseas for longer periods of education in universities or foreign laboratories (Kikuchi, interview).

Sony sends some researchers to Santa Barbara University in California, to the University of Illinois and to Stanford. Some are sent to Ireland and to Grenoble in France. Many of those who have been overseas become managers on their return. During their time abroad, they send monthly reports to the Research Centre by E-mail. Above all, they are encouraged to develop an extensive network of friends (Le Bellégo, interview).

The president of the University of Illinois often comes to Sony asking for financial support in exchange for joint research projects, despite increasingly restrictive US policies regarding foreign involvement in US universities. Not long ago, Sony granted 13 million dollars over a five-year period to a new chair called the John Barlin Chair. A good friend of Dr Kikuchi, Professor Honia, became the first holder of this chair.

Among other universities, MIT and Stanford are gradually closing their doors to Sony, due to government requirements. In the past, when Dr Kikuchi established university contacts, Sony, for instance, paid a yearly membership fee of 5,000 dollars to Stanford's Electronics Affiliates Program. Since then, the membership fee has multiplied a few times and the reaction has become cooler when Sony's researchers want to join in. Open refusals are becoming more frequent. Still, Sony has the right to send three engineers there each year. Sony also has the right to all publications and Dr Kikuchi can go there as often as he wishes (Kikuchi, interview).

Openness to foreign researchers
Due to the increasing closedness of US universities, Dr Kikuchi has initiated a new approach to university interaction. By offering a sabbatical chair within the Sony Research Centre, famous foreign professors can be attracted. During 1993, Professor Hans Queisser from the Max Planck institute in Germany enjoyed this invitation. Former Research Director Dr Kikuchi states that 'we are sincerely interested in maintaining a friendly and long-lasting relationship with excellent Western researchers. Their uniqueness of ideas is lacking in Japan'. Sony also offers a summer internship to promising Western scholars, who can pursue their research at the Sony Research Centre.

Overseas R&D units
In the late 1980s, Sony began to expand overseas R&D facilities in order to shorten development-cycle time and to make better use of global R&D capabilities.[91] There are five different development centres, located in Europe. In the US, Sony Engineering and Manufacturing America (SEMA) alone has three technology centres, working in close co-operation with Japan. By sending Japanese engineers to SEMA for a year or more, they acquire new skills that they can bring back to Japan. These are all very localized, with an emphasis on scientific research and open exchange of information with universities. Hierarchy is very low in these centres. 'By moving the designers between Japan, the US and Europe, they learn from each other' (Gérard, interview).

Sony's strategic alliances
Trans Com., an American company engaged in design, manufacturing and installation of audio visual entertainment systems for commercial aircraft, was acquired in 1989.[92] Sony Electronic Publishing Company in the US specialzies in the development and manufacture of game and multimedia software; Sony Tektronix Corporation is an R&D-intensive joint venture between Sony Corp. and Tektronix Inc. in the US that designs and manufactures measuring instruments; Materials Research Corporation, a US company, was acquired in 1990 by Sony and Anelva.[93] It pursues design, manufacture and sales of thin film processing equipment and high purity metals; In November 1991, Sony invested in the US General Major, which is a subsidiary of Apple Computer; for the development of CD-ROM drives, Sony has a joint venture with Philips and they also have shared patents in this field.[94]

In the field of GSM phones, Sony used to rebadge phones manufactured by Siemens. In 1995, however, the two companies started a joint development for next-generation phones.[95]

In order to catch up in liquid crystal display technology, in 1995 Sony joined with TI in developing a screen with higher resolution and less power consumption that current LCDs. While Sony brings in its innovation and mass production expertise, TI contributes with a unique mirror chip technology – developed with assistance from the US Defense Department, but never successfully commercialized. Sony and TI also have co-operated in micro-controllers and semiconductors.[96]

In an alliance with Sony and Philips, Samsung Electronics has developed a PALPLUS system television which is capable of receiving broadcast signals both for traditional televisions and wide-screen televisions.[97]

Seagate and Sony have agreed to develop and market a new disk drive based on Pre-Embossed Rigid Magnetic (PERM) media.[98]

A joint team with Sony and Microsoft engineers develops prototypes of hardware for video on demand systems.[99]

According to Reuters News Service (1995), Sony and Oracle are jointly investing in a project on the next-generation broadcast technology.

NTT, Sony and AT&T have created a $5.7 million joint venture, NTT Fan Inc, to develop General Magic technology-based network services. Sony provides the terminals, AT&T the know-how and NTT the facilities.[100]

Sony Software Corp and PC Financial Network, an on-line discount brokerage unit of Donaldson, Lufkin and Jenrette, has agreed to develop an online trading system to be used on personal communicators using the General Magic alliance's Magic Cap operating system.[101]

A larger group af companies including Sony, HP, Mitsubishi, Verbatim, Philips, Ricoh and Yamaha have created an alliance to develop a re-writable CD technology.[102]

Sony and Oki are co-developing a quarter micron process technology.[103]

Sony and Nissan jointly developed the world's most advanced lithium-ion battery, to be used in Nissan's hybrid electric vehicle in 1998.[104]

In close co-operation with Sanyo, Sony developed a unique low-temperature polysilicon display.[105]

Sony, Nintendo, Sega Enterprises, NEC, IBM and Oracle have formed a joint venture called Navio for the development of software to make a new blend of Netscape Navigator into smaller, modular software that can be easily integrated into less powerful hardware of non-PC devices.[106]

In an alliance with Intel, Sony Music is developing video streaming technology for the Internet, enabling Web surfers to tune in to music video broadcasts on the net. Sony and Intel also conduct joint development of both hardware and software for Sony's new home-use television-based PC model.[107]

In a mega-joint project, Sony, Fujitsu, Hitachi, Maxell, Sharp, Sanyo, Olympus and Philips develop the next-generation magneto-optical disc.[108]

AT&T and Sony jointly develop video compression and multiplexing technologies for higher transmission quality.[109]

Toyota's Additional Sources of Technology

University interaction
From when Toyoda Automatic Loom was established in 1926 (from which Toyota was spun off in 1937), personal links to university professors played a

major role in product development.[110] Even though product development in those days usually was tantamount to duplicating and modifying foreign technology, Kiichiro Toyoda ensured that the finest university professors and engineers were involved. Since then, Toyota has been actively engaged in joint research with universities and research organizations when tackling unfamiliar fields.

> Co-operative research with universities is done from the Central Research and Development Laboratories. Our researchers can do some of their work in the universities and they also have very free communication with a large number[111] of professors (Kageyama, interview).

The development of a three-ply leaf spring in 1954 was possible through help from professors at Tokyo University. Now that Toyota is ahead of the domestic universities in many fields, it has developed close ties with and supports professorships at a large number of universities overseas, such as the University of London, Harvard University, Massachusetts Institute of Technology, Columbia University, the University of Michigan, Rockefeller University and the Art Centre College of Design. Between 30 and 60 employees per year are offered the possibility to go to one of them, sometimes as degree students and sometimes as visiting researchers (Noda, interview).

In Japan, the establishment of the Toyota Technological Institute aims at attracting seasoned professionals from Japanese industry and engaging them in joint research projects stretching across industrial and academic lines. One requirement is to have been employed continuously for at least two years at a Japanese company. The studies are highly interdisciplinary, including mechanical engineering, electronic data-processing engineering and materials engineering. Experiments and practical exercises are often conducted within Toyota's production facilities. In 1984, a graduate program was added, which keeps a strong emphasis on interdisciplinary research.

Overseas Design Centres

Advanced styling design seems mainly to be done at Calty Design Research in Newport Beach, California, where 50 designers co-operate with the Japanese design divisions (Nakajima, interview). A second overseas design centre, located in Brussels, Belgium, 'focuses on information collection from the European market and has extensive exchange of information with design centres in the US, Europe and Japan', according to Mohri-san, who has just returned from Belgium, where he managed a technical centre, also located in Brussels.

Ohtani-san, who has worked for Toyota Deutschland, adds that 'it belongs to the tasks of every expatriated Toyota member to give detailed reports on recent car models and new colour trends'.

Overseas Technical Centres

These support vehicle development and production in Japan through intensive observation of competitors. Vehicles are dismantled and examined and relevant technical information is collected on parts, materials and innovative technologies. For the purpose of country-specific certification, usually regarding emissions, Toyota's own vehicles may also be evaluated in such centres. In the US, the Toyota Technical Centre in Ann Arbor, Michigan, acts as head office for the other centres in Detroit, Los Angeles, San Francisco and Phoenix – in all, counting 300 employees (Kageyama, interview). It also advises the product planning division on future product development. Toyota Motor Corporation owns 80% of the technical centre and two members of the Toyota Group, Aisin Seiki and Nippondenso, also have an equity participation.

In Europe, the main technical centre is located in Brussels, but there are sub-operations in Derby in the UK and Cologne and Hannover in Germany, all of which total some 100 employees (Nakajima, interview).

Toyota's strategic alliances

Since 1984, Toyota Motor has had a joint venture (called NUMMI) in the US with GM for development and production of 1600 cc cars.

Ford has teamed up with Toyota for the development of speed control systems.[112]

Toyota is developing an off-road vehicle jointly with Hino Motors.[113]

US-based Delco Motors develops an electromagnetic induction recharging system for automobiles in co-operation with Toyota.[114]

Toyota has entered a joint R&D agreement with Daimler Benz, with the goal of reducing each of the companies' R&D and mass-production costs, while maintaining product quality.[115]

Through a joint venture with Hamilton Standard in Connecticut, Toyota has developed an airplane engine to be available in 1998.[116]

The luxury division of Toyota has a partnership with Shell Oil to study how to get gasoline to Lexus owners whose tanks are nearing empty.[117]

Toyota is teaming up with Mitsubishi, Nippon Oil and Family Mart to undertake research on a new integrated circuit card sustem for expressway toll collection.[118]

A joint venture has been planned with Matsushita for the development and manufacturing of batteries for electric vehicles.[119]

Now that the case-study companies have been located in their surrounding R&D networks, detailed descriptions of their intracorporate R&D actors and activities will follow, and be examplified with three R&D projects.

The intracorporate impact of acquiring extracorporate know-how will be in focus.

NOTES

1. Cf. Håkansson (1987, 1989, 1990); Imai, *et al.* (1985); Kodama (1991, 1992a); Laage-Hellman (1989); Nonaka (1988a, 1988b, 1990, 1993, 1994); Van Dierdonck *et al.* (1991).

2. Cf. MITI (1992a, 1992b); Sheard (1992a); US Committee on Finance (1992); Lawrence (1991).
3. Cf. Fujikura (1992, 209); MAP (1991).
4. The book that became most popular in Japan during the Meiji period was Samuel Smiles's moralist 'Self-Help', which argued that neither rank, nor status were necessary for industrial expansion, but rather hard work, self-improvement, perseverance and thrift (Wilkinson 1990, 59).
5. See, for example, Fruin (1992, 90); Vogel (1979, 107); Whitley (1992, 173).
6. In an interview with Dr Nakada, who was present at Sumitomo's 300 year anniversary, he noted that the presidents of different member companies sat in a certain order, relating to their ranking based on seniority rather than on actual financial importance of the company. NEC only came somewhere in the middle, although its turnover by far outperforms Sumitomo Mining, which had the number one position in the ranking. Some observers, however, describe them as 'structured in an egalitarian manner with no single component controlling the network' (Whitley 1990, 55).
7. See, for example, Imai (1989a, 123; 1990, 18); Okumura (1991, 2-3).
8. Mitsubishi, Mitsui, Sumitomo, Fuyo, Dai-Ichi Kangyo and Sanwa are the six most important groups, but there are also several smaller kinyu shudan in the Japanese economy (Dodwell 1992/93). In 1988, a total of 194 companies were members of one of these presidents' council (Okumura 1991, 2).
9. The equivalent number in 1970 was 371 firms (Gerlach 1992b, 95).
10. Cf. Howard (1990, 94); Nakamura (1987, 28); Sakai (1990, 40-5).
11. There are other types of keiretsu as well, such as ryutsu (or distribution), keiretsu and shihon (or capital) keiretsu, based on the flow of capital instead of the flow of product materials and goods (Gerlach 1992c, 68-9). These types of keiretsu are excluded from our study, as their impact on R&D is of considerably lesser importance than that of kinyu and kigyo keiretsu. A more extensive examination of Japanese corporate networks has been made in a separate paper (Harryson, 1994).
12. Fruin (1992, 20); Gerlach (1992b, 95); Okumura (1991, 2).
13. E.g. Aoki (1988, 224); Dodwell (1990, 9); Goto (1982, 55); Kester (1991, 68); Van Wolferen (1989, 46).
14. Cf. Japan-U.S Business Council (1992, 26); Fujigane (1991, 29).
15. This statement is supported by publications, interviews and discussions on the topic with, e.g., Professors Abegglen, Gregory, Kusunoki, Teramoto and Yawata.
16. Cf. Ballon (1992, 102-103); Vogel (1979, 94-96).
17. Anchordoguy (1990, 59); Irimajiri (1992, 23); Makino (1992, 19); McKelvey (1993, 209); Sheard (1992d, 5); Whitley (1990, 53). For Western short-term vs. Japanese long-term goals, see also Ballon (1992, 83).
18. Around 1800 out of 2,350 large companies hold shareholders' meetings on one and the same day in June every year. In 1992, Sony closed its shareholders' meeting within 10 minutes, which in Japan signifies that it was very successful. Source: Sunaga, interview.
19. See for example Powell (1991, 38); Makino (1992, 19); Nakatani (1992, 27); Irimajiri (1992, 23).
20. 'UK R&D Scoreboard', an analysis based mostly on Standard and Poor's data, financed by Britain's Department of Trade and Industry.
21. Ballon (1992, 117, 151); Gerlach (1992a, 16; 1992b, 107).
22. Encountering a crisis in 1973, Mazda was offered financial and managerial support by the Sumitomo Group (Womack *et al.* 1990, 68).
23. Gerlach (1992a, 32; 1992b, 105); Nakatani (1984, 244); Sheard (1992d).
24. Ferguson (1990, 63); McKelvey (1993, 209); Nakatani (1990, 156; 1992, 27); Whitley (1990, 53).
25. Frankel (1991, 123) concludes in an extensive study that the cost of capital was lower in Japan than in the US during the 1970s and 1980s, and that group-affiliated companies were able to borrow capital more cheaply than non-keiretsu companies. However, he suggests that the cost advantage will disappear in the 1990s.
26. Badaracco (1991, 94); Japan Foreign Trade Council (1992, 9).
27. Cf. theoretical perspective in Chapter 1.

28. Also about 200 women are hired every year, but mostly for internal office supporting functions.
29. Cf. Anchordoguy (1990, 59); MAP (1991, 8); Nakatani (1990, 157-8; Whitley (1990, 56; 1992, 30).
30. According to data provided by Gerlach (1992b, 109), keiretsu firms that had a major mainframe computer producer in their own group bought three times the number of computers from this company that they did from producers linked to other groups.
31. Usually, there are strong buyer-supplier relationships among members of the same kinyu keiretsu. In 1987, trade between Mitsui's members accounted for 17.2% of the group's total trade (Anchordoguy 1990, 59).
32. Cf. Japan-US Business Council (1992, 10); Lamming (1993); Nichiguchi (1994); Smitka (1991); Whitley (1992, 27).
33. Aoki (1988, 210); Jones (1990, 9-10); Lamming (1993); Mitsubishi Research Institute (1987); Samuels (1994, 22); Waldenberger (1992, 276).
34. Cf. Clark and Fujimoto (1991, 140); Howard (1990, 94-96); Lamming (1993); Perrow (1993, 120); Sheard (1992b, 19).
35. Cf. Cutts (1992, 48); Lincoln (1992, 52); Samuels (1994, 26); Teramoto *et al.* (1993, 74-6); Whitley (1990, 53; 1992, 27; Womack *et al.* (1990, 61).
36. (Prof. Kodama; Dr Mori; Prof. Odagiri; Takahashi, T.;) various discussions at a workshop of the European Institute of Japanese Studies on: 'Corporate Technology Strategies in Japan', August 17-19, 1994.
37. The equivalent number in March 1985 was 3,688 executives. Source: *Kigyo Keiretsu Soran* (Corporate Keiretsu Data Book) by Toyo Keizai Inc.
38. Cf. Howard (1990, 96); Jones (1990, 7); Nakatani (1990, 158); Teramoto *et al.* (1993, 76); Womack *et al.* (1990, 146-8).
39. Assemblers call these engineers 'guest engineers', whereas the suppliers see themselves as 'hostage engineers'. In effect, their help is taken for granted, being a *sine qua non* for long-term business (Fujimoto, discussion).
40. Cf. Gerlach (1992b, 108); Itami (1987, 101-2); Lincoln (1992, 52).
41. Cf. Nakamura (1987, 22-8); Teramoto *et al.* (1993, 69-71); Whitley (1990, 53).
42. For instance Johnson (1990); Sakai (1990) and Thoburn and Takashima (1992, 116) see the suppliers' situation as very disadvantageous. Cutts (1992, 50) and Sheard (1992b, 24) suggest that rather than parent firms 'exploiting' subcontractors by shifting risks on to them, quite the opposite might be the case, with parent firms absorbing some (but for incentive reasons not all) of the risks faced by parts suppliers. Womack *et al.* (1990, 149) state that the supplier 'keeps all the profits derived from own cost-saving innovations and kaizen activities' (cf. Jones 1990, 8). Aoki (1988, 204-5) proposes that the subcontracting group formed by the major contracting firm and its satellite firms is a mutually rewarding and efficient economic institution.
43. Cf. Kodama (1986; 1992b); Howard (1990, 96); Gerlach (1992a, 35).
44. *Gijutsu no jidai ni ikiru*, 1983, p. 51
45. Cf. Makino (1992, 19); Orru (1993, 179); Sakai (1990, 39); Teramoto *et al.* (1993, 76); Waldenberger (1992, 276).
46. Quoted in Ackenhusen and Ghoshal (1992, 14).
47. The Toride plant is interlinked with the other Canon manufacturing plants via a satellite CAD network, thus assuring the rapid transfer of new designs and best practices (Emura, interview; cf. Friedland 1994, 78).
48. Cf. Dodwell (1992/93, 245); Gerlach (1992b, 106).
49. Although this is clearly stated in the annual report (SONY 1992c, 30), Toyoo Gyohten, the present Chairman of the Bank of Tokyo, said in an interview (94.05.31) that his bank had no such ties with Sony and that Sony never would want to be put in such a situation.
50. Dr Le Bellégo, who is working as a researcher in the Sony Corporation Research Centre, states that he is 'very surprised by the total openness and trust towards some suppliers. Dai Nippon Printing's engineers receive an incredible amount of technological information on the process of developing and manufacturing an entire transistor, even though they only supply our transistor structures'.
51. These affiliated suppliers usually become first-tier suppliers in Sony's kigyo keiretsu.
52. Dodwell (1992/93, 271-5).

53. According to an official MITI study, presented in Fruin (1991, 272).
54. Previously, the good reputation of Toyota used to enable the company to attract good engineers, but today it experiences recruitment problems, partly due to its isolated location in a city which is entirely dominated by the company (Mohri, interview).
55. The fact that Toyota can maintain stronger and longer-term supplier relationships with better JIT deliveries and more integrated product development than other automotive companies is, above all, due to a finely-tuned purchase forecasting that usually never diverges by more than ten per cent from actual orders. Source (Fujimoto, discussion).
56. The automobile department of Toyoda Automatic Loom was established in 1933.
57. The tie-ups with Hino in 1967 and with Daihatsu in 1968 were encouraged and arranged by MITI (Cusumano 1989, 23).
58. In 1991 as many as three out of every eight yen of Toyota's profits stemmed from non-operating sources, i.e., financial activities (Quinn 1992, 195).
59. Some of these are not included in the above figure, due to a lack of information.
60. Cf. Dodwell (1992/93, 21).
61. Sten Bergman, Science and Technology Counsellor, Embassy of Sweden in Tokyo.
62. Kikuchi; Lewis; Nishibe; Miyamoto, Nishisawa (Prof.), interviews.
63. See, for example, Dore (1983); Fransman (1990); Hollomon (1982, 617-18); Orru (1993, 186); Peck (1990, 243); Sigurdson (1986); Teramoto (1987, 159); Toda and Sugiyama (1984); Watanabe et al. (1991, 111); Whitley (1992, 126-27).
64. Cf. Dore (1983, 1); Gerybadze (1993, 143-6); PLAN (1994, 46); Tatsuno (1990, 75); Watanabe et al. (1991, 111-13).
65. Sony uses compound semi-conductors for their junction lasers, which are key components of CD players (Kikuchi, interview).
66. One of Sony's key researchers in the MITI program relating to Metal Organic Chemical Vapour Deposition technology, Dr Mori, received his PhD from Tokyo University for this work (SONY 1992a, 17).
67. 'MITI is sponsoring interesting fundamental research that would not have been done at Sony otherwise' (Le Bellégo, interview).
68. A Charge-Coupled Device is an 'electronic eye' that converts light energy into electrical signals, mainly used in video cameras.
69. *JIJI Press Newswire* (16.01.95).
70. Applying researchers may come from MITI, universities and also from companies. Researchers from Sony have received support from this kyo kai for research on, *inter alia*, compound semi-conductors and on compound semi-conductor production technology (Kikuchi, interview).
71. Sunaga, interview.
72. *Nikkan Kogyo Shimbun* (03.05.95).
73. Arnfalk; Brunsell; Irie; Kjellgren; Nanao; Nannichi; Nishisawa, J.; Rubber.
74. 'Il ne s'agit donc plus, pour les Japonais, de copier des produits finis élaborés à l'étranger; il s'agit de maîtriser en amont les réseaux d'information, qui constituent le substrat virtuel dont les Japonais sauront tirer, mieux que d'autres, des produits industriels compétitifs' (PLAN 1994, 157).
75. According to statistics presented by Professor Odagiri at a workshop of the European Institute of Japanese Studies on: 'Corporate Technology Strategies in Japan', August 17-19, 1994, Japanese overseas R&D laboratories employ 7,000 researchers. At the same conference, Professor Sigurdson stated that he had counted 264 Japanese R&D facilities in Europe alone.
76. Steppers constitute a core technology in the production of semiconductors and FLC displays.
77. Tokyo University, Keio and the University of Electrocommunications.
78. Due to shortage of resources and a redundancy of projects, four other projects were discontinued at the same time, but the somewhat younger researchers of these projects chose to obey Canon's request and moved to the more product-oriented development activities of a business group.
79. As a consequence of the obligation to generate patent-applications, these two researchers eventually cut their funding ties with Canon as well (Anonymous C, interview).
80. In 1990, approximately twenty researchers of the Canon Research Centre were sent to domestic universities (Bergquist, interview).

81. Cf. Dodwell (1992/93, 258).
82. Quotations are from Canon Chronicle, no. 172, March-April 1993, p. 13.
83. Quoted in Friedland (1994, 73).
84. After a few years of research duties within Canon in Japan, Kozato-san was offered the possibility to spend two years at the University of London. He then took part in the establishment of the Research Centre in Surrey and the recruiting of researchers. After four years in Surrey, he was transferred back to Japan, where he now is managing overseas R&D (Kozato, interview).
85. At least $140 million (Johnstone 1994, 97).
86. Cf. Friedland 1994, 73, 78); Dodwell (1992/93, 259). Canon owns NeXT hardware manufacturing in the US (Bergquist, interview).
87. Canon also does Original Equipment Manufacturing of certain Kodak copiers and printers. Canon has an 84% world manufacturing share in desktop laser printer engines even though its brand share in the laser printer business is minuscule (cf. Prahalad and Hamel 1990, 85).
88. *Nikkei Sangyo Shimbun* (31.01.97).
89. *Multimedia Futures* (20.05.96).
90. It was previously called Sony Magnetic Products, Inc. (SONY 1992a, 13).
91. Cf. Malnight and Yoshino (1990, 5).
92. Cf. SONY (1992c, 45).
93. Anelva is controlled by NEC (Ferguson 1990, 62).
94. Cf. (Collinson 1993, 298; Malnight and Yoshino 1990, 5-6; Schlender 1992, 22). When Philips developed the CD technology, it shared the know-how with Sony in exchange for an agreement to accept its standard (Lewis 1990, 35).
95. *Nikkan Kogyo Shimbun* (31.01.95).
96. *Nikkei Weekly* (06.03.95).
97. *Korea Economic Weekly* (12.05.95).
98. Newsbytes News Network (27.01.95)
99. *Electronic Times* (26.01.95); *Nihon Keizai Shimbun* (23.01.95); and Reuters (1995).
100. *CMP Publications* (1995).
101. Reuters News Service (August 29, 1995).
102. *Office Equipment and Products* (01.05.97).
103. *Electronics Weekly* (13.12.95).
104. *Electronic Buyer's News* (26.05.97).
105. *Electronic Engineering Times* (07.10.96).
106. *Electronic Engineering Times* (02.09.96).
107. *APT* (18.1.96); *Network News* (31.07.96) and Reuters (1996).
108. *JIJI Press Newswire* (17.07.96).
109. *Multimedia Futures* (22.04.96).
110. A classmate of Kiichiro Toyoda, the founder of Toyota Motor, became a professor at the University of Tokyo where he gave courses on automotive engineering. He, professor Kumabe, and many other professors came to play a great role in the development of engines and vehicles. During 1931 they acquired and tested foreign engine components and, at the same time, helped local firms to copy them. In 1932, a Chevrolet engine was purchased and copied. Already in 1934, the first improvement over the Chevrolet engine was made (Cusumano 1989, 58-64).
111. More than 25 professors at any given time (Nakajima, interview).
112. *JIJI Press Newswire* (21.07.95).
113. *Nikkan Kogyo Shimbun* (27.12.95).
114. *Nihon Keizai Shimbun* (13.12.95).
115. *Japan Industrial Journal* (04.09.95).
116. *Nikkan Kogyo Shimbun* (06.06.97).
117. *Tribune Business News* (1997).
118. *JIJI Press Newswire* (16.10.96).
119. *Nihon Keizai Shimbun* (27.08.96); *Electronic Engineering Times* (27.05.96).

4   Canon Inc.[1]

INTRODUCTION

Canon Inc.[2] was founded in 1937 as a camera manufacturer that attempted to emulate, and as soon as possible overtake, Leica, which in those days was in the forefront of its industry. In 1962, Dr Keizo Yamaji, now Vice Chairman, found a way of circumventing Xerox's patented xerography and entered the copier business. In 1991, office automation equipment accounted for 75% of total sales. Canon maintains 80% of the world market for laser printer engines.

Johnstone (1994, 97) argues that, measured by number of US patents awarded, 'Canon can claim to be the world's most consistently creative company'. In 1988, Canon filed more patents in the US than any other company, Japanese or American.[3] Through risky but seemingly successful diversification, it is today five times Nikon's size, from being equally large a few decades ago. Canon has thus experienced impressive growth, from a total of 25,607 employees in 1982 to 62,700 in 1991.[4]

Some 6,000 engineers are engaged in the quest for getting new products to the market at the parent company, which numbers approximately 26,000 people.[5] Kazuo Tanaka, who is in charge of the training of researchers and engineers, states that close to 100% of them go through an initial training program that includes approximately two months of production and three months of sales. However, it seems that work on production lines is done only when an increase in production output can find an outlet on the market.[6]

INTRAORGANIZATIONAL ASPECTS OF R&D AND TECHNOLOGY

Business Groups and R&D- related Headquarters

Canon Inc. consists of 18 Business Groups that are supported by 16 headquarters, five of which perform the administrative tasks of finance and accounting, personnel and organization, general affairs, corporate communications, and social and cultural programmes. The Traffic and Distribution HQ and the Planning and Marketing HQ support and coordinate sales and distribution of each Business Group's Planning and Marketing Centre.

Approximately 4,000 of Canon's 6,000 engineers are located in Shimomaruko, close to Tokyo, where most of the HQs and three of the Product Operations are found. 'Seventy per cent of our engineers are located in production' (Toyosaki, interview).[7] The number of researchers and engineers that pursue research in the Canon Research Centre has diminished to approximately 200 from more than 300 in 1992.[8]

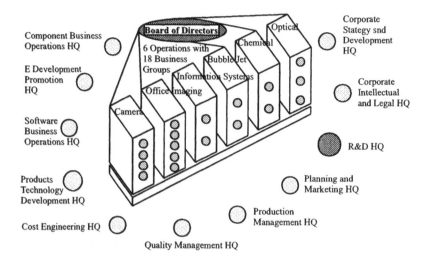

Figure 4.1   Canon's Microcosm of Headquarters and Product Operations

Twenty-seven directors are members of the board. These are the senior general managers of each headquarters, Product Operation and of the most important production plants. The senior general manager that heads one or several Business Groups is also a member of the board of directors.

To begin with, it will be examined how some of the HQs are linked to Canon's R&D activities.

R&D Headquarters is the lead unit within Canon's R&D system, supporting and coordinating all other research and development functions. It performs international coordination of R&D and long-term strategic planning of future products as well as allocation of researchers to different operations and projects.

The Advanced Technology Division is an internal intelligence agency that has six engineers dispatched around the world for technology scanning activities.

Apart from its R&D Planning and Administration Centre, the R&D HQ administrates three research centres that focus on Nanotechnology and Imaging Technology. Its primary coordinating mechanism is offered by the HQ, described below.

The Corporate Strategy and Development HQ, directly attached to top management, assures the preparation of future development plans and formulates visions that support these plans. Furthermore, it performs their translation into catchy slogans that are hammered into all employees via speeches, pamphlets, newsletters etc. This HQ also ensures that Business Groups and divisions at all levels set goals in accordance with top-management visions and that managers at lower levels translate the guidelines of the overall visions when they formulate visions with more tangible and specific goals for their own divisions, groups or projects.[9] This HQ also plays a key role in the evaluation of Business Group leaders, division managers and project leaders. The key performance criteria is the extent to which their achieved goals correspond to the visions, not their individual P&L (profit and loss) result.

The R&D HQ also supports and supervises the Research activities of the Canon Research Centre. Dr Mitarai, who headed this HQ and its five different centres until early 1993, is now the President of Canon Inc.[10] The R&D HQ is located in Shin-Kawasaki, ten minutes away from Shimomaruko. It shares premises with Hitachi, which has two thirds of the office space, and some facilities are in common.

The Canon Research Centre: Patents as Source and Driving Force of Innovation

> At Canon, the easiest way to prove your competence is to write patents. (Yasokawa, interview)

The Canon Research Centre is located in Atsugi, which is approximately one hour away, by car or by train, from the HQ in Shimomaruko. Founded in 1986, it is the locus of Canon's most upstream research activities, but seems to conduct much applied research and development, transforming applied research results horizontally into new products.

> A lot of trial-and-error of prototypes is done here and many of the engineers are transferred to product development in Shimomaruko after a year. (Anonymous researcher E, interview)

The prototypes are usually put together without designs. Applications are promoted more than scientific thinking. Then they are tested and modified until they work. Another anonymous (C) researcher considers the main function of the Research Centre to be recruiting. Graduates from the best universities are attracted to the possibility of doing advanced scientific research. However, after one year of employment, most of the researchers are requested to assume more product-oriented activities, often located in development centres of the business groups. Most researchers seem to be rotated against their wills.[11]

The main source of inspiration for innovation is patent screening. Patent mapping and filing are core activities in the Research Centre:

> All engineers and researchers spend each Tuesday reading patent applications of competing companies. In intensive brain-storming meetings they try to identify the competitors' direction of research and create inspiration for new patent applications and product ideas (Anonymous researcher E, interview).

Most of the researchers at the Canon Research Centre are requested to submit between eight and twelve patent applications each year.[12] Development engineers and production engineers are said to generate more patent applications than researchers do.[13] The application procedure is largely supported either by members of the Corporate Intellectual Property and Legal Headquarters or by private consultants, who specialize in specific areas.

> In the last year, I have filed at least ten patent applications. This obligation is a company policy that helps us to be both productive and creative. The application procedure requires us to explain the technical details and to give possible practical uses, which is a good way to promote creative thinking and spread the results of it. As soon as we join Canon Inc., we are taught to think in terms of patenting and how to do it. (Senior Researcher Tanaka, interview)

An engineer receives ¥3,000 for each patent applied for with some extra bonus if the patent is registered. 'The amount is symbolic' (Emura, interview). The most important incentive for researchers to generate patent applications – apart from the fact that they have to – is that they are allowed to publish an article for each application that they register. The pressure to generate patents is so strong that it has caused several researchers to leave.

A Keen Eye for Optics, Production and Bright Ideas

At an initial stage, everybody has to pass a highly compressed three-month full-time course in optics. Other important training topics are cross-industry exchange, IPR, manufacturing technology and production. The Manufacturing Technology Training Centre constantly offers 100 courses in 11 different production fields. Some training is also geared towards unique thinking and generation of bright ideas, for better understanding and acquisition of Western individualistic thinking. Dr Mitarai, Senior Managing Director of R&D[14] states that:

> Japanese students receive enough group-oriented discipline in school. When they enter Canon, we encourage them to become more individualistic and independent. Moreover we want to be able to accommodate researchers who come from other countries.

In 1993, Canon employed approximately five foreigners, two within R&D. Foreign researchers are usually highly specialized in an area for which Canon has a commercial application in mind. As an example, Dr Albrecht, who acquired a PhD in solid-state physics focusing on Langmuir Blodgett (LB) films, at the University of Ulm in Germany, joined the Canon Research Centre in 1990. Three ordinary researchers work with him on a permanent basis to relate his research to a larger group of researchers who work on a high-capacity tera-bit (a trillion bits) memory system. The goal is to fuse Dr Albrecht's LB film technology with Scanning Tunnelling Microscopy technology.[15]

A second research laboratory was inaugurated in Kyoto in mid-1993 which focuses on energy- and environment-related research.

A perhaps un-Japanese characteristic that Canon claims to have is their openness towards people from other companies, in particular towards re-searchers. CTO Takahashi-san states that:

> this is an advantage of Canon, because these people have different cultures, training and experience. Canon has a culture that accepts these differences, which promotes the flow of people to Canon.

Yasokawa-san, who initially worked for Nomura Securities, agrees that 'those who come from other companies are not discriminated against regarding pro-motion'. To take an example, Vice President Tanaka worked for another com-pany before joining Canon. The practice of senior hiring mainly aims at breaking routines and mainstream thinking.

An Array of HQ-units Support the Innovation Process

The Products Technology Development HQ was established in Shimomaruko to gather related technologies from unrelated business groups, thus assuring a better coordination with broader fusion and exploitation of core technologies, and with less duplication of activities across Business Groups. A second pur-pose of this HQ is to act as possible sponsor of promising technologies that cannot find applications and funding within Canon's existing product groups. Once such a technology has developed into a marketable product, it becomes a new Business Group that is integrated into one of Canon's six Product Opera-tions. Apart from that, this HQ does usually not pursue any development proj-ects of its own, but supports the projects of other Headquarters and Business Groups.

The 1,000 engineers of the Products Technology Development HQ are grouped in four different development centres, the majority of which relate to copying machine technology. Takahashi-san, who was the former Director and senior general manager of the Products Technology Development HQ is now the CTO of Canon.

The Software Business Operations HQ heads all activities that relate to soft-ware research, conducted in eight different centres. The location of these cen-tres are in Shin-Kawasaki, but some of their development activities take place in the Canon Research Centre in Atsugi.

The Component Business Operations HQ focuses on the development of production technology for semiconductors and FLC displays, but also runs projects on solar cells and magnetic optical discs.[16] It counts some 1,000 engi-neers, who are divided into the four interrelated activities. The majority of the members is at the headquarters in Hiratsuka, located two hours away from Shimomaruko. Most of all new product projects come to this HQ for trial production, after having been developed in the Products Technology Development HQ, or in the Canon Research Centre. Later, when the product is ready for marketing and the trial production line yields an output of adequate quality, the HQ 'pushes' the whole project horizontally into a new Business Group, which is joined by most of the previous project members.

The Production Management HQ plays an important role in shortening the lead-time of development projects. Before a project reaches the trial production stage, production engineers usually join the project for a certain time in order to improve the manufacturability of the product. Second, these engineers bring knowledge that is related to the product back to the plant before it arrives, thus preparing for shorter startup times.

Quality Management HQ supports and supervises all quality control and thus plays an important role in the innovation process. Before going on to a new development stage, the project leader needs the approval of this HQ.

The Planning and Marketing HQ is not strongly linked to the Business Groups, but mainly takes care of small markets that do not have any sales function of their own. The marketing link is thus rather weak as it is mainly taken care of by each independent Canon Sales organization, located in most countries in the world.[17] Each Business Group has a Planning and Marketing Centre of its own that does sales forecasting and coordinates sales to the independent sales units.

Now that we are familiar with those HQs that are linked to R&D activities, a deeper penetration will be made of how a Product Operation is divided into Business Groups which, in turn, consist of three different centres, linked to or directly located in an assembly plant.

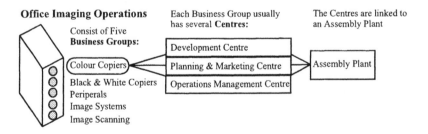

Figure 4.2   Example of a Product Operation at Canon

Each Business Group consists of a development centre, a Planning and Marketing Centre and what could be labelled an Operations Management Centre, that has links to one of Canon's eleven assembly plants and assures cost engineering, quality management, production management and intellectual property matters that are related to production technology. A Business Group thus works much like an independent company, managing planning of new products, their development and finally also their manufacturing and part of their marketing.

Interlinking Market Needs

Market feedback is usually not gathered by specialized marketing people, but rather by dispatching development engineers to the Planning and Marketing Centre of their Business Group.

CTO Takahashi-san does not think that there is much good co-operation between the Planning and Marketing Centres of the Business Groups and the independent Canon Sales companies around the world, an opinion that is supported by many other interviewees. Product planning is largely controlled by the development engineers themselves, which he considers a good approach when technology is developing quickly.

> A design engineer is of course using both copiers and fax machines. Therefore, he knows what to design without being in contact with the market. The dark side of this approach is 'over development'. I personally think that many of our products are becoming too complicated with sometimes too many functions. (Takahashi, interview)

This belief seems to be widely supported within the company. Tanaka-san stresses that, especially within office automation equipment, it is more important to observe competitors than listen to customer needs: 'we are all users of this equipment anyway'. Other Product Operations like, for example, the Camera Operation, organize focused group discussions with customers to get their opinions on cameras and camcorders.

Product Planning Usually Assumed by Engineers

> At Canon Inc., we do not have many company members with background from business schools. Instead, we let our engineers move into planning and marketing divisions, in order to gain experience there. Afterwards, these engineers are better at bringing back knowledge from the market to the team. (Kawashima, interview)

In order to strengthen market linkages of Canon's R&D efforts, R&D members participate along with those of marketing organizations in semi-annual international product strategy meetings and sometimes in itinerant meetings at principal sales subsidiaries. Most planning and marketing functions are staffed by engineers who have been transferred from a research, development, or production-plant function. These members get ample in-house training in marketing as well as in sales techniques.

Using the Power of Rotation for Knowledge-creation

> The atmosphere is very relaxed and informal in our Research Centre, compared to the rest
> of the company. We don't even wear the company uniform and rotate a lot within the
> building to get to know as many people as possible. (Senior researcher C, interview)

In order to accelerate knowledge creation within the Research Centre, monthly
brainstorming meetings are held between researchers and production engineers in one of the two frequently-used brain-storming rooms of the building.
No marketing experts normally take part in these meetings, although their purpose is to generate new product concepts (Bergquist, interview). To promote
the spread of knowledge within the centre, most of the approximate 200 engineers and researchers are relocated so as to get new neighbouring colleagues
every six months.

Inter-functional job rotation within each of the 18 business groups is also
frequent, in particular between the aforementioned centres of development,
planning and marketing and production. In contrast, rotation of personnel does
not occur frequently between different Business Groups of Canon Inc. When it
happens, it is usually on an exchange basis. The reason of this is that the company has mostly experienced expansion and therefore could not afford to have
its members leave their Business Groups, which always have been short of
manpower and function as small companies themselves.

Both senior engineer Tanaka and chief engineer Kawashima state that for
startup projects, based upon entirely new technologies, it is very common that
the involved engineers at the Canon Research Centre are transferred to Planning and Marketing, or to headquarters related to manufacturing.

Know-who for Effective (Dif)fusion of Technologies

Spread and fusion of technologies is, according to Takahashi-san, current
CTO, possible mainly because Canon started as a camera manufacturer, diversifying into copiers and other office equipment. This expansive diversification
caused people, who knew each other well from working closely together, to
spread throughout the organization. As a result, communication remains
strong within intracorporate networks of key persons. For example, Endo
(who invented the Bubble Jet), Kondo (who developed Canon's toners), and
Saito (who lead Canon's Liquid Developing methods)[18] all used to work very
closely together, mainly in one common office, before Canon's massive expansion drove them apart.

PUSHING SCIENTIFIC RESULTS DIRECTLY TO THE FACTORY FLOOR

The Role of the Chief Engineer

Each development centre consists of several development divisions that are headed by division managers who have the rank of general managers. The chief of the development centre has the rank of senior general manager. He is supervised and supported by the aforementioned R&D HQ. Development projects are headed by chief engineers, who may be senior engineers or, for large projects, general managers of a development division. The chief engineer borrows engineering resources from the different divisions of one or several Development Centres (Takahashi; Toyosaki, interviews).

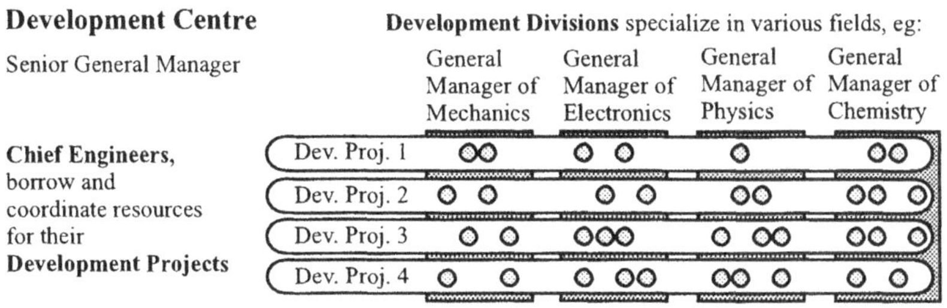

Development Centre — **Development Divisions** specialize in various fields, eg:

Senior General Manager

	General Manager of Mechanics	General Manager of Electronics	General Manager of Physics	General Manager of Chemistry
Chief Engineers, borrow and coordinate resources for their **Development Projects**	Dev. Proj. 1			
	Dev. Proj. 2			
	Dev. Proj. 3			
	Dev. Proj. 4			

Figure 4.3   A Development Centre and its Cross-divisional Projects

Each vertical technology-organization is run by a general manager, who is in charge of setting development targets, directing the development and evaluating the probability of success, but the actual development of a product-project is represented by the horizontal line, cutting across all technology fields. This is the team/task force that gathers engineers from the different development divisions. Normally, each development project consists of several sub-projects, organized quite similarly to the above matrix, but on a smaller scale.

The chief engineer is in charge of the progress of his development project and of meeting targets, mainly in terms of launchability or productability. He takes both time-schedule and costs into consideration. Economic calculations are usually done, or at least strongly supported, by the product-planning division of the Business Group in question.

Team members report both to the chief engineer and to their general manager, i.e., the manager of their home division. The general manager has to know what his engineers are doing, how well they are doing it, and whether the task is good for their education. General managers lend their engineers to specific projects of chief engineers. Once assigned to a project, it is the chief engineer who gives the orders. The general manager stays informed about all projects in which his division is involved. It is also his duty to know about other related projects, even if he is not directly involved in them.

The chief engineer is in charge of setting up the concept of the product and of realizing this concept. The general manager is in charge of his division's technology and the education of his engineers.

The average age of a project chief engineer is approximately 35 for an average-sized product-project. Larger teams have older leaders. For an important product, the chief engineer may be a general manager. Due to their executive director functions, senior general managers are usually not team leaders.

A chief engineer of a large project usually reports directly to the senior general manager, who heads the development centre, instead of reporting to the various general managers. The reason why a chief engineer does not have to respect the traditional hierarchical levels is that 'his development project is independent of the permanent organization so he can talk directly to whom he wants' (Takahashi, interview). However, they still have to negotiate with the general managers of the related divisions and technologies for the allocation of personnel.

'In the final stages when deadlines are severe, many of our engineers may work 18 hours a day' (Yasokawa, interview). The chief engineer may request a specific deadline, but the chief executive of the development centre in question also has a say in judging whether this deadline is possible or not.

Usually, a senior general manager has previously worked as a general manager. Above all, he is required to have rich experience as a chief engineer and good technological capabilities.

Birth and Evolution of a Task Force

The idea usually originates from the Product Planning Division of the Business Group in question. This is the only organization that actually manages planning of new products. The goal is that every company member should routinely be involved in product planning. 'Ideas about new products do not go from top to the bottom at Canon. We get visions from the top, but most ideas come from below' (Yasokawa, interview). 'Sometimes the market provides us with an idea for a product that we adopt and improve' (Takahashi, interview).

The development process can be divided into six steps, as depicted in Figure 4.4.

According to Kawashima-san, collaboration with suppliers is usual in stages D and E. Sometimes it already occurs at the stage B or C, depending on what technology the suppliers in question have. Due to problems of confidentiality, suppliers are rarely invited to join Canon's offices. Still, Takahashi-san emphasizes that 'by actively working together with suppliers we achieve strength.' Equipment manufacturers do join the development teams, but only in the manufacturing plants.

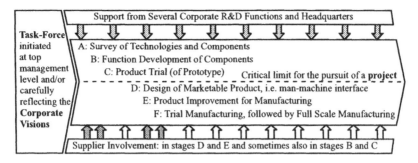

Figure 4.4   Canon's Product Development Process

Stages A and B are usually, or at least to some extent, carried out in the Canon Research Centre in Atsugi, but more often they have no specific location at all. In effect, they are performed by a task force, the members of which are dispersed in the organization and usually appointed directly by the company president. One person may be involved in several task forces and phases. Fully assigned participants do not seem to exist at these stages. Instead, task force participants continue to belong to their specific home divisions. The actual mission of a task force is usually the result of top management decisions, but it may also be formulated at lower levels. Most important in its formulation is that it reflects the corporate visions that diffuse from the top to the bottom of the company, formulated by the aforementioned Corporate Strategy and Development HQ. Clearly stated goals seem to penetrate all development activities.

> The main purpose of the visions is to coordinate all our corporate activities at all possible levels towards a common goal and to push technology towards its limits by translation into seemingly impossible goals. (Senoir Researcher Bergquist, interview)

Time-scales vary according to the nature of the project. The process as a whole normally takes four years from stages A to F. Stage A is usually relatively short (one week to two months), but often continues throughout the entire process, in case a new technology should emerge on the market. B is almost fully overlapped by C, which is the most critical and difficult stage that has to be accomplished in order to secure commercialization. Hence, products that have reached stage D will normally also reach the market. Production engineers from the Production Management HQ are usually involved in the task force already at stages B and C, 'which are mainly based upon trial-and-error' (Takahashi, interview). Their involvement aims at preparing for the F-stage as early as possible.

The fact that many different divisions and operations can be represented in one and the same task force, seems to facilitate vertical integration of competence developed within a certain field both upstream and downstream, as well as horizontal integration between different Product Operations. One example of this is that the cartridge developed for a personal copier came to be used in laser beam printers, facsimile machines and micrographic equipment.

Model renewals of already existing products only pass through the D-stage and forwards. The average elapsed time from D to launch of product is two years. This part of the innovation process usually requires many more resources than the initial part.

If the number of people involved has grown to 100 at this stage, a handful of these will work on the project on a full time basis and all participants will still belong to their home divisions. The actors that are said to be most frequently involved are those from intellectual property: quality engineering; cost engineering; production management; products technology development, assisting with, for example, computer aided design; and the Canon Research Centre.

Takahashi-san emphasizes the importance of patent aspects. Several patent attorneys, with individual areas of expertise, are more or less continuously on loan from the intellectual property headquarters.

When mechanical design is started, this is usually done in co-operation with designers who bring in aspects of ergonomics, look and layout. Environmental, service and ease-of maintenance aspects are included by the quality management headquarters.

Managing the Transfer from Research to Product Development

As long as the probability of success is considered to be less than 50%, the activities related to the task force or its emerging project will be kept in the R&D centre. If stages A, B and C are successfully accomplished and if the probability of success is considered to exceed 50%, the pursuit of stages D and E is started, usually in the development centre of a Business Group, which implies that the task force develops into a more concrete development project. This transfer is, however, only possible if the Business Group in question agrees to sponsor the project.

The chief engineer and the involved general managers decide upon the probability of success.[19] As long as they judge the probability to be between 50 and 80%, the product is improved and developed in stages A, B and C. When they are convinced that it exceeds 80%, the project is moved on to stage D. Once it has reached this stage, the project will usually not be stopped and is very likely to result in commercialization, unless market trends should change.[20] If so, attempts will be made at least to incorporate the core technologies of the project into a commercialized product. A more frequent source of changes is competition. If a competitor launches or plans to launch a rival product, then the specified targets of a project may also change at stage D.

Trial manufacturing is a phase where flexibility is still important and not all technologies in use are confirmed for final application. Gradually, as production, methods, equipment and materials are confirmed at acceptable levels of reliability and price, a full-scale production line emerges, which thus is usually an improved trial production line. It often happens that the product in question is commercialized before completion of the full-scale manufacturing line. In these cases, production is assured through the trial production line, labelled intermediate manufacturing.

Some engineers only participate in stages A, B, and C, but not in D or E. However, most participants remain. Takahashi-san says that of seven to eight participants at stage A, approximately five will remain at D and E.

There are always several projects running in each development centre. Engineers usually take part in several projects at the same time. Their general manager may sometimes withdraw an engineer from one project in order to assign him on a full-time basis to another project instead.

Usually, the Operation Management activities that take place in stages E and F require many more resources than the previous development stages, with perhaps twice the amount of engineers involved compared to stage C.

Interlinking Production

Hiraishi-san, general manager of Production Division 1 at the Toride Plant, describes their interaction with other corporate functions. On average, one engineer from the Planning and Marketing Centre of the related Business Group comes three times a month to his plant for a stay of anything from three hours to an entire day. He mainly reports on customer complaints and future products. Hiraishi-san considers interaction with related development activities to be more important and intensive:

> A whole team of 10 to 20 engineers comes from the development centre in question. On average, they come three times per month, but for much longer stays than the planning and marketing engineer. One to three days is usual, but there are many cases in which they have stayed for more than a month. One development engineer stayed for a whole year before he returned to his development centre, but nobody remains here for the entire time of production.

Hiraishi-san usually goes to the related Business Groups in Shimomaruko on a monthly basis for meetings both with the Planning and Marketing Centre and the development centre.

Competing Development Teams Working in Parallel

> We don't think that internal competition is bad for the company. (Takahashi, interview)

Stage A is research, so there are no specific teams, but rather many members pursuing research with a common goal. At stage B, the development of components, Takahashi-san says that they have two or three task forces working on different components but targeting the same application and thus competing with each other. At stage C, Product Trial, there is only one team in 70-80% of the cases. In the remaining 20-30% of the cases, there are two teams.

The fact that teams are competing does not totally prevent co-operation, because the competition is not fierce at this early stage where the final probability is not yet so high. Also, There are no special rewards for the teams at this stage (Takahashi, interview).

The dividing up of different teams is based upon a time perspective. This means that some teams have short-term objectives, and some teams long-term perspectives, sometimes working on different technologies, but aiming at the same application. Hence, they work in parallel to solve one problem, but both solutions are needed. Therefore, 'they are often rather helping each other than competing' (Kawashima, interview).

When Kawashima-san was in charge of new materials for the copying machine business, he had two groups working on somewhat different materials, both aiming at the same application.

When the two teams had developed their respective technologies, Kawashima-san joined the two teams at a technical meeting at which he presided. Together, these two teams were to decide upon the best technology.

By actually letting the teams decide, Kawashima-san ensured that the decision was factual, and that everybody in the teams was satisfied. Internal consensus and co-operation thus seem to be more important than competition. 'Competition is the major driving force among our teams, but we are competing more with other companies than within Canon' (Kawashima, interview).

DEVELOPING FERROELECTRIC LIQUID CRYSTAL DISPLAYS

In brief, Canon started to do research on Flat Panel Displays in 1982, then focusing on TFT technology. Later in the same year, Takahashi-san, who had a senior position within the Copying Machine Business of Canon, initiated a task force of three people, the mission of which was to identify a future key technology. For three years, the task force kept working with different types of displays. The projects were in stages A, B and C but never made it to D:

> We were three people when the project on new display technologies started and when we had reached stage C we had grown to ten engineers. However, failing to move on to stage D, the team was trimmed down to three members again. (Takahashi, interview)

They realized the need to look for other methods and began co-operating with external parties. In 1995, the FLCD project counted close to 200 researchers and engineers, headed by chief engineer Kawashima at the Display Development Centre in Hiratsuka, where intermediate[21] manufacturing has been running since the beginning of 1993. Although the core of the project now is in Hiratsuka, some of its activities take place in Shimomaruko and in Atsugi, but also in Australia and in the US.

This case study will follow the entire innovation process, from initial acquisition of the technology to development and production of FLC displays.

External Sourcing of a Breakthrough Technology

Dr Kanbe joined Canon Inc. in 1977, after acquiring his Ph.D in solid state physics. To begin with, he worked two months in a calculator production line and then spent two months in the inspection line of a camera production line. He was then sent to support research on thermal printing technology, before his first position was decided: to develop a toner development process for copiers. After having finished this project and successfully accomplished another three-year research project, his closest chief, Takahashi-san, charged him with a new mission: to find the future key technology of Canon. In 1982, Canon created a small task-force of three engineers that searched for a future key technology, headed by Dr Kanbe who was a chief engineer within the Copying Machine Business at Canon. Three overall visions were given by division manager Takahashi to the task force, indicating important fields of the future:

- High Definition;
- High Image Quality; and
- High Density of Information.

With these visionary directives in mind, the task force decided to concentrate on future display technologies. Dr Kanbe was aware of the FLC discovery from having read the Applied Physics Letter that reported on the technology in 1980, written by the inventors Dr Lagerwall from Sweden and Dr Clark from the US.[22] In 1983, Dr Kanbe suggested to his chief, division manager Takahashi, that he go and see the inventors. The reason of this suggestion was that their discovery of a new bistable liquid crystal technology could possibly be used in panel displays. Neither Takahashi nor Dr Kanbe were familiar with liquid crystal technology at that time, but the initial meeting in the US was successful and a co-operative relationship was established between Canon and the two scientists. At this stage, the task force of Dr Kanbe was put to work on FLC technology.

Dr Kanbe had samples of FLC compound prepared by engineers in the Central Research Laboratory and asked previous production-engineer colleagues in the Component Development Centre to prepare glass plate prototypes. A lot of trial-and-error of the resulting components followed and a small FLC display prototype was eventually presented to Takahashi, who encouraged and supported a presentation to upper management. After some hesitation, the pursuit of the task force was allowed.

Later that year (1984) negotiations were started with Chalmers University of Technology and, in 1985, an agreement was reached by which Canon was granted exclusive rights to two fundamental patents held by the scientists.[23]

Since then, both Dr Clark and Dr Lagerwall come at least twice a year to Canon, so as to bring additional scientific progress into the project. Through participation in associations for display technology and by scanning various research reports, Canon learnt that Seiko also worked on FLCD.

> These associations are very open so any of our researchers could go there. I think that both Dr Kanbe and Takahashi-san participated in their meetings. During the following two years, we also found out that several other companies were running FLCD projects. (Yasokawa, interview)

From 1983 and onwards, Canon thus had a task force working on FLC, running in parallel with the TFT development task force. They both succeeded in stages A, B, C and made applications to go on to stage D. However, having two competing task forces in stage D would have required large amounts of money and people. So far, the limited R&D activities of the task forces had mainly taken place in Shimomaruko, but larger facilities would be required to go from trial to real manufacturing. It was clear that one task force would have to be discontinued. The question was which one. According to Takahashi, Canon would have continued the pursuit of the two projects in parallel if their resources had been less scarce:

> The TFT Group had good results, but so did the competitors within this area. Especially threatening were the big companies Matsushita, Toshiba, Sharp and Casio. They all had the resources to be capable of price dumping, a scenario to be expected when so many large companies were competing, especially as the two latter companies were notorious for price dumping. We felt that our chances of being profitable would be small in this field.

Both projects were at this time striving to succeed in stage C and did not yet have any clear application. Therefore, different Business Groups were approached to obtain resources for the pursuit of the projects. The Camera Development Division was quite interested in TFT, but concentrated at that stage so strongly on the development of 8mm video cameras that it could not afford to sponsor the TFT project. A Copying Machine Business Group was interested in the FLC technology and also had the necessary resources to sponsor the project.

> FLCD would be a unique technology, if we pursued the development of Super High Resolution Displays. We wanted to be different. (Takahashi, interview)

A meeting was called for, at which approximately eight persons participated. These included senior general managers of Camera and of Office Imaging Products and their concerned general managers plus senior vice manager of R&D headquarters Endo. The deputy leaders of the FLC and TFT projects, Dr Kanbe and Yoshihara made presentations of their rival technologies. After two half-day meetings with ample argumentation, the members agreed to join the two development projects. However, there was a disagreement on which technology to choose. Three reasons made FLC the final choice:

1. TFT had many competitors and would be unprofitable because of price dumping;
2. There was no business group to sponsor the future development fees of TFT. So far, the Camera Group had sponsored the TFT project, but they felt that this technology was going to be unprofitable. In addition, the Camera Group wanted to concentrate on the development of 8mm video cameras;
3. The FLC group was supported by those working with business machines,[24] who had it in mind to develop a filing system in the future with magnetic optical discs and digital copiers. They would therefore be main sponsors of the group, if FLC were to be the selected technology.

Furthermore, it was suggested that if Takahashi worked exclusively on the FLC project, then he would be supported. The day after Takahashi agreed, Dr Yamaji, who at that time was president of Canon, announced the choice of FLC. Until that day, Takahashi had been the deputy senior general manager of the development division for Office Equipment. Now, at the end of 1985, he was assigned as chief engineer of what had turned from a task force into an FLC project. The core of this project's activities were now transferred to Hiratsuka, totalling some 50 engineers, of which approximately one-third became related to the FLC project.

The TFT project was not entirely abandoned. Some of its key participants joined the FLC project and the others continued working on TFT on a smaller scale within a Camera Group (Ando; Yasokawa, interviews).

An additional research agreement was signed with the inventors, in order to provide the necessary competencies in material design and other related research activities. Some FLC technology also seems to have been sourced from Bell Laboratories. For further support in the development of liquid crystal material, Canon established joint development with a supplier and maintained co-operation contracts with three professors at two domestic universities: Tokyo Institute of Technology and Saitama University (Anonymous C; Kanbe, interviews). In this context, Dr Kanbe states that

> We can go freely to these universities to have free discussions with the professors and researchers there. We also conduct joint experiments.

Changing Chief Engineers

In early 1988, the technology was mature enough to be moved into stage D. But as the yen was continually appreciating, the economic conditions became bad for Canon Inc. If this had not happened, Takahashi-san would have asked for ¥10,000,000,000 (then equivalent to approximately $80,000,000), in order to build new facilities, invest in new equipment and expand the development team. Now, this was not possible. Instead, Dr Yamaji told Takahashi that he was spending too much and that he had to earn some money. Consequently, he was sent back to the Copying Machine Business Operations, where he strongly reinforced sales with the development of colour copiers.

Still, the technology was mature enough to be moved into stage D. By late 1988, Kawashima became chief engineer of the FLC display project.

The Multicompetent Project Coordinator

Chief engineer Kawashima majored in Physics and, before joining Canon, did research in physics at a state laboratory. When he joined Canon in 1970, he first went through the traditional manufacturing and sales rotation program, and then started his career in the Canon Research Centre to develop photo sensors. Three years later, he started to work on materials for copying machines.

> My official location was at the Research Centre, but in fact I was serving rather as a link between our laboratory and the development centre of a Copying Machine Business Group. (Kawashima, interview)

When stage F (trial and final production) started in 1980, Kawashima was moved to the production plant in question, where he stayed for two years until production was stable, and was then moved to a development centre of silicon drums, where he spent a few years in the chemical division. After this period, he was put in charge of a Magnetic Optical Discs project, related to Optical Products Operations.

In 1988, his project was moved to the development centre of the Component Business Operation Headquarters. At this stage, he was also assigned as chief engineer of the FLC project and had an assisting position to Dr Kondo, the senior general manager of the entire Component Business Operations.

In the organization chart below (Figure 4.5), Kawashima has thus both the role of assisting senior general manager of the entire development centre, and the chief engineer assignment of FLCD. Consequently, his position of project-leadership is stronger than those of chiefs A, B and C, which enables him to mobilize and allocate resources more effectively within the development centre.

As depicted below, the development centre consists of four divisions run by General Managers who focus on the four different technological fields of mechanics, electronics, physics and chemistry.

After a few years, the FLCD project expanded to a Display Business Operations Centre, for which Kawashima became the senior general manager. At this stage, Kawashima's second Chief Engineer position (of Magnetic Optical Discs) was transferred to another engineer so that he could concentrate fully on the FLCD project. The project had now developed into three different sub-projects, focusing on, respectively:

1. Materials; in particular, alignment of crystals;
2. Production technologies: panel manufacturing and high-precision mounting techniques; and
3. Interface: the connection of computers to the FLC displays, mainly software engineering.

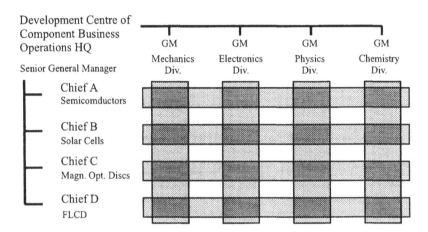

Figure 4.5   Development Centre of Component Business Operations HQ

A fourth small group was assigned the task of developing a shock-resistant casing for the display.

The Display Business Operations Centre was still attached to the Component Business Operations HQ, but financial resources were obtained from the Colour Copier Machine Business Group, to which Takahashi was assigned between 1988 and 1992. During this period, some of his engineers were transferred from their development centre to the FLC project.

Takahashi and Dr Kondo, who are said to be the strong supporters of FLC, both have their roots in the Management Group of Office Equipment. This is also the case of Vice Chairman Dr Yamaji. The relationship between these engineers appears to be very strong.

Visionary Guidance and Proactive Patenting of Progress

Guiding visions were set by the Corporate Strategy and Development HQ. The overall vision that was used to motivate involved engineers and researchers was the picture of a large flat FLC display that covered the wall of a living room and was used for High Definition Television, supported by the slogan 'Big and Fine' (Kanbe, interview). A perhaps more realistic vision was 'same product as our competitors with different technology', meaning that they should achieve at least the same size, weight and power consumption[25] as competing TFT products from, e.g., Sharp and Matsushita, but adding the advantages of FLC technology in terms of high resolution, low blurring and low flicker. The tangible goals that were set from this second vision thus prescribed a specific size, thickness, weight, power consumption and price.

Patent engineers were constantly involved in the different sub-projects, ensuring that all concepts and technologies that emerged from the original invention were protected through elaborate walls of patents. Already in 1992, Canon held close to 150 patents in the US, related to FLC technology. Apart from offering protection of R&D efforts, Canon would get revenues through second-stage licensing.

Tapping and Fusing the Right Corporate Skills

In May 1992, Takahashi was dispatched from his (Colour Copier) Business Group to take charge of the Products Technology Development Headquarters, a core mission of which is to support other Development Centres. In his new position, an important role of Takahashi was to give support and advice to the FLC project. Furthermore, engineers were dispatched from his HQ, to provide technical assistance. Considerable synergies seem to have existed within the Component Business Operations HQ, partly between flat panel displays and solar cell panels, and also with semiconductor production technology.[26] Tanaka-san stated that

> Canon's experience in development of aligners and steppers has been of great use to us when developing production equipment for FLCD. Also, a lot of the work that our material engineers in the Canon Research Centre have done on toners and on optical products has greatly benefited our development of FLC materials.

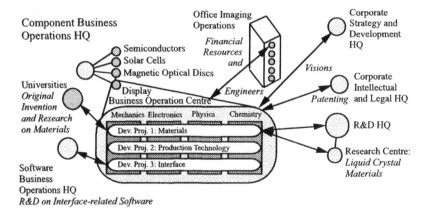

Figure 4.6   Initial Key Actors in the Development of FLCD

Figure 4.6 depicts the three parallel R&D activities and the key actors of what had grown from FLCD task-force, via FLCD project, to a Display Business Operations Centre.

Transferring Critical Competencies to the Factory Floor

> Right now, we are at the stage of putting the product into the market. We therefore need production engineering expertise in order to prepare for full scale manufacturing. Consequently, we have recently invited some production engineering specialists into the team (Kawashima, interview).

A large part of the R&D activities took place outside of the centre – projects 1 and 3 in particular. Research on liquid crystal materials was (and is continually) pursued in the Canon Research Centre in Atsugi, initially involving approximately ten researchers. As the project advanced, most of these researchers were dispatched to the Display Business Operations Centre, where more applied and strongly production-oriented development activities were required.

Some time before production engineers from the Production Management HQ joined the Display Business Operations Centre, some of its engineers used to visit the production engineers at the HQ to get help with and prepare for computer aided manufacturing. The Display Business Operations Centre itself is very production-oriented and thus enjoys ample support from those Headquarters that relate to operations management, i.e., Cost Engineering HQ, Quality Management HQ and Production Management HQ. Trial manufacturing, intermediate manufacturing and full-scale manufacturing is done in the same plant and with the same equipment.

As soon as the trial production line started to yield non-defective prototype displays in 1990, a Planning and Marketing group of approximately five engineers was formed and dispatched to the Planning and Marketing HQ in Shinjuku,[27] where they were joined by a few marketing experts.

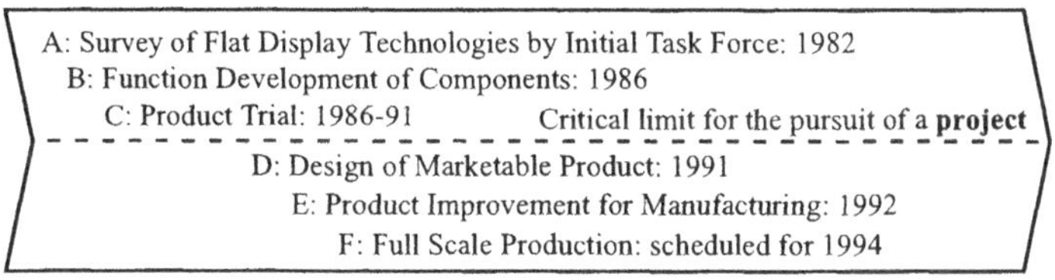

A: Survey of Flat Display Technologies by Initial Task Force: 1982
  B: Function Development of Components: 1986
    C: Product Trial: 1986-91   Critical limit for the pursuit of a **project**
    ——————————————————————————————————
      D: Design of Marketable Product: 1991
        E: Product Improvement for Manufacturing: 1992
          F: Full Scale Production: scheduled for 1994

Figure 4.7   The Development Process of FLC Displays

From the picture above, we can see that phases are continuous, once they have started. This implies that, apart from the first four years of research, all different phases overlapped and were run in parallel.

In April 1993, the Component Business Operations HQ was dissolved and its four development activities were transferred to new HQs: the solar cell project went to the new Research Centre in Kobe; the project on magnetic optical discs joined a memory products project of the Products Technology Development Headquarters. The Display Business Operations Centre and the Semiconductor development project were transferred to the R&D HQ in Shin-Kawasaki. But as 'reorganizations do not necessarily affect the locus of our activities' (Toyosaki, interview), the trial (or intermediary) production lines are still located in Hiratsuka.

Seamless Communication in the Emerging FLC Group

The Display Business Operations Centre numbered, in early 1993, some 100 engineers that were involved in one or several of the three projects. Now that the task force had developed into several official projects, a large number of these engineers were administratively assigned to the Display Business Operations Centre and thus formally transferred to Hiratsuka. Initially, most engineers were mobilized from within the Component Business Operation. Later on, as stage C was completed, some engineers were newly recruited and a large majority 'immigrated', partly from other Headquarters, from the development centre of the Colour Copier business group and, above all, from the Canon Research Centre. As the date of commercialization approached, some persons from the Planning and Marketing HQ joined the centre. Communication floated very freely between the three groups.

> Our open office layout provides us with the advantage of sharing information about a problem. Basically, all members get involved in the problem-solving process. Our goal is to have no barriers at all, neither between task forces, teams and technology fields, nor between research and development. I think that this approach is typical of most Japanese companies. (Kawashima, interview)

Kawashima-san states that 'there are no strong hierarchical levels, preventing communication. All team members feel free to talk to me as long as we are dealing with an urgent project'. The main flow of communication seems to be within the project team and is, for this reason, not strong with external divisions, like for example the Central Research Laboratory. Instead, transfer of knowledge seems to take place through immigration of engineers from these units:

> Knowledge from external divisions is brought in, whenever necessary, by moving in members from these divisions. As a result, a project team is not in a rigid form but rather transitory and flexible through the continuous moving in and out of members. (Kawashima, interview)

When Tanaka joined Canon in 1986, her first two years consisted of testing and measuring the results of extensive trial-and-error activities of liquid crystal materials. In 1988, she changed field and started to develop software for the display-computer interface. Then in 1990, she was dispatched to the Planning and Marketing HQ in Shinjuku to undertake market intelligence activities.

These activities, that relate to her previous development of interface software, mainly consist of observing what competing display companies offer and identifying what computer companies and other potential customers need and want.

Adding specialized Know-how From Universities, Suppliers and Overseas Labs

Senior researcher Miyata joined the material analysis division of the Canon Research Centre in 1989, but was quite soon dispatched to Tokyo University, where he acquired new skills in material evaluation. On his return to the Canon Research Centre, he was assigned to the new generation FLC task force, for which he now works three days a week, commuting between the two centres. He also remains in close contact with researchers at the university to secure further scientific know-how transfer.

As FLC displays have never been mass-produced before, a lot of manufacturing know-how together with new equipment is necessary. This is done in close interaction with suppliers. Key suppliers were involved as soon as the pilot production line began to develop in Hiratsuka in 1988.

> We studied the technology together, which was advantageous for all of us. The key suppliers could acquire more knowledge on our FLC technology and its development and we could build know-how within production technology. (Senior Researcher Tanaka, interview)

Intimate contacts were maintained with several suppliers of equivalent equipment, with the purpose of keeping updated on the latest production technologies and increasing the competitive pressure on the suppliers.

Suppliers are involved in each of the projects' core technologies, i.e. FLC materials; molecular alignment; cell fabrication; drivers and controllers; and interface. Tanaka-san states that there are several different layers of suppliers and that approximately ten of the suppliers are not involved in the actual development work, but simply offer materials and equipment. Another ten suppliers, labelled 'co-developers', are closely involved in the development activities of all the aforementioned core technologies. Only a few of these are said to be financially affiliated with Canon. Tanaka-san further mentions that:

> we have a special organization for information-sharing with our co-development suppliers that we use if they have advanced technological skills that are interesting to us.

If necessary, Canon engineers will go directly to the 'co-development supplier,' but usually only for stays of one or two days. In the case of equipment suppliers, it is more common that they come to the location of the equipment in Canon's facilities. Visits of three days in a week are usual in intensive periods. For specific information on FLC technology, the involved R&D divisions organized separate meetings with a limited number of technologically advanced suppliers. Equipment was not purchased until it had been confirmed for full-scale manufacturing, which left Canon with the flexibility to try different production technologies throughout the project. When a business relationship had been established, the supplier was also invited to Canon's monthly kyoryoku-kai,[28] i.e., the technology co-operation councils.

Software engineering activities aiming at the interface of FLC displays with computers were partly pursued in the Software Business Operations HQ in Shin-Kawasaki. However, the larger part of the software development activities was (and is still) made in the Canon Information Systems Research in Sydney. Additional software support was provided by the labs in the UK and the US Deputy chief engineer Dr Kanbe states that

> Some of our engineers go to Australia five-six times a year. This lab strongly supports our development of software simulation programs and interface electronics. Our R&D labs in the US and in the UK also give us support in these fields.

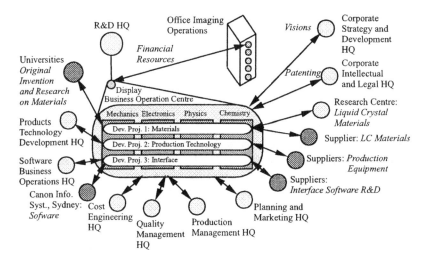

Figure 4.8   Main Contributors to the Development of FLC Displays

Keeping a Close Eye on Competitors

Senior researcher Tanaka knows of three associations, or societies, for display technology in which Canon engineers participate: the International FLC Symposium; the International Society for Information Displays and the Japanese Display Society.

> We are rather passive members of these societies and use them mainly for information gathering. Active participation with presentations and publications of scientific papers is too time consuming. (Tanaka, interview)

Observing the competition is possible in several ways. Tanaka uses computer manufacturers as a source of information regarding flat panel display competitors. 'As the computer company is the potential customer of newly developed displays, it will know of any improvement or problem that a manufacturer like Sharp and Matsushita may have'.

Tanaka-san also mentions the importance of scanning research reports, press releases and going to fairs. As an example, Canon takes part in the FLC symposium of Chalmers University of Technology. A third way is networking with friends from the university. In the FLC group, Tanaka knows of at least three persons who have such contacts within competing companies:

> Most of the information that goes through these channels is of course two-way. Competitors usually get to know just as much about us as we about them.

As of late 1994, the FLC group had grown to a 200-person operation. Ninety per cent of all members were located directly in the Display Business Operation Centre. Eight per cent of the engineers were still located in the R&D HQ, where they did some interface development and coordinated those software development activities that took place overseas. The remaining two per cent were researchers of the Canon Research Centre, working on next-generation FLC materials.

FLCD: Financial Disaster and Corporate Success Story

Although commercial production has been running for several years now, and the size of the displays has kept increasing, they do still not enjoy any significant sales volumes. The barrier is the high sales price. Still, this price is not likely to cover even half of the actual costs, given the impressive investments that Takahashi-san pushed through the Board to make commercial production possible.

Given the financial disaster of this project, most Western organizations would probably have fired Takahashi-san, or 'punished' (see Chapter 8) him with a lateral move. At Canon, he was promoted to CTO after completion of this project. Why? The answer resides in the holistic network approach taken both to T&I and to performance evaluation. Although the FLCD-project investments may never be covered through pure sales of FLC displays, the unique production technologies and skills that were acquired and created throughout the project have already been propagated across the company.

As a consequence, Canon is today the world-wide leader in TFT display manufacturing equipment (i.e., of a competing product). The patents (now over 200) that were awarded during the project will certainly protect Canon's position as unchallanged master of ultrafine precision in both crystal displays and in additional related manufacturing equipment.

NOTES

1. Canon Inc. has figured in a large number of articles and publications, the most important of which are: Gregory (1988); The Canon Handbook (1987); Yamanouchi (1987; 1989); Nonaka and Yamanouchi (1989); and Sigurdson and Anderson (1991). Friedland (1994, 72) reports that Canon is attacking its industry's recession by launching radically new products like the new display technology, FLCD – a high-risk project that will be penetrated in this study.
2. Its forerunner, Precision Optical, set up its first plant in 1936 (Canon Chronicle, no. 172, March-April 1993, p. 13).
3. Nonaka and Kenney (1991, 70); cf. IVA (1993, 48).
4. Cf. Canon (1992); Friedland (1994, 74).
5. Most of the numbers indicated in the case were given by Mr Toyosaki, manager, corporate communications. In 1982, the number of engineers was 2,000. Cf. Dodwell (1992/93, 258); Friedland (1994, 75-6).
6. When Miyata joined Canon in 1989 as a researcher, he did three months of sales, but no production due to declining sales figures (Miyata, interview).
7. Seventy per cent of all engineers thus pursue activities that relate to development and improvement of trial-, pilot-, intermediate-, and full-scale manufacturing lines.
8. This does not mean that they are fired. Those who accept to be transferred to development and production activities are allowed to stay. Those who refuse usually go back to universities, or in some cases to other companies (Anonymous C, interview).
9. An example of such a vision, formulated by the manager of the Canon Research Centre in Shin Kawasaki, is 'Outward Research', meaning that all group managers and their researchers only should do research activities that reach outward, i.e. that result in commercialized products (Bergquist, interview).
10. Dr Mitarai is the son of Canon's founder. He has spent 17 years in the US, doing initial studies at the University of Pennsylvania, working for Hewlett Packard, and acquiring a PhD at MIT, with some of the research conducted at Stanford (Bergquist; Emura; Toyosaki, interviews). There is a clear relation between important product innovations and top management positions. Dr Mitarai was the key factor in the development of laser printers as was Kitamura-san, who now is Director and in charge of all computer and information systems activities. His educational background is applied physics at MIT. Endo-san invented the bubble-jet printer and is presently the Senior General Manager of R&D, which seems to be the third highest position ranking directly after Chairman and President in most Japanese companies.
11. Of the 25 engineers who joined the Canon Research Centre in 1989, 12 were left in mid 1994, but most of these remaining researchers are engaged in applied, or rather production-oriented, R&D (Miyata, interview).
12. Several engineers have left Canon due to the strong pressure to file patent applications. 'Our Research Director says it's OK to leave Canon for a university position, as long as the relationship with Canon remains strong' (Anonymous C, interview).
13. Between 80 and 90% of patents applied for are related to production technology, generated within the product operations (Toyosaki, interview; cf. Canon 1987).
14. Quoted in Canon Chronicle no. 172, March-April 1993, p. 12.
15. Apart from high-capacity memory systems, LB film technology has many other applications, mainly in integrated circuits, but also in thin display technology and medical equipment (Canon Chronicle 172, p. 14).
16. Projects frequently change location within the seemingly organic organization of Canon Inc. The Component Business Operations HQ has disappeared in recent organization charts. Projects on solar cells are now (1994) located in the E-Development HQ in Kyoto. FLC and semiconductor projects are still in Hiratsuka, but operating as individual centres, headed by the R&D HQ. The project on magnetic optical discs has been moved to the Products Technology Development HQ (Toyosaki; Yasokawa; Bergquist, interviews).
17. As of mid-1993, there were 195 Canon Sales subsidiaries (Toyosaki, interview).
18. These three technologies all relate to office automation equipment.
19. They discuss the matter of probability with all engineers involved in the project.
20. Takahashi-san states however that 'if it's an innovative product, we can't do market research,

due to the speed of development of our competitors'.
21.   Cf. Figure 4.4.
22.   The invention was partly based on previous research that had been conducted at Harvard University and at Université Paris-Sud in France. The discovery of Clark and Lagerwall at Chalmers University of Technology enabled very fast switching speed and bistability in ferroelectric liquid crystals, which, at least theoretically, had major implications for FLC displays. The main obstacles resided in manufacturing techniques.
23.   According to Ando-san, the Japanese representative Director of INVENTURE, a Swedish company that specialises in commercialising technology, the Swedish manager, Mr Lagergren, noticed Chalmer's discovery of FLC technology in the early 1980s: 'At that time, we could not find any interested buyer of the technology in the West. Not even ABB or Ericsson in Sweden were interested. Then, in 1983, we made a survey in Japan which showed that the Japanese firms all thought the FLC technology was a dream and nothing else. Later, in 1985, as Seiko made an FLC prototype, the interest for FLC grew big in Japan and Canon purchased the FLC patent . . . Out of natural reasons, Canon immediately closed their doors, as they had purchased the technology. They could however send some people to the University of Colorado and to Chalmers University, but as the patent is almost pure fundamental physics, Canon had to create the related applied technology itself. This has been done through a lot of extremely hard trial-and-error efforts . . . The most direct help that Canon will get is with problems that are entirely related to the science of physics. In these cases, Professor Lagerwall and Professor Clark are keen to help, as this actually also advances them in their own research' (Ando, interview).
24.   Now called the Office Imaging Products Operation.
25.   These three factors represent weaknesses of FLC technology, compared to competing products: TFT, CRT and LC displays (source: Canon, 1991; various interviews and research reports). In mid-1994, a size of 24 inches was achieved, which was twice the size of the average TFT display.
26.   Both semiconductors and FLC panels require high-precision mounting techniques. Canon seems to have a well-developed competence in steppers and aligners, that are two important pieces of equipment in high precision manufacturing processes.
27.   Relocated to Shimomaruko in June 1993 (Tanaka, interview).
28.   See Chapter 3 for further discussions on kyoryoku-kai.

5　Sony Corporation

INTRODUCTION[1]

> I usually say that we are a bunch of crazy people at Sony. We have the curiosity always to ask why, why, why and the courage to do things which nobody tried before. Conservative people only do things which others have done in the past. Sony's success is based on the fact that we never tried to follow tradition. (Akio Morita, interview)

In May 1946, Masaru Ibuka and Akio Morita founded Tokyo Tsushin Kogyo, which in 1958 was listed on the Tokyo Stock Exchange as Sony Corporation, after its successful launch of the world's first compact transistor radio. A long success story followed, with continuous expansion and profitability until fiscal year 1991, for which Sony projected its first operating loss. In order to improve profitability and reduce vulnerability to changing economic conditions, Sony diversified into the information and telecommunications industries in the mid-1980s,[2] and into the service and software industries in the late 1980s.[3]

One hundred and twenty thousand people work for Sony Corporation world-wide. Twenty thousand of those are located in the Tokyo area within administration, sales and R&D. Sony has some 80 production subsidiaries in the world, half of which are located in Japan. In a world-wide perspective, only 40% of Sony's employees are Japanese. Itami (1987, 102) states that Sony's core competence[4] is product development. This chapter will focus on structural, organizational and managerial factors which have allowed Sony to 'reign unchallenged as the most consistently inventive consumer electronics enterprise on the planet' (Schlender 1992, 22).[5]

INTRAORGANIZATIONAL ASPECTS OF R&D AND TECHNOLOGY

Sony's Business Groups as Incubators of Innovation Through Open Sharing of Technologies and Skills

Owing to its large size, Sony Corporation is divided into 19 *Jigyobu*, generally translated as 'business group'.[6] The business groups function as profit centres, the managers of which also belong to the board of directors.

Each business group has a product-planning section of its own, housed in the strongly product-oriented development division, which is the core of the entire business group. Instead of being science-oriented themselves, these development divisions operate in a highly organic manner.

They partly function as incubators of technologies that have spread from the Research Centre and are already being applied in products, but they also have responsibility for the development of next-generation products in their markets within a three-year perspective. When new technological competence is needed, they may borrow engineers from other business groups' development divisions. An open recruiting system, the so called *shanai koubo* system, authorizes project leaders to borrow engineers from any business group, without requiring approval from division managers.

Business groups can also send their engineers to some of the research labs to acquire new technologies and competencies. Much of the development work is related to the improvement of production technology. Each business group also has its own manufacturing plants.

The R&D System

Sony's R&D activities are organized in three levels, beginning upstream with a Research Centre, pursuing medium- and long-term research. Corporate Research Laboratories handle the practical application of the Research Centre's activities, thus linking them to the development divisions of the business groups, which mainly carry out the development of production technology and house the large majority of engineers.

In all, approximately 9,000 engineers and scientists work within Sony Corporation.[7] At the Sony Research Centre, main activities focus on medium- and long-range research on electronic materials and devices. Some 250 researchers work there, 75% of whom are physicists, but there are also some chemists and mechanical engineers. More than 60 of the researchers are top foreign scientists, working on a quasi-permanent basis with one-year contracts. They are all discouraged from adapting Japanese habits and instead encouraged to keep and disseminate their Western style of conducting scientific research (Kikuchi, interview).

The work ethic is rather severe by Western standards. In 1993, the number of holidays was augmented from 17 to 22 per year. In practice, 12 'compulsory' holidays of the 22 are taken and the rest are kept as a reserve in case of illness, as no other compensation is available for those who have to stay at home. Dr Le Bellégo, a foreign scientist at Sony, comments on his colleagues: 'My Japanese colleagues are extremely patient, but quite inefficient when it comes to research, which I believe has to do with their lack of individualistic thinking'.[8]

The Director of the Research Centre is officially in charge of all R&D activities. He handles recruitment and allocation of researchers. As for the research budget, he makes a bi-annual presentation to the board of directors, including the president of Sony, of how much money he needs and for what purposes. The board argues about the amount, but less so about the allocation.

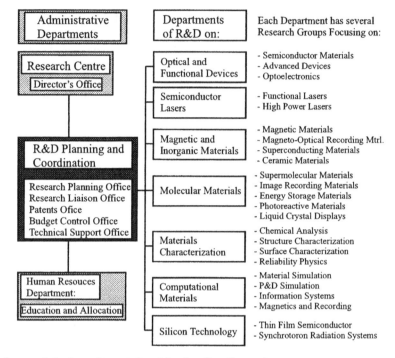

Source: Author's own interpretation of data from Sony Corporation

Figure 5.1   Organization of the Sony Corporation Research Centre

Sony Corporate Research Laboratories pursue applied research on optical, magnetic, audio-visual and advanced product technologies, often linking R&D activities of the Research Centre to product-oriented development. Approximately 600 engineers with backgrounds in mechanics, electronics, optics and sound processing are dispersed throughout the different research departments, all of which are located in the HQ buildings in Tokyo. The main purpose of these departments is to support and educate the engineers of the aforementioned development divisions and sometimes to serve as a link between the development divisions and the Research Centre.[9]

The R&D Planning and Coordination Group manages all the strategic R&D activity of each research laboratory, relevant to the overall Sony Corporation. The rather organic organization of this group will be described later on.

Patent Mapping for Strategic Management of Technology

In the early 1970s, Chairman Morita decided that Sony should put more emphasis on patent applications. Today, researchers receive extensive information on procedures for obtaining patents. Chances of promotion increase with the number of generated patents. The encouragement of patenting is a Japanese way of accelerating creativity.[10]

> It is true that most Japanese companies try to encourage or even push their engineers to file patents. At Sony, too, we stimulate our engineers to think about patents and there is strong competition in this field, even within the company. (Kikuchi, interview)

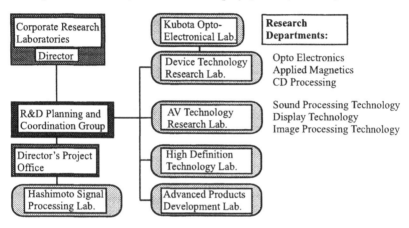

Source: Author's own interpretation of data from Sony Corporation

Figure 5.2   Sony Corporate Research Laboratories

At Sony, a patenting division organizes a monthly meeting which gathers between 10 and 15 persons, including the director of research and even the president of Sony. At this meeting, participants analyse their own patents and possible applications, their relation to Sony Corporation's goals, other companies' patents, and possible future trends. President Ohga enquires how much money is made from different patents and sometimes orders to drop the less profitable ones. In the past, patents generated a tremendous income to Sony, but now, former CTO Dr Kikuchi claims that the costs of maintaining these patents are almost as large as their income. He thinks that

> it is quite possible to increase the number of patents. There still is a strong race among our engineers to generate patents and they still serve as a mode of evaluation both for them and for their chiefs, but our major concern now is to increase the quality of our patents instead. It is a fundamental part of the Sony education to ensure that our engineers and especially our managers always think about the possibility of patenting what they are doing and that they know how to do this.

Sony's engineers write weekly reports on their research activities. Their division managers read these and write new reports to the research director. Sometimes when reading these, Dr Kikuchi discovers important findings, whereupon he urges the manager in question to file a patent, who then goes to the patenting division to push for 'his' finding to be patented. The inventor would only be contacted for a technological matter, if at all necessary. At the HQ, the patenting division consists of senior engineers with some experience in research who function as a link between the actual researcher and Sony's in-house patent attorneys. 'Only the patent attorneys have the legal knowledge and language to accomplish an entire process of applying for and filing a patent. They also have the necessary connections at the Patent Office' (Kikuchi, interview).

Market Needs as Primary Source of Inspiration for Innovation

> We always have to see the market by ourselves. That's why we move around, read books, journals and catalogues on consumer products, even if they are sometimes unrelated to our business. Scientific publications and conferences may also provide good sources of inspiration for innovation. (Morita, interview)

More than 70% of all R&D expenses is not related to the research director's budget, but financed through business groups. This market-driven research is maintained through the practice of internal sponsoring of individual researchers projects. Initially, researchers have some liberty in choosing fields of research, but after a certain period of time, they must find a sponsor for their research. In order to attract sponsoring, their department manager orders them to prepare a so-called *technical sample*, usually with a very demanding time deadline.

Once the technical sample is prepared, the researcher must identify and convince a business group – sometimes one of the product groups and sometimes the Semiconductor Group and the Production Technology Group in Atsugi – that is willing to sponsor further research. If this succeeds, the researcher develops his technical sample further into an *engineering sample*, which will be demonstrated to the sponsoring business group.

If the demonstration is successful and the business group has or can have a commercial use for the product, the researcher will be sponsored to develop a *commercial sample*,[11] again with a very strict deadline, but commonly also with the support of new engineers, usually with production expertise,[12] added to the project. At the end of this stage, the entire team may be transferred to Atsugi for the development of a prototype production line. The finished commercial sample is presented to the board, after which commercial production starts. Through this system, 'research always finds an application, or else it will be discontinued early on' (Le Bellégo, interview). Cases in which inventors have been unable to find a sponsor within the existing business groups,[13] have caused the creation of a new group called the Business Development Division, which supports the development of entirely new businesses.

Proactive Product Planning Through Global Market Feedback

There is no central marketing entity within Sony. Each one of Sony's product groups has a market information-gathering function, apart from development and production of products. Pure consumer marketing is totally divested to Sony's sales subsidiaries.

Twice a year, the marketing companies send their product planners to so-called line-up meetings in Japan, where negotiations are hammered out and where marketing people identify new opportunities with arguments like: 'If we had this model, we could sell this amount per year.' It is a process of persuading the production groups to produce what they want (Kawakami, interview).

Usually each business group has a resident Japanese product planner in each important market, who 'is in daily contact with the development division of his product group'. The resident Japanese product planners are located in Sony's overseas sales subsidiaries. So-called Sector Offices were set up quite recently in Europe – for example, the Audio Sector Office in Amsterdam and the Video Sector Office in Brussels. Some resident Japanese at these offices have pan-European responsibility on product matters, and feed back strategic market information to their the development division of their business group.

> Sony is always trying to shorten the cycle-time between the identification of a customer need and the launch of a modified product on the market. In many types of products, we are down below six months, as long as the modifications do not require a total redesign. (Kawakami, interview)

When a product planner comes to the line-up meeting, he has to be very persuasive, giving detailed information on the size of the opportunity and on his promotional plans. If he can make a good case, he will convince the engineers to develop and produce the product that he wants. These meetings, e.g., the Audio Group line-up, usually involve 50 people. Engineers from each engineering group, their managers and the top managers of the business group as a whole take part. As competition for production time in the factories is severe, representatives of the Production Control Group and the Scheduling Group also take part in order to prepare for planning and scheduling of all production.

Product Planners Understand Both Technology and the Market

Expatriated product planners are in most cases engineers, as they must understand the engineering capabilities of their development divisions back in Japan and be able to weigh the business opportunities that the subsidiaries bring to them and communicate these strategic considerations to division managers in Japan. They usually go to Japan on a monthly basis.

In order to get reliable customer feedback on certain products, registers are kept on the most fanatic and dedicated Sony customers, who usually buy each new product launched by Sony. Sometimes, new products are sent to some of these customers with an invitation to come to Sony after some period of testing. A division within the Audio Group has a register of dedicated customers with specifically outstanding listening expertise, and tests their reactions to new audio systems. As Mr House joined Sony Japan with prior sales experience from the UK, he was astonished to discover a unique degree of 'customer fanaticism':

> Some customers are so fanatically interested in our products that they know more about them than myself and many other Sony members. These experts often feel free to write to us or even to come to Sony, telling us what changes should be made with the next generation of a product. I have never seen such a dedication in the UK.

All new entrants, including researchers, who arrive at Sony get acquainted with the corporate culture through training programs. According to Dr Kikuchi, the most important part of their education is to sell products in a Sony shop, which they do for one to three months, at least twice during the first two years at Sony.[14] If the market demand should fall and Sony experience over-capacity within development or production, engineers may be sent back to sales again on a temporary basis. 'In addition to the necessary acquisition of customer needs, our company members realize Sony's vulnerability in respect of changing-market demand' (Kikuchi, interview). Therefore, 'even researchers in the Research Centre are well informed about customer needs, which makes Sony's research quite market-oriented' (Le Bellégo, interview). One month of manufacturing in a Sony plant is also included in the training of all new company members.

Interaction with sales units is intensive, as exemplified by Miho Fuji, who demonstrates products in the Sony Building on the Ginza. This is an important Sony outlet in Tokyo that also has the largest Sony showroom, exhibiting all major Sony products that are available on the market:

> Five days a week we have meetings with people from the marketing and advertising department to discuss customer reactions. Development engineers often take part in these meetings as well. The project leader of a new product always comes to see us before his product is launched, so that he can explain its characteristics. Two months after the launch, he comes back to get feedback on customer reactions.

The showroom staff writes two different monthly reports: one on the number of visitors, their questions, complaints and positive impressions; and a similar one, relating to telephone contacts. The reports are sent to some 30 R&D departments, product groups and marketing departments.

Institutionalized Job Rotation for Diffusion of Skills and Development of Multicompetent Engineers

> The transfer of researchers is like breathing: both necessary and natural. Interaction be-

tween our Research Centre and production in Atsugi is frequent. Many of our engineers start their career in the Research Centre, where they usually spend three years doing fundamental research and experiments. We give these engineers some time for doing research. Even if it doesn't always bring results, it is fundamental for their training and understanding of technology. After these three years, we carefully judge their situations and usually ask them to try something new, that offers more practical application of their knowledge. (Kikuchi, interview)

To most researchers, the Research Centre offers more a period of education than a long-term opportunity. Approximately 50% of the engineers leave after three years and 80% of them have left after ten years. Once they have left research, they usually do not come back. Dr Le Bellégo, states that as he arrived as a foreign researcher at the Sony Research Centre, a group of 50 researchers was doing research on integrated circuits, mainly based on trial-and-error. All of a sudden and much to his surprise, the entire group was transferred to Sony's production plant of semiconductors in Atsugi. When he was working as a researcher in France, the greatest loss of information occurred in the junctions between research, development and production. In contrast,

what strikes me most at Sony is that not only the product, but the entire team is transferred from research to production. It is clear that such a transfer does not come naturally to researchers and requires rather strong managerial intervention, but the benefits are considerable.

Researchers are transferred on very short notice whenever necessary. In some cases, this occurs at a very early stage, like in a project on perpendicular magnetic recording. The project, which was initiated in the Magnetic Materials Research Group of the Research Centre, spread to a Corporate Research Laboratory – the Device Technology Research Laboratory – where a similar project was set up in the Applied Magnetics Research Department to work on a practical application of perpendicular magnetic recording. This department also co-operated with Sony Precision Magnetic Corporation, a principal subsidiary. Research went on in parallel for a while, with frequent interaction between fundamental and applied research. When an engineering sample was prepared and presented to top management, Vice President Ohga (now President) became very eager to incorporate the research results into a marketable product. He ordered the R&D Planning and Coordination Group to try to accelerate the transfer from research to product development.

The R&D planning and coordination group consequently ordered the Magnetic Materials Research Group of the Research Centre, together with its manager, to move to the Sendai Technology Centre, a production plant, to develop a trial production line. Researchers from the Sendai Technology Centre, development engineers from the Applied Magnetics Research Department and some production engineers from Sony Precision Magnetics Corporation in Atsugi were added, thus forming a new perpendicular magnetic recording group. They succeeded in developing some prototypes, but results were unsatisfactory due to problems of precision. As this was a problem of rather fundamental research, half the group was sent back to the Molecular Materials Research Department of the Research Centre to solve it.

Not until a few years later could a satisfactory level of precision be achieved,[15] and half the group of researchers joined the Sendai group again to continue the development of a production line, which finally resulted in successful production of the by-now well-known metal tape. For this accomplishment, the Molecular Materials Research Department received the President's Award jointly with the Sendai Technology Centre.

Dr Seto, who was a key person in the research work, had already first-hand experience of magnetic tape production as he had initially worked in Sony's Tape Plant in Sendai, before joining the Molecular Materials Department in the Research Centre. His research was done in close co-operation with the Tohoku University in Sendai, where he also obtained his PhD.[16] Today, he is concurrently the manager of the Molecular Materials and the Materials Characterization Departments (depicted in Figure 5.1).

Researchers who Refuse to Transfer to Production Should Stay in the University

Rotation of engineers is not only project-related, but more or less institutionalized every three years, after which a development engineer may be asked to join a production plant or sometimes to work for another business group.[17] More science-oriented researchers are also usually rotated between different Research Centres. Close to 7,000 of all engineers and scientists work in Atsugi, where the majority of all innovations are produced. Here, the Semiconductor Group and the Production Technology Group have division labs covering mid-term R&D projects, but are also responsible for in-house support of R&D. Hence, many of the aforementioned engineering- and commercial samples of the Research Centre are being sponsored by these two groups, thus ensuring the transfer of technology into production. Semiconductor production has grown to a core business within Sony, more than 50% of which is sold to other manufacturers.

Senior researcher Fujima, who spent many years doing research on the abovementioned junction lasers and rapidly became the manager of that research group, is now working in the semiconductor group of the Atsugi plant, where he is responsible of both production and sales of junction lasers. Dr Kikuchi discovered his 'hidden potentiality' and has always found him to be both competent and charismatic, but it took two months to convince him to leave research and go to Atsugi.

> An old friend of mine breaks the pattern of transfer. He has spent his entire life in the Research Centre working on crystal physics. In his case this was all right because he is world famous in his field and had, in other words, no hidden potential for doing other things. (Kikuchi, interview)

Until 1993, Sony Corporation recruited close to 1,000 new members each year. Approximately 700 of these were engineers, mainly specialized in electronics and mechanics. 'Depending on their character, I carefully judged whether to send newly recruited engineers directly to the 'flow' of our Corporate Research Laboratories, or to the Research Centre' (Kikuchi, interview). Apart from the foreign researchers, Ph.Ds are rarely employed,[18] as they are found to be less flexible, to dislike job rotation, and want to stay within their field of specialization instead.

> When we were developing the CCD, a Ph.D was included in the development team. As we had finished the research stage, it was time to move the team to the Atsugi Plant to go on with the production stage. However, our Ph.D, who also was the key researcher, disliked the idea of being transferred to production. I managed to find him a new position within the Research Centre that he fortunately accepted. Otherwise he would have had to go back to the academic world. (Kikuchi, interview)

In this project, 35 of the original 45 researchers followed the project to trial production in Atsugi, and only three of these came back to the Research Centre afterwards.

During his time as research director, Dr Kikuchi hired five or six Ph.Ds, but had difficulties in finding any with both excellent scientific skills and the flexibility to change areas and levels of research. He holds that those who do not have this flexibility should stay in the universities.

Turning the Research Centre into a Factory Floor

In the case of the CD player, Sony and Philips had agreed upon 1982 as the launching date. Due to Sony's use of compound semiconductors in the junctional lasers, which constitute the core of a CD player, the process technology was very complicated. All research on compound semiconductors and junctional lasers was done within the Research Centre, which had both the competence and the instruments to develop prototypes. Dr Kikuchi realized that it would be impossible to develop such a complicated production line in Atsugi before the launching date. Therefore, he decided to develop a small production line in the actual Research Centre, despite the strong protests of the subordinate researchers. Hence, the first two years of production of junctional lasers were made in the Research Centre and the critical launching date was maintained. A full-scale production line was prepared in Atsugi in parallel, where production continued afterwards.

The use of junctional laser technology eventually spread to many other product areas like optical disc memories and satellite receivers. In fact, Sony organizes for knowledge diffusion in many other ways than direct transfer of researchers. These ways are described in the following section.

PROMOTING KNOW-WHO TO SUPPORT THE INNOVATION PROCESS

> The critical factor of any R&D management is to make sure that researchers, development engineers and product group managers meet as much as possible so that both competencies and technologies can spread throughout the organization. (Kikuchi, interview)

The Research Planning and Coordination Group Secures Sharing and Transfer of Technology

The Research Planning and Coordination Group is the key actor in the management of all T&I activities within Sony Corporation. This group is working as an executive committee, directly reporting to the President of Sony on a weekly basis. Hence, even the Research Director is subordinate to the orders of this group, which is formally located in the Research Centre, but is also connected to the Corporate Research Laboratories and supervises all Peripheral R&D Units as well (Kikuchi; Le Bellégo, interviews). Through this group, all important R&D activities are coordinated by top management. The direct involvement of the President or the Chairman is emphasized by Dr Kikuchi:

> Here at Sony, most of what we do depends mainly on human relations and is coordinated by Ohga-san or Morita-san themselves.

Every Tuesday morning, the Research Planning and Coordination Group organizes a visit to one or several of Sony's most interesting R&D projects. Afterwards, a long lunch meeting is held among the members, i.e., 18 top managers, usually including the Chairman, the President, the Research Director and the managers of the most important product and marketing groups. Discussions on both technical and strategic R&D issues take place. On the first Tuesday of each month, the lunch is followed by a Research Report Meeting, which is also organized by the Research Planning and Coordination Group. In a first session from 13:00, focused presentations, limited to 15 minutes, are made by R&D managers on their specific research achievements and the possible practical applications of these achievements. These presentations are not technology-oriented, but aim at strategic decisions on whether the project shall be kept in the Research Centre, or transferred to a product group's development division.

> During such a session, the manager of Optical and Functional Devices made a brief presentation of his division's achievements within a new Low Pressure Chemical Vapour Deposition technology and its possible application on VLSI. President Iwama asked the director of the semiconductor group what he thought about buying this technology. The director was reluctant and found it too expensive, but Iwama-san said 'I would like to order you to put this technology into your products, because it will increase the competitiveness of Sony's semiconductor lasers. (Kikuchi, interview)

The second session, starting at 15:00, is open to a broader spectrum of researchers than the top-level managers and research directors. Without time re-strictions, any researcher may lead a technology- and science-oriented discussion, much like a less formal version of the Technology Symposia, de-scribed later on.

For a long time, Dr Kikuchi served as Research Director and concurrently presided over the Research Planning and Coordination Group. His most fre-quently used method of spreading the technologies of his Research Centre was to invite one of the product group managers, quite informally, to make a pres-entation on an ongoing project and 'make them feel appetite for our technol-ogy'. Thanks to the above lunch meetings, he knew these managers and their technological needs, but also their needs vis à vis the market. If the invited manager became interested in the technology, he would send a few skilled en-gineers from his business group to join the research group, twelve to six months before the project's research stage was ended. These engineers would then play a key role in the transfer of the project, by setting up a similar project in their business group's development division and continuing with a practical application of the technology in question.

During his presidency of the Research Planning and Coordination Group, Dr Kikuchi made frequent individual visits to product group managers to dis-cuss certain technologies and their strategic importance for the future of their business groups. He would then report on the outcome of these discussions di-rectly to Chairman Morita. The Research Planning and Coordination Group organizes a large number of less regular forums of interaction, a few of which will be mentioned below:

Open-house Meetings Bring Together People from the Entire Innovation Process

Open-house Meetings, held at least twice a year, gather up to 1,000 group and division managers, aged between 30 and 45, from the entire corporation's key divisions. Managers of research divisions and their different research group leaders – sales, development and production managers of all product groups; patent engineers and patent attorneys – all get together at the Research Centre where 'every single door is open' so that everybody can walk around freely and ask all the questions they want, related to present and possible future research projects and technologies. At the same time, researchers can upgrade their knowledge on market needs and requirements from production. Open-house meetings last two days, opening with a talk by Chairman Morita and ending with a stand-up beer party for everybody, held in three large halls. 'In addition, this is an excellent occasion for our company members to keep track of each other's positions and whereabouts' (Kikuchi, interview).

Technology Exchange Forums Link Technology Seeds to Market Needs

Technology Exchange Forums offer an extensive presentation of Sony's technological capabilities to all product, marketing and sales managers, who are
potential buyers of technologies or sponsors of research projects. This yearly
forum usually fills several floors of the HQ building with booths, displaying all
available technologies, components and ongoing research projects. Not only
are the Research Centre's divisions and groups present, but all peripheral R&D
units within Sony Corporation as well as all development divisions of the different product groups and the research departments of the Corporate Research
Laboratories display, explain and demonstrate what they have to sell. Individual researchers hoping to find a sponsor exhibit their embryos. Hence, the primary goal is to find practical applications for existing technologies and
competencies as well as enhance their cross-fertilization. The best presentation, or the most promising technology, is commended by the President.

Each important sales group also has a booth of experts, displaying sales volumes, trends and anticipations for their respective products. Dr Kikuchi emphasizes the importance of giving researchers and development engineers
access to market expertise.

Technology Symposia Merge Available Scientific Skills into Corporate Brain-storming Processes

Technology Symposia focus on very specific technological, and often also scientific, problems. Taking place every three months, they gather between 150
and 200 engineers and scientists. Between 13:00 and 18:00, three or four scientific problems are presented, usually by the company's absolutely top chemists and physicists. The Chairman of Sony moderates the subsequent
discussions, the main purpose of which is to engage all participants in a large-
scale brain-storming process, aiming at solutions to the problems. Know-who
is another important purpose, fulfilled through a stand-up beer party after
18:00.

Know-who is actually considered to be at least as important as know-how.
By fostering a network of strong personal relationships within Sony, individual knowledge becomes more accessible. Dr Kikuchi launched a 'three
phone-calls' slogan, meaning that the manager or member of a new development project should always try to identify persons with past experience in the
field of the development project, by calling at least three colleagues before
starting off. These calls usually start the necessary chain-reaction to identify
and learn from the relevant experience.

Within two weeks, key persons can be mobilized from anywhere in the
world to join a new development project. 'Finding the absolutely best candidate for a project or position is the most important factor in determining the
chances of success'.[19] Also, if a project manager should perform poorly, he

would be removed instantly.[20] If necessary, a research project can also be stopped or change directions at any time, depending on its chances of finding a commercial application. Closing down a project is perfectly acceptable at Sony. 'As project leaders are very famous and respected people, they do not lose face when discontinuing a project, but sometimes become even more famous instead' (Kikuchi, interview).

The Commitment of a Big Mistake is Critical for your Promotion as Long as Nobody Repeats it

> I have always encouraged our people to be curious and find new applications for our technologies and new uses for our products. Trying new things is risky, but our policy is: don't care if you make a mistake, but don't do the same mistake again. In this way, we encourage new approaches. (Chairman Morita, interview)

Job rotation and transfer of engineers reflect the promotion criteria quite well. It is essential for higher promotee to have prior experience with turning an invention into a commercialized innovation by being engaged in the research, development and production of a product; to be open-minded and able to communicate freely; to be able to set clear goals; and, finally, to have a good sense of the market. In an interview with Akio Morita, he stresses the importance of having foresight:

> Dr Kikuchi is an important person within Sony. Not only is he an excellent scientist, but he also is a good businessman and, above all, has a good foresight. These are all focal points of a perfect Research Director.

Dr Kikuchi's successor, Yamada-san, began his career in the Research Centre, was then sent to a Corporate Research Laboratory and was finally requested to run a semiconductor manufacturing plant in Sendai. In 1994, he became Sony's new Research Director.

Perhaps most important of all, employees are particularly encouraged to share experience from failures, thereby preventing their repetition instead of sweeping them under the carpet. In an interview with Akio Morita, he stated:

> At Sony, you can only be promoted to manager if you are known for a success *and* for a failure that you have committed so that everybody can learn from it instead of possibly repeating the same mistake that caused the failure.

This approach promotes a lot of trial-and-error, which has led to serendipitous discoveries of great importance, including the historic high-frequency transistor. Through theoretical calculations and advanced scientific methods, Bell Labs was attempting to find a new transistor technology with a frequency of 20 MHz instead of the original 15 MHz. Senior researcher Esaki, who joined Sony at that time, applied a traditional trial-and-error approach to the problem. One morning, his assistant was measuring characteristics of failed high-frequency transistors and discovered the peculiar characteristic of negative resistance, which eventually came to be called the electron tunnelling effect and led to the development of the tunnel diode.[21] 'Only Sony tried the stupid and unscientific approach that led to this discovery' (Kikuchi, interview).[22]

Dedication to Perform and Diffuse New Results

Dedication seems to be inherent among the company members, perhaps while fostered by managers.[23] 'When an engineer or a researcher is ordered to do something, he will do anything to succeed and to keep the deadline'. Dr Le Bellégo, senior researcher in the Research Centre, states further that – quite in contrast to his experience in the West – researchers do not keep their results secret and personal at Sony:

> as soon as you have some results, you write and talk about them. In the West, research efforts and results are quite personal, but here at Sony, there is no name attached to research results. My results, for instance, were presented by a Japanese colleague without even informing me about it.

DEVELOPING THE MINIDISCMAN (MD) THROUGH CORPORATE-WIDE TECHNOLOGY FUSION

> The driving force of our rapid innovation is the conviction that if we lose money, we can always recover, but if we lose time, we can't. Therefore, time has always been a critical issue at Sony. (Morita, interview)

In the mid-1980s, Sony had started to lose some market share in its portable audio products line, mainly because of rapid imitation by competitors. In response, Sony accelerated the pace of innovation, thus proliferating its product line to recover market share (cf. Deschamps and Nayak 1992, 39). The perhaps most radical innovation of all was the MiniDiscman, as this introduced a new media format on the market. We now turn to the description of how it was developed.

The Audio Development Group has been working on other disc recording technologies than the traditional CD, since 1983. The main focus of development department manager Tsurushima and group manager Yoshida was to develop a recordable CD player. Additional groups started to work on competing technologies, and, in 1986, four different groups were working in parallel, all headed by Tsurushima-san. The Digital Audio Tape (DAT) technology emerged from one of the groups and, by 1987, another group had developed a prototype of a recordable CD player. At that time the Digital Audio Cassette technology caused strong resistance from the software producers, who believed that the music industry would suffer if digital technology replaced the analogue cassette. Therefore, Sony did not announce the recordable CD. Instead, a time-consuming war with the software industry started, and Sony eventually purchased CBS in 1988.

In late 1989, several of the aforementioned technologies merged into the MD proposal, as a result of a discussion with top management, in which President Ohga expressed great enthusiasm (Tsurushima, interview). As a consequence, the MD team was staffed with several know-how carriers from the discontinued technology projects and could therefore get a very quick start.

Its main advantage compared to cassette-type Walkmans was that it allowed for instantaneous random access to specific selections, just like the CD, but it would also be recordable and much more shock-resistant than the traditional CD. The reason of this proposal was however not technology driven, but instead based upon market considerations. From the beginning, the company knew what kind of product it wanted to make. The proposal was to replace the analogue cassette with a portable audio format. Sony already knew that the cassette market was declining. A study made by Sony Music in Japan indicated that as many as 80% of all CD records never left their homes and that an equivalent percentage of all cassettes was listened to outside of the home, a clear confirmation of an already well-known fact that portable applications of the CD player business never had succeeded.

It was time to develop a successor to the audiocassette that would beat both the conventional Walkman as well as the Discman, i.e., the portable CD. Hence, the project attempted to fulfil a perceived market need with the MD technology, but also competed with other Sony products.

An additional consumer survey was made in Japan by Young Laboratories,[24] a Sony-affiliated market research institute, aiming at identifying what customers liked about the traditional audio cassette and what they felt should be improved. This study confirmed the expected advantage of random access, versatility and shock resistance.

The MiniDiscman Team: an Amoebic Mass of Networkers

> Hundreds, if not thousands of people are directly or indirectly involved in the MD project. It is hard to define a true core of the project. Rather, it's an amoebic mass of moving people that interact with each other. (Kawakami, interview)

Senior General Manager of the Audio Development Group, Tsurushima, officially became in charge of the MD project, and of the other projects going on in his group of close to a hundred engineers. In practice, Yoshida led the MD technology development group, which consisted of ten engineers in its initial phase. As the project progressed, five more engineers were added, but the group never exceeded 15 full-time members up to 1987. Yoshida was concurrently in charge of the development of a Car Navigation System, a project of 30 engineers, but the synergies between the two projects were important as Monolithic Microwave ICs[25] and HIFET semiconductor devices constitute core technologies in both of the products.

Another project of Tsurushima's development division was developing a Digital Data Storage system. In 1987, this evolved into a joint project with Hewlett Packard, which mainly provided the software development part. Together, Sony and HP set a new standard called DDS.

Because the strict deadline set by President Ohga of November 1992 – the tenth anniversary of the CD – there was no time for developing entirely new technologies for the MD. Instead, the disc mechanism of the MiniDiscman was based on the previously-developed digital technology used in Sony's different CD players and the DDS.

Making Effective Use of Available Technologies and Skills

In effect, most technologies were already available in development divisions of different business groups. Hence, Yoshida acquired these technologies both by sending his engineers to the respective development divisions and by borrowing engineers directly from the divisions, who would 'drop in for a few days, but never stay on a permanent basis'. In this sense, there was no permanent transfer of engineers. 'All technologies were assembled in the MD Group, but in order to succeed, constant interaction with other groups and labs was necessary' (Yoshida, interview). The development divisions for Optical Pickups, Playback-Only Optical Discs, and Recordable Optical Discs were strongly involved. The business groups involved were the Semiconductor Group, the General Audio Group, the Mobile Electronics Group, and the Audio Group.

A small-sized optical disc technology was already developed for the Digital Data Storage system that was adopted by the MD group. But in order to have a smaller disc format than that of the traditional CD, the sound would have to be compressed before being stored in the disc and then decompressed before reaching human ears. This called for sophisticated Audio Sound Compression Technology, which had to be developed by the Algorithm Group in the AV Technology Research Laboratory. Also, in order to reduce space and complexity, Direct Overwriting was requested. The Device Technology Research Laboratory solved this through further development of an existing Magnetic Field Overwrite Technology. The most important actors in the development process of the MD are depicted below, after which their contributions to the innovation process will be described.[26]

Joint Efforts in Six Business Groups and Six Labs, Divisions and Departments Made an Impossible Lead-time Possible

The recordable MD uses magnetic field modulation, a technology which originally was developed for the CD-MO, i.e., a recordable magneto-optical version of the CD. The CD-MO technology already had a perpendicular magnetic head and flexible disc drive, which allowed for adequate recording density.

Two key improvements were, however, necessary: First, the magnetic layer of the disc had to be thinner, thus reducing weight and the price of the music software. For this purpose, an amorphous perpendicularly magnetized ultra thin layer of terbium, ferrite and cobalt was developed, which allowed for more than one million repetitive recordings without decreasing sound quality. The original magnetic material technology had already been transferred from the Research Centre to more applied development in 1983. As the requirements of repeated recording reliability arose, Dr Kikuchi intervened on President Ohga's advice and took the problem back to the Department of Magnetic and Inorganic Materials of the Research Centre:[27]

> First, I brought a few researchers to a development department and talked to the people working in the more practical field to let them understand correctly what the problem was in practice. Then we analysed the problem partly from a strategic point of view and also from a scientific point of view. It was clear that we had to think at a 'molecular' level. If you look carefully, some molecules are long and others short. What we needed was a uniform length of the molecules. Therefore, I brought the problem back to the Research Centre, where I called the physicists and the chemists to my office to let them understand the strategic importance of the problem, telling them that they *had to* learn what we should do to achieve uniform distribution of the molecule length, to achieve higher recording reliability of the disc. (Kikuchi, interview)

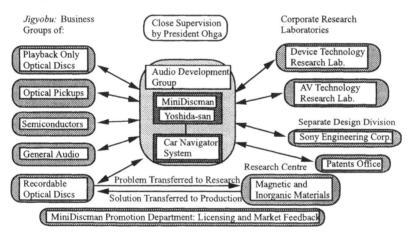

Source: Author's own interpretation of data from Sony Corporation

Figure 5.3   Main Actors in the Development of the MiniDiscman (MD)

Eventually, a new magnetic thin film was prepared and the technology was brought back to development. Second, the magnetic head had to be lighter and smaller with lower energy consumption. This could be achieved through miniaturization of the existing head, thanks to the thinner magnetic film that could operate in weaker magnetic fields. A problem of temperature increase during operation was solved by increasing the frequency of magnetic flux reversals. Playback-Only Optical Discs are with few exceptions based upon the established CD technology. Both of the Optical Disc Business Groups focused on the development of production lines.

The Applied Magnetics Research Department of the Device Technology Research Lab (Figure 5.2) worked on Direct Overwriting. Again, much thanks to the thinner magnetic film and its ability to operate in weaker magnetic fields, the development of a Magnetic Field Modulation Overwrite Process was possible. Consequently, the traditional space-requiring arrangement with a magnetic head which emitted an opposing magnetic field for erasure could be abandoned. One single recording head overwrites the signal directly, instead of first having it erased by an additional magnetic head. Hence, the size of the MD player could be further reduced.

By combining the previously developed CD pickup technology with sophisticated magnetic recording technology, the MD pickup can read both optical and magnetic signals. Hence, magneto-optical recordable MiniDiscs and playback-only MiniDiscs can be played back with one and the same pickup, which further reduces size.

The AV Technology Research Lab (Figure 5.2) delivered critical sound-processing technology. As the MD only measures 64 mm in diameter, it only holds one fifth of a CD's information. Hence, music that is converted into digital signals must be compressed to one-fifth of the original quantity of information. By using Sony's Adaptive TRansform Acoustic Coding (ATRAC) system, which was designed specifically for high-fidelity audio,[28] adequate sound compression could be achieved, without sacrificing high-level sound quality.

The Semiconductor Group developed a Shock-Resistant Memory that continuously keeps three seconds of music stored. Hence, if the MD optical pickup misses any signals due to shocks or vibrations, this will not be perceived by the listener as long as the pickup can recommence reading within three seconds. As these signals still are in a compressed stage, the MD can in fact be rattled like a cocktail shaker up to 15 seconds, without the music being affected. A similar technology was already in development for the CD, whereby the MD Memory Chip could be developed within a year.

Although the final MD project started as late as 1990, President Ohga demanded that the MD be launched by November 1992. There was no time for developing a prototype line before putting together a final production line. Production engineers from the General Audio Group were in constant interaction with Yoshida's group from the beginning of the project, supporting the development of a hardware production line, i.e., for the MiniDiscman itself. This production line started when a barrack type of the MD was ready, i.e., a functioning mechanism mounted on a plate, but without any casing. The casing was designed in parallel by Sony Engineering Corp.

The Patents Office was in close interaction with Yoshida's group during the entire innovation process, thus offering protection of arising intellectual property and, to some extent, supporting licensing negotiations that were run in parallel with competitors like Sharp, Sanyo and Matsushita. The MD Promotion Department started an aggressive licensing process immediately after Sony's official announcement of the MD technology in May 1991. 'Technology development was not important in the MD project. The critical factor was to establish the MD format as a world standard' (Yoshida, interview). Two years later, the number of licensees totalled 53 companies with 64 licensing agreements, 32 of which were hardware-related, 18 pre-recorded software and 14 MD blank media. Some of its work will be described below. Yoshida-san emphasizes his role as a coordinator:

> The mobilization of resources is like a flow within Sony. No boundaries for co-operation exist and doors are always open. My primary task is not technology-oriented, but to coordinate engineers and to motivate them by setting clear goals.

Innovation Would Never Happen without Setting New Industry Standards

Kawakami-san was called back on very short notice from the US to become manager of the MD Promotion Department, organized as a sub-division of the Audio Development Group. Its primary purpose was to promote technology licensing and software production overseas and to coordinate these activities with the product launch. It produced a lot of 'educational material' and arranged events for the audio trade,[29] dealers and customers, the main mission being to convince key partners to produce MiniDisc products and the software industry to produce music on MD format, both in Japan and overseas.

Two persons were appointed to establish links with music software producers overseas, one in New York and one in London. Both were in daily communication with Kawakami-san, but not having any tangible prototype to demonstrate, they failed in their efforts to convince the software producers and went back to Japan, where they stayed until Yoshida-san's group had developed prototypes.

An extensive market research study was prepared in May 1992 by a private market research company in the US for Sony Software Corporation, US. The study measured a large number of aspects (Lieberman 1992, 1): initial purchase interest and market potential of the MD; Perceptions about the benefits of the MD such as size, compactness, portability, random access, durability, shock-resistance, recording capability and digital sound quality; and attitude toward the MD as a purchasing complement to CDs.

A final mission of the survey was to measure the awareness of Philip's Digital Compact Cassette system (DCC) versus the MD system. 'The research that was being done was rather to confirm what we already knew, but we needed good studies to convince the software manufacturers and to back up what we wanted to do' (House, interview).

Early customer feedback was interlinked through the establishment of a monitor program. Short before launching the new MiniDiscman, Sony Music of Japan advertised a campaign of lending MDs, addressed to an existing list of highly 'sony-dedicated' customers. An MD was sent to those who were first to notify their interest, with an invitation to come to the Sony HQ building, a few weeks after reception, for a focused group discussion.

After the first line-up meeting of the MD, a modified version was on the market within four months, due in large part to President Ohga's strong personal involvement in the product.

Dedication to Innovation in Creative Chaos

I wanted one more year to develop the MiniDiscman, but Ohga-san refused. When pressure is that strong, hierarchies within the group are abandoned and younger engineers can even tell older ones what they think. This chaos is confusing, but in a positive way. (Project Manager Yoshida, interview)

'President Ohga drove us crazy by setting hard deadlines and monitoring us carefully' (Kawakami, interview). The emphatic support of President Ohga also encouraged instant mobilization of resources.[30]

Owing to the strict deadline set by President Ohga and also to his own strong belief in the MD, the development project received the status of 'corporate project', which permitted an entirely different resource mobilization.[31] A steering committee was formed in late 1989, which consisted of Tsurushima-san, the Senior General Managers of the most involved Business Groups and of President Ohga, who headed the committee.

As Tsurushima and Yoshida were backed up by this powerful committee, it became easier to encourage the large number of interrelated engineers to co-operate. At some points, the project involved close to 300 engineers and 20 researchers of the Research Centre.

Approximately 20 key persons from the related units gathered on a monthly basis to discuss the advancement of the project's interrelated parts with Tsurushima and Yoshida. President Ohga usually participated at these meetings as well.

'Although we made a lot of sacrifices and had an average of a hundred hours overtime per month, we missed the target by almost a month' (Yoshida, interview). The core team of project leaders were all described as powerful personalities with large prior experience from the development of the CD and the DAT. To them, the development of the MD was a logical next step to make. In addition 'these engineers are all fanatically dedicated, as if their genes were made of music notes' (Kawakami, interview);

The fact that Philips was working on a rival product pushed us to focus our efforts within the Sony Corporation. To have a clearly visible competitor definitely helps us to become more organized and coordinated. (Kawakami, interview)

Global Networking to Miniaturize the Next-generation MD

Improved versions of the MD are underway. By shortening the wavelength of the optical pickup, higher density optical recording and playback would be possible, which would miniaturize all optical disc products. The Research Centre is now working on the development of a miniature blue laser, the wavelength of which is half that of currently used semiconductor lasers. After four years of research at Sony, Tamada was sent to Stamford University, where he majored in optics. He is now managing the Blue Laser Research Project, in close co-operation with the Thin Film Semiconductor Research Group.

Similarly, another researcher of semiconductor lasers within Sony went to the Faculty of Physics at the University of East Anglia in the UK. His instructor, Professor Davies, was deeply involved in basic research on optical physics in regard of the II-VI semiconductor:

> It was significant for me that I could learn new measurement methods and their backgrounds . . . It was a pleasure that I could get to know the way of thinking of foreign people through my life and studies there and could have the opportunity to meet and work with Professor Davies and many other researchers. This experience will stimulate me in my future research activities and I will endeavour to make use of it. (Nakano, quoted in SONY 1992a, 51)

Back in the Research Centre, he joined Tamada's project attempting to apply his research on the II-VI semiconductor to the development of a blue laser.

Other research is being conducted in parallel, as a shorter-wavelength optical pickup will call for new recording materials. Dr Hashimoto, who joined Sony in 1981, is in charge of the Magneto-Optical Recording Material Research Group. His research on artificially layered film, with an achieved thickness of less than 1,000 Ångström, may be a promising candidate for the prospective blue light laser. Recently, he received his Ph.D from Nagoya University, where some of the research was conducted in parallel.

Another technology that may support high-, or even ultra-high-, density optical recording is that of Photochemical Hole Burning (PHB). In the pursuit of this technology, Sony joined MITI's Photo-Reactive Material Project in 1986 and hired a Tokyo University graduate who specialized in the field.[32] His research within the Research Center and the MITI project was supervised by his old professor at Tokyo University, where he recently received his Ph.D.[33]

Monolithic Microwave ICs largely contribute to the performance of the MD.[34] Today's generation is produced in the Semiconductor Group in Atsugi, but one MMIC project was transferred back to the Research Centre in 1989, for further circuit density and miniaturization. Another challenge is to increase the frequency of the MMIC. Fujita joined Sony's Research Centre in 1986, and was in 1989 sent to the University of Rochester in New York State to study optical sampling, which makes possible the measurement of ultra-high frequencies. On his return, a year later, he was engaged in the MMIC project to design and develop an ultra-high-speed MMIC.

As an initial result of the technological improvements in terms of component and IC reduction, Sony launched a 40% smaller and 45% lighter version of the MiniDiscman in November 1993, with recording capability, now called MD Walkman.

Needless to say, Sony has not given up on reducing size further, while continuing the performance increase.

NOTES

1. The books by Kikuchi (1983) and by Morita (1988) provided a good introduction to Sony, before writing the case.
2. Multi-function telephone sets and teleconference systems were launched in 1985, and Sony's first engineering work station, NEWS, was put on the market in 1987 (Dodwell 1992/93, 245).
3. CBS Records was bought in 1988 and a purchase of Columbia Pictures Entertainment followed in November 1989 (Dodwell, 1992/93).
4. In a more technology-oriented perspective, Miyazaki (1994, 289) suggests that Sony's core competence is opto-electronics.
5. In each of the last few years, Sony has unleashed close to 1,000 new products and devices, 800 of which have been improved versions of the previous year's model, with the rest aimed at creating new markets (cf. Schlender 1992, 23). Ohbora *et al.* (1992, 59) state that Sony launched 182 new products in 1990, or almost one new product per business day.
6. In April 1994, Sony Corporation's eleven-year old structure of 19 product groups and marketing groups was replaced with a flatter corporate structure, consisting of three large Group Companies and five Division Companies. To this author's knowledge, this reorganization will not cause any important changes of the R&D structure presented here (Sony, 1994).
7. Four hundred of these engineers are women, a remarkably high number for a Japanese company.
8. 'Still today, Japanese researchers are less good than European or American ones' (Kikuchi, interview).
9. In a recent discussion with Dr Kikuchi, he states that the Corporate Research Laboratories have been organizationally merged with the Research Centre.
10. The department in which Dr Le Bellégo is working with 50 researchers was awarded 60 patents in 1993. The number of initial applications was many times higher (Le Bellégo, interview).
11. A technical sample is a very raw 'barrack-prototype' without any box around it. The commercial sample has the same function, but is designed in a more presentable shape, which usually requires that components in use are miniaturized, if possible, and put into a presentable metal shell.
12. Before a project is transferred from research to production, it is a frequently used practice that production engineers from the 'receiving' production group are integrated into the project team.
13. Perhaps the most famous example of a scientist that did not succeed in finding funding for his invention is Dr Doi's project with NEWS computer workstations. No existing business or product group could handle his prospective product, but Dr Doi could finally get the support of the Business Development Division and is today the Senior General Manager of Sony's Computer Group, a 400-employee operation. He is also Director of the Sony Computer Science Laboratory Inc. (cf. Sony undated; 1989, 19).
14. These numbers are supported by several interviewees (Eda; Hayashi; Kikuchi).
15. This technology called for combinations of scientific methods and tools like Reflection High Energy Electron Diffraction analysis and a Multi-Source Sputtering System.
16. It is very common practice in Japan to gain a Ph.D for rather applied research conducted entirely within the company to which the researcher in question belongs. Dr Aso, for example,

received his Ph.D from Hokkaido University for his work in the Research Centre on amorphous ribbons, a project that was initiated by the MITI supported Research Development Corporation of Japan (SONY 1992a, 13).

17. Sugyama-san, manager of corporate communications, tried to arrange interviews for the author with key persons in the development of Sony's Camcorder CCD TR55. This however failed as all those involved in the project, which ended more than five years ago, were dispersed throughout Sony's organization, working in totally new areas for new Business Groups.

18. 'When we need a specific expertise for an important project, we do hire Ph.Ds in our research centre. However, it is necessary that he accepts to leave his speciality and is flexible enough to work in new, more product-oriented areas; otherwise his contributions to Sony will be of limited value' (Kikuchi, interview). More commonly, Sony's researchers remain in contact with their universities to conduct joint research, thus gaining their Ph.D for rather applied research.

19. The former President of Sony Corporation, Iwama-san, is said to have remembered everything about a person's characteristics, and used to select all project leaders and managers himself, calling them back from wherever they were at very short notice. Owing to Sony's increased size and to President Ohga's stronger focus on business instead of technology, he is less directly involved than Iwama-san was (Kikuchi, interview).

20. In this respect, 'Sony has a combination of Japanese style lifetime employment and the American way of dealing with key persons' (ibid.).

21. Thanks to this discovery, Leo Esaki was awarded the Nobel Prize 17 years later (Morita 1988, 162).

22. Similarly, Quinn (1992, 288) reports that the discovery of the Triniton television system was possible thanks to a young engineer's mistake while experimenting to find an alternative approach to RCA's system.

23. President Iwama, who was a strong supporter of the CCD project, unfortunately passed away in 1982, before the CCD was launched on the market. In commemoration of his strong leadership, his project members mounted a CCD device on his gravestone. 'They hoped that, through this 'electronic eye', Mr Iwama would continue to watch over them' (Sony 1989, 14).

24. This institute, which also does trend-tracking, subscribes to 'every magazine and journal on the map' (Kawakami, interview).

25. MMICs have, for quite a long time, been successfully applied to low-noise amplifiers (SONY 1992a, 24). Before joining the Audio Development Group, Yoshida-san developed such an amplifier. His project was conducted partly in the Research Centre and partly in a more product-oriented Audio Laboratory (Yoshida, interview).

26. In a recent interview, Tsurushima-san states that the number of actors in the above picture would be double, if indirectly related ones were also counted.

27. This transfer happened before it was clear that the technology would find an application in the MD.

28. To a large extent based upon ultra-high-frequency technology, which has applications in, among other areas, amplifiers and satellite decoders, i.e., the key technology fields of chief engineer Yoshida.

29. For instance, music label executives, distributors and wholesalers (Lieberman, 1992).

30. As the MD was developed within a Business Group, there was no need of developing technical, engineering or commercial samples to raise funds for further research.

31. In Sony's history, there have been three other corporate projects: Betamax, 8mm Camcorder and the CD player (Tsurushima, interview).

32. As he was born already in 1956, he most probably spent several years in a national research laboratory, before joining Sony.

33. Cf. SONY (1992a, 28-31).

34. They are also essential parts of satellite receivers, like those used in Sony's Car Navigation System.

6   Toyota Motor Corporation

BRIEF INTRODUCTION

Toyota Motor Corporation(TMC)[1] makes 28 passenger car models and 9 commercial models in Japan. During fiscal year 1992, 2.23 million Toyota vehicles were registered in Japan and 1.7 million vehicles were exported overseas. With an 8.6% share of the world market based on production, Toyota Motor was in 1990 the second largest automobile manufacturer in the world, following General Motors, which had 8.7% (Dodwell 1992, 270). Its domestic share was 32.6%, followed by Nissan's 20.0% (Japan Almanac 1993, 134).

In December 1992, Toyota Motor had 72,533 employees, but the group's total number was close to 200,000 employees, including some 170 subsidiaries. Consolidated net sales for fiscal year 1992 were ¥10,163,376, out of which approximately 70% accounted for sales of motor vehicles.

INTRAORGANIZATIONAL ASPECTS OF R&D AND TECHNOLOGY

The Research and Development Group

Excluding overseas operations, described in Chapter 3, there are 11,500 engineers and researchers related to the Research and Development Group of Toyota Motor, which is headed by the Technical Centre at Toyota headquarters, located in Toyota City. Here, some 9,700 engineers belong to an R&D Group which is split into three vehicle development centres, one component and system development centre and a large number of supporting and administrative functions, e.g. technical information, intellectual property, material research and prototype production. The component and system development centre is technology-oriented, concentrating on advanced engineering of components and large vehicle systems, which are to be integrated in entire vehicles by the three vehicle centres.

The Central Research and Development Laboratory is Organized for Technology Fusion across the whole Toyota Group

The Toyota Central Research and Development Laboratoy, Inc. is a spun-off independent company of the Toyota Group with some 900 researchers and engineers,[2] who mainly do basic research on components. Researchers are not exposed to the imperatives of job-rotation. Instead, they have long-term careers within the centre, which allows for extensive specialization.

Toyota Motor is the largest owner, but equity is also held among other Toyota Group companies. In 1980, a matrix organization divided its research into basic groups of specialized areas such as combustion, heat, materials and electronics. The purpose of this organization is to facilitate coordinated collaboration among the laboratory staff when it works together on special new technology projects, in which several technology areas are fused.

For some of the research collaboration with universities is common. Research projects are commissioned from Toyota Motor or from other stakeholders like Nippondenso to the R&D centre, which has its own profit responsibility. Sixty-five to 70% of all its activities are commissioned by the Higashi-Fuji research centre, described below.

R&D of electronic technology systems (e.g. ABS brake-systems), engines and new materials is done in the Higashi-Fuji Technical Centre, where approximately 1,800 engineers are employed. A second activity is advanced engineering development of body, chassis, engines and drive trains. Third, there is the research and advanced development planning division, where, for example, motor sport activities are planned and supported. Approximately 20% of Toyota's total university interaction is with Higashi-Fuji, the remaining 80% being concentrated on the aforementioned Toyota Central R&D Laboratory.

All R&D projects are preceded by project proposals that are submitted to the members of the board of Toyota. Once a project is close to completion and approved by the board members, the entire project is moved to the Component and System Development Centre, or directly to a Development Centre. The technology transfer is not heavily dependant on human transfer. Hane-san estimates that approximately 90% of all researchers in Higashi-Fuji stay for their entire career in the Technical Centre. The remaining ten per cent are transferred with their project.[3] It is the goal of TMC to increase the share of transfer to 30% of the researchers.

Advanced engineering development and commercial product development of basic components is, to a large extent, done by parts suppliers. Commercial product development of vehicles is largely assisted by body makers who also have some R&D capacity. Both suppliers and body makers interact directly with the head office technical centre and with Higashi-Fuji technical centre. Some suppliers also interact directly with the spun-off Toyota Central R&D Laboratories (mentioned in chapter 3).

Figure 6.1 depicts the interconnections and contributions of each domestic unit in the R&D system. The activities and interlinkages of the Component and System Development Centre and of the three Vehicle Development Centres in the Head Office Technical Centre are more thoroughly described later on.

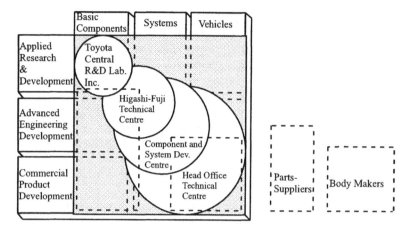

Source: Author's own arrangement of data provided by TMC

Figure 6.1   The Toyota R&D System's Domestic Actors

Previously, there was no clear distinction between advanced engineering of components or systems and current, or commercial, engineering of vehicles. At Toyota, this was all done within one large development centre. Today, Toyota clearly distinguishes between basic R&D, advanced development and commercial development. Different time perspectives of the development of components, parts assembled in systems, and entire vehicles is the main cause of the separation. In most cases, these activities also take place in different geographical locations.

Many other actors are involved in the development of a new vehicle than those in Figure 6.1. Development of advanced styling designs is conducted at the Tokyo Design Centre, but most of Toyota's advanced styling design seems to be created at the aforementioned Calty Design Research in California (Chapter 3).

As a complement to the proving grounds at the head office and those at Higashi-Fuji, the Shibetsu proving ground in Hokkaido permits automobile testing in a cold environment and at very high speed. Another proving ground centre in Arizona tests vehicle performance at high speed and high temperature.

Frequent Travelling and Video Conferencing Tie the Toyota R&D System Together

Intensive communication aims at linking the different units together, including those described in Chapter 3:

> Within Japan, the use of video phones is extensive and when personal interaction is necessary, we can always use one of our helicopters to go to the Higashi-Fuji Technical Centre.

Also, we have daily flights between Toyota City, Tokyo and the Shibetsu Technical Proving Ground in Hokkaido with our jet shuttle. (Mohri, Head of Project Mgmt., interview)

Video board meetings are frequent with the technical Centre in Ann Arbor, Michigan and the design centre in California. Sometimes these conferences are three-way, connecting the two to HQ in Toyota City. The technical centre and the design centre in Brussels have no video connection to Japan yet. Instead, a lot of travelling is necessary. Managers of overseas R&D subsidiaries usually go to Japan once a year, but including all members of the subsidiary, there will always be someone who goes back to Japan every month. During a two-year period, there are usually five or six peaks in the development work. At each of these peaks, several engineers go from the R&D centres in the US and Europe to Japan and *vice versa*.

A Satellite-structured New Product Development System Allows Technology Development and Project Management to Coexist

The new product development system is based upon three vehicle development centres, all of which have between six and ten chief engineers, each in charge of a specific vehicle. A vehicle development centre takes care of each specific category of vehicles: rear-wheel drive (1,500 engineers), front-wheel drive (1,800 engineers) and multipurpose and commercial vehicles (1,300 engineers). A centre consists of a few fixed divisions, indicated in Figure 6.2, which support its chief engineers. Their activity is commercial development of vehicles. Needless to say, there is a continuous competition against time in these centres.

Two additional activities – material R&D and prototype production – are pursued within the vehicle development centres, but are organized as independent divisions with only one manager each. A larger number of surrounding divisions, altogether comprising some 3,000 engineers, support all of the development centres.

The technical administration division handles resource allocation and an engineering administration division gathers and channels technical information regarding vehicle design, acting much as a link to overseas technical centres. One on-site design division and one in Tokyo handle styling design, partly through their own R&D and partly through interaction with the design offices in Belgium and in California. Protection and application of patents is assumed by the intellectual property division.

Extensive support is also given by the component and system development centre, which has a total of 2,100 engineers. Their areas of expertise are engine and drive-train components, electronic parts, electronic systems and semiconductors. This is where most advanced development of components and systems is done. It is located on the same premises as the three vehicle development centres, but acts as a separate unit in close interaction with all three.

Previously, this unit was entirely integrated in one large vehicle development centre. There is a high time pressure here too, but the focus is on components and systems, i.e. technology development, rather than on product development as is the case with the vehicle development centres. Hence, Toyota has separated these and other activities in a 'satellite-structured' new product development system so as to increase technological expertise without slowing down the speed of product development by having separate, but co-existing structures, one focusing on technology and the other focusing on project management.

The Component and System Development Centre is said to have deeper hierarchical levels than the central R&D laboratory and the Higashi-Fuji research centre, which more enjoy individual freedom of research activities, or R&D activities in small groups in the latter case.

Marrying Specialization with Skills Diffusion

This newly introduced development system intends to enhance expertise within the divisions. Engineers are not requested to change working fields as frequently as before, in order to reduce the drawbacks of too frequent job rotation. A body engineer, for instance, may now stay for five to seven years within the body engineering group of one vehicle development centre, where he will work with the same type of parts all the time, but on different vehicles and for different chief engineers. An engineer frequently works on several projects at the same time. He reports both to the division manager of the body engineering group and to the chief engineer who 'borrows his services'. A multiple reporting system, in which both the manager of a division and the chief engineer and possibly also a superior general manager get reports from one and the same subordinate engineer, is a delicate matter, as stated by Mohri-san, Head of Project Management:

> Our multiple reporting system is good for the spread of information, but it may also confuse the engineers and result in a 'who is my boss syndrome'. It is like a double-edged sword, *ryoba no yaiba*. When I master it and have two edges to cut with, I can kill you more easily, but if I don't master it, I may cut myself instead.

A fact which increases the 'who is my boss syndrome', but also encourages greater spread of information, is that approximately half of all engineers assigned to the project of a chief engineer are concurrently involved in other projects to dissipate their skills as widely as possible.

Figure 6.2 depicts the three vehicle development centres with those units that support their development activities.

The closeness of the prototype production division makes possible early involvement of production engineering and manufacturing. Prototype production lines are developed here and, usually, the same lines are used in mass production, so as to minimize time-to-market.

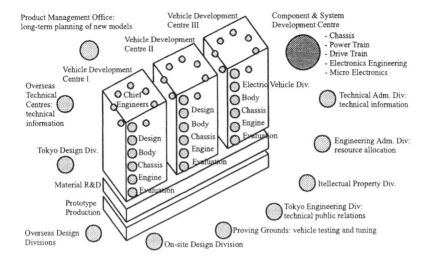

Source: Author's own interpretation of data provided by TMC

Figure 6.2   Toyota's New Product Development System

Sakakibara-san, General Manager of the Tahara Plant, states that 'the vehicle development centres' prototype production division is in charge of automation of my plant, I'm not'. Product development thus seems to have the leading role within Toyota.

Linking Every Customer Complaint to the Source of the Defect

An extensive and finely detailed sales network may be the largest contributor to this interlinkage. According to Mohri-san, 'one of the most important factors underlying Toyota Motor's success is our strong sales organization, domestically and overseas'. In Japan, Toyota has five different dealer networks with a total of 310 automobile dealers who operate approximately 5,200 sales and service outlets. Overseas, the number of distributors is 158, who operate 7,187 sales outlets. Sales managers return to Japan four times a year on average.

Considering these numbers together with Toyota's efforts to establish a relationship of close co-operation and trust with both distributors and dealers, the company appears to have succeeded in drawing itself close to the market. As a result, systematic collection of market information and quick feedback to product development flows seamlessly.

Customer complaints about defects are reported via retailers to the quality control group, or directly to the research and development group. A second route for feedback is that received directly from customers to the customer relations group. In either case an important customer complaint is always immediately linked to the source of a defect.

Overseas marketing is coordinated from the Tokyo office and domestic marketing is done at the Nagoya HQ.

> Marketing departments have information which is really important to the vehicle development centres. In order for them to make good products, they interact frequently with our market researchers, who really know what the customers want. In some cases, development engineers may even do some sales themselves. (Noda, interview)

Toyota's top management directors pay frequent visits to both distributors and dealers, in order to set development strategies which respond better to market needs. For 32 years, Toyota Motor Corporation and Toyota Motor Sales were two independent organizations, but in 1982, a merger of the two aimed at a stronger integration of marketing and sales into product development.

Training and Job Rotation Bring Every Engineer to the Customer

According to rules issued by the human resources department, everybody has to change functions within ten years. On average, managers change functions every three years and engineers every five years. All newly recruited engineers must spend an initial training period of three months doing sales for a Toyota dealer and another three months on the line in a production plant. Take Noda-san for example: after his six months of sales and production, he spent 13 years in three different departments: the sales, systems and legal departments. He was then sent to Harvard University for one year, mainly to develop a network of connections. All costs were paid, and he remained on Toyota's payroll during the course of studies. Presently, he is working within the industrial affairs division.

Experienced development engineers tend to move between research, development and production, rather than into other corporate functions like marketing. Toyota attempts to develop a system which allows engineers to stay longer within the same function, so as to develop expertise rather than become generalists. To some extent, this is already possible within the vehicle development centres, as indicated above. According to Mohri-san, the engineers themselves would like this to spread to other departments as well.

For overseas managers, the tendency is reversed. Technical managers usually stay for three years before they are sent back, but marketing and sales management usually stay for five years on average. Mohri-san means that 'a shorter stay is necessary for expatriated engineers. They get behind in technology and innovation if they stay away too long'.

MANAGING COMPLEXITY IN SEAMLESS INNOVATION PROCESSES

The Chief Engineers are True Champions of Innovation

Approximately 20 chief engineers are housed in the product management office, but belong to one of the three development centres, where they manage Toyota's different vehicle projects. Mohri-san states that for Toyota, the most important qualities of a chief engineer are technical know-how, authority, leadership and, above all, visionary dreams. Translation of the initial visionary concept into smaller part concepts and then again into yet smaller tasks is an equally important task of the chief engineer.

> Chief engineers are hard-working, admired super-engineers, who discuss and exchange ideas with members of all departments that are related to the development and production of their vehicles. (Mohri, interview)

At any given time, the chief engineer has no other assignment than to develop one specific vehicle. He cannot sit on the board at the same time, but some of the present directors at the Technical Centre have previous experience as chief engineers.

Some vehicle development projects have mobilized more than 1,000 engineers.[4] The chief engineer has little or no time for paper work. Instead, he is always actively involved in the different development phases, and intervenes if necessary.

Strong internal competition between different chief engineers and their competing models appears to increase the pace of innovation. Even though all chief engineers are located in one large Product Management Office, they hardly communicate with each other, due to the intense internal competition. Instead, their assistants exchange a lot of information.[5]

Formally, a chief engineer is at the same level as a division manager, but informally his authority is greater. His age is between 38 and 50. Conflicts of authority between the chief engineers and the division manager are rare. The overall reason is that the division manager seems to respect the greater informal authority of the chief engineer, which is based upon several factors:

- Everybody, including division managers, seems to acknowledge a unique excellence among chief engineers;
- Each chief engineer reports directly to and receives orders directly from top management. Consequently, any instruction given by a chief engineer is regarded as the reflection of top management;
- Each single drawing of a vehicle must have a signature of approval from the chief engineer in question, which makes him a key person in all development divisions.

- Chief engineers have a strong impact on the performance evaluation of all those engineers who participate in his projects.

Figure 6.3 depicts the three aforementioned Vehicle Development Centres, which respectively have functional divisions for styling design, body design, chassis design, engine design and evaluation. Moreover, they share the divisions for materials and prototype production. (The centres develop a larger number of vehicles than those indicated in Figure 6.3.)

Chief engineers negotiate with the respective division managers for the allocation of engineers, but are then in charge of these engineers through the aforementioned mechanisms. Although the engineers are assigned to a chief engineer, they remain in their home divisions, where the division manager ensures their education. The division manager also has a joint responsibility together with the relevant chief engineers to evaluate his engineers, but before making a final decision of whom to promote, they also consult both the subordinates and the colleagues of the engineers in question.

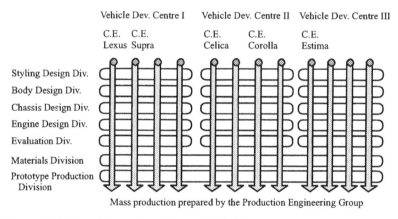

Mass production prepared by the Production Engineering Group

Source: Author's own interpretation of data provided by TMC

Figure 6.3   Toyota's Cross-divisional Vehicle Development Projects

The fact that several divisions along the innovation process are involved concurrently does not mean that the various activities are performed by one and the same team. Instead, concurrent engineering seems to be based on continuous exchange of information between the individual divisions. (Hane; Kageyama; Nakajima; Tsurusawa, interviews).

The description below of the new product development process will describe how the interactive consulting process is managed and also bring additional key-actors into the picture.

Networking Between Marketing and Sales, R&D and Production

A highly interactive consulting process, including the research and advanced development planning division from the Higashi-Fuji Technical Centre, the component and system development centre, the product planning division, design divisions and offices, the marketing group and the production engineering group, precedes the development process. The chief engineer of a development project organizes the information-gathering and heads the process in which each division and group gives opinions on the project. Approximately 20 to 30 deputy chief engineers are assigned to support the chief engineer throughout a project. R&D results, design trends and ideas, customer complaints and requests from overseas distributors are presented, sometimes in individual meetings and sometimes in large group meetings. The production engineering group is also consulted to obtain opinions on design for easy manufacturing and assembly.

The result of this interactive process is a proposal for development, which is further reviewed by the chief engineer, who includes much of his own vision before he presents the proposal to top management's product planning committee. If top management gives approval, the proposal finally becomes a product concept including concrete criteria, such as vehicle size, performance requirements, prize and targeted customer group.

The chief engineer prepares an instruction for development which he, or one of his deputies, presents to the relevant vehicle development centre. This is the base of the next four stages in the innovation process: styling design, body and component design, prototype production and testing and evaluation. Development results from these steps are continuously fed back to the chief engineer, who continues to consult the above groups and divisions. At any time, he may revise the instruction for development. Once testing and evaluation of a prototype is satisfactory, a request for production is prepared and given to the production engineering group, which is well prepared thanks to the continuous bilateral consulting. As soon as two pilot runs have been successfully completed, mass production starts, as depicted in Figure 6.4.

The Proactive Involvement of Production Engineering Secures a Seamless Transfer to Manufacturing

The interlinkage of production is mainly taken care of by the production engineering group. This group acts as an integrated part of the development process, by letting some of its engineers participate from concept generation to the design of prototypes, thus supporting design for manufacturing.

Already in August of 1937, when Toyota Motor was founded, executive vice president Kiichiro Toyoda is said to have decided that the manufacturing department and the engineering department should work in close cooperation, and the respective managers of each department were given simultaneous managerial control of the other department. Sakakibara-san states that 'co-operation between R&D departments and production departments has kept increasing. Now, I meet with people from R&D every day'. He often sends his people to the development teams at a very early stage in order to prepare for a seamless transfer to production:

> For instance, 18 months before marketing the new Soarer and Supra, a small project team was formed, which included both development team leaders and group leaders from production engineering, who were asked to participate, already from the prototype stage, in developing the new models.

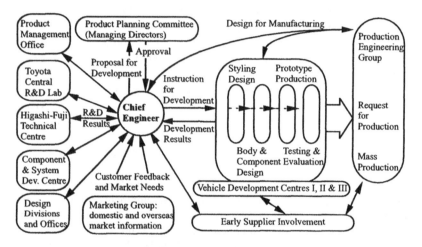

Source: Author's own arrangement of data provided by TMC

Figure 6.4   Toyota Motor's New Product Development Process

Powerful Visions Support Alignment and Creative Involvement

The use of visions penetrates the entire development process. Initially, top management proposes an overall vision, capturing the corporate goals, which is disintegrated and further disseminated by the chief engineers. Hence, the overall corporate goal is translated into development efforts and extended throughout the corporation.

Everybody involved in the process seems to respect the leadership role of product development and there seem to be few barriers between departments, 'thanks to the chief engineer, who acts as a coach and inspires people to join and help, instead of merely giving orders' (Mohri, interview). The highly interactive and flexible process relies upon an organic group, continuously gathered, coordinated and, eventually, dissolved by the chief engineer.

Even when mass production has started, development and incremental improvements continue to flow. In a way, the entire workforce is involved in product and process improvements. Not only engineers, but also production-line workers are engaged in some 6,800 quality control circles. In 1991, they submitted 2,076,077 suggestions, or 35.6 suggestions per company member, out of which as many as 98% were adopted and rewarded. Company slogans like 'good thinking, good products' strive to encourage the creative involvement of each company member.

A Collective Committment to the Final Deadline Replaces Excessive Project Scheduling

As opposed to many Western automobile manufacturers, there is no large scheduling or timing department that supervises and schedules all development projects. Scheduling is not a big issue at Toyota,[6] where only a few milestones are set up by the chief engineer. Instead of having numerous detailed deadlines, only the launching date is firmly set and agreed upon by everybody. In this approach of overall consensus on only a few important milestones, internal flexibility is great. Hence, if one stage of the development process takes longer than expected, the next stage can more easily be reduced in length through acceleration and more extensive overlapping.[7] The importance of time is well understood by everybody, and all those concerned almost seem to be 'programmed' to accept that development cycles for model renewals last four years.

Shameless Copying Paves the Way For World-wide Leadership

In order to promote creativity, Toyota practices a 'sempai system', much like the German 'Meister system', in which the inexperienced learn from the old experts, mainly by watching. This has proved to be a good way of acquiring tacit knowledge. In the trainee programme mentioned earlier, newly recruited engineers are guided through the most important corporate functions – marketing and production – which they both observe and practise. Another example, at a different level, is when competing vehicles are observed, thoroughly evaluated, and possibly copied before in-house inventive design is begun.

The practice of initial product development through indirect technology transfer, or reverse engineering, is deeply rooted within Toyota Motor Corporation. Since the early 1930s, Kiichiro Toyoda was confident that he would be able to duplicate and combine the superior features of Ford, Chevrolet and Chrysler. Discovering that this practice enabled rapid and extensive development of competence among his engineers, it has remained a tradition within the company notwithstanding a steady increase of in-house capacity in R&D[8]

A good analogy is when young painters copy famous originals in museums and later become good artists themselves. It is too difficult to explain how to become a good painter, so you have to start by copying, before you understand how to produce a masterpiece yourself. (Mohri, interview)

DEVELOPING THE LEXUS – DECLARING WAR WITH GERMANY

As a result of an export restraint agreement in 1981, the number of complete exported vehicles from Japan to the US was limited. Furthermore, as the yen appreciation never seemed to reach an end, it became a natural consequence for the large manufacturers to move their car models up-market, aiming for higher profit margins per vehicle. Honda was the first manufacturer to move in this direction, in the mid-1980s, by the introduction of the Accura and its new dealer network. Nissan and Toyota quickly followed suit, both aiming further up-market than the Accura. This case will explore Toyota Motor's efforts in the development of the Lexus LS 400.[9]

Product Planning: Ambition Increased over Time

In late 1983, a product planning meeting was held to discuss a successor of the Cresida (called Mark II in Japan). The chief engineer of the Camry had already been allowed to develop a 2.5 litre engine, which would move his car into the intermediate luxury car market. The original plan at this meeting was to develop something better, and a V6 engine of somewhat more than three litres was approved by Toyota's managing directors. Still, this was much more modest than what eventually came to be the Lexus. The price and quality was to be higher-market than for previous models, but the initial purpose was not to compete directly with the high-class products of Mercedes Benz and BMW.

A project team was formed and in February 1984, Jinbo, a veteran product manager, was officially assigned the role of project manager, or chief engineer. He was provided with an initial vision from top management 'to develop a model which is attractive both to current Cresida users and to luxury sedan users'. The target market was the American high-end segment. Of Toyota's 3.4 million vehicles produced in 1984, 24% was exported to the US.

Acquiring Strategic Market Needs Through Cocktail Parties

An ordinary project has relatively few members and scarce resources in the beginning, and increases progressively as the project advances. However, in this case, Jinbo decided to invest a lot of resources in the planning and early development stages, so as to solve as many problems as possible upstream. In May 1985, he headed a study team that went to America to do initial market research. Members from several divisions were included in the team: the product management office (a division that mainly contains chief engineers), the product planning division and a design division.[10] At this point it had not been decided whether the car would be an up-scaled Cresida, or something totally different. As this was no ordinary replacement model, which usually is developed every four years, no rigid time deadlines were set. Rather, this was a new concept aiming at a new segment. Therefore, it was judged necessary to spend more time and resources on concept-generation. Lead-time was not yet the significant issue.

Although the team was not entirely marketing oriented, its assignment was to study the American luxury car market in Los Angeles, New York and San Francisco. Ample visits were made to dealers of Mercedes Benz, BMW, Volvo, Audi, and other up-market cars. In the summer of 1985, Jinbo's team, Toyota's American marketing unit and the overseas planning department from HQ in Japan jointly arranged initial cocktail parties and would, later on, conduct focused group discussions with 21 owners of the previously mentioned luxury cars, as well as some American equivalents.

The study was highly instructive to Toyota. European luxury cars, with Mercedes and BMW on top, were given the highest scores, both in terms of prestige and dealer satisfaction. American cars came in second place, and Japanese cars ranked the lowest, not due to reliability, nor to design, but to lack of prestige. Furthermore, a luxury car was seen not only as a means of transportation, but as evidence of the owner's success. The important factors were status image, high performance, high quality, distinct differentiation from other cars, dealer attitude and location and design of the outlets. Luxury car users all wanted to be treated as VIPs in these aspects.

Proactive Elimination of Potential Client Dissatisfaction

Jinbo and some other team members left after one month, but his study group of designers stayed in America. They rented a luxury house in LA to get the feeling of a luxury-oriented Californian. A lot of time and resources was also spent on exploring what the luxury car owners and dealers were *dissatisfied* with and what additional functions and options they would see as valuable improvements.[11]

In January 1986, Jinbo presented a product development proposal of the car to the product planning committee, consisting of top managing directors, which officially approved it. At this point, they finally decided that the car should not be an extension of Cresida, but a totally new strategic product, destined to become Toyota's new flagship. Chairman Eiji Toyoda summarized the project in a wide, yet goal-oriented vision: 'Making an ultimate luxury car by injecting Toyota's fifty-year experience and skills in automobile development and manufacturing into the project'.

From this point and onwards, the project was called the 'F-project', F meaning flagship. Hence, they decided to go all the way through and not take the risk of making compromises. The new flagship would eventually form a totally new product platform that was epoch-making in Toyota's global strategy.

The Empowered Chief Engineer Emphasized Performance

In February 1986, Jinbo was promoted to director of product development. According to Toyota's rules, a director could not concurrently be a chief engineer.[12] Suzuki, a veteran body engineer,[13] was at this time product manager in charge of Toyota's overall product line. It was his duty to prepare a list of candidates for Jinbo's successor. However, this list was overruled and Suzuki himself was assigned as chief engineer of the F-project. In this way Toyota assured that the chief engineer of their most important project was a particularly respected 'heavyweight' product manager with strong authority. The major decision makers of these promotions were Sasaki, head of the product manager office and Matsumoto, Executive Vice President in charge of technology.

Sasaki told Suzuki to front-load the project by spending a lot of time and resources on the concept generation phase. Matsumoto asked him to 'make a truly epoch-making car' and emphasized that such a task would require more than internal efforts within the vehicle development centre. The goal of the F-project, completely different from earlier Toyota projects, was thus a new platform positioned close to top-level luxury cars. The problem was that the time left for Suzuki was very limited. This was the first luxury car for Toyota in the American market, which also meant that they would have to set up at least one hundred new dealers.

The front-loading strategy, with a lot of market information gathered in the early concept-formation stage, left Suzuki with two visionary concept guidelines: the car should enrich the minds of its users; and the users' sentimental attachment to the car should increase over time, meaning that the car should do more than merely arouse initial enthusiasm that could fade away over time. Suzuki ensured that the above visionary and rather abstract concepts were translated into more tangible product concepts, and then further supervised translations into yet more detailed numerical targets and engineering drawings. The abstract initial concept was first translated into the general guidelines of (1) high functionality; (2) warmth, sophistication and nobility, and also (3) to overcome the trade-off between 1 and 2. These three guidelines became the basic philosophy in the development of the Lexus. They were further translated into 5 criteria, taking into account the results of the marketing research:

1. High performance in road-holding, comfort, speed, etc.;
2. Image of high prestige and status;
3. Sense of high quality;
4. High resale value; and
5. Safety.

Benchmarking and Reverse Engineering World-class Performance

Market research indicated that image was the most important criterion and that technological features were of less importance. Suzuki, however, realized that Toyota with its present image would never be able to compete with Mercedes Benz and BMW solely based on this factor, and decided to put highest emphasis on performance. In this sense he overruled the market voice, arguing that, for a late-comer, a focus on high performance was necessary. The name of the new game was distinctive superiority in functional performance. Accordingly, he set very high quality and performance targets based on Mercedes Benz and BMW. Among the top models of these two companies are the MB 420 SE and the BMW 735i, which were designated as target vehicles to be emulated and, if possible, even outperformed through incremental improvement of all their key technology criteria.[14] This benchmarking yielded the following specific and very demanding targets:

- Maximum speed: 250 km/h;
- Maximum fuel consumption: 25.5 mpg;
- Quietness (noise and vibration): 100 km/h – 53 dB; 200 km/h-73 dB;
- Cd-value: 0.28-0.29; and
- Weight: 1710 kg.

As a consequence of these targets, a lot of trade-offs had to be solved. To be able to meet the speed-target at the same time as that of fuel-consumption, the car had to be light. But a light car is normally noisy. 'Autobahn speed' was very important for the image, even though probably few of the drivers would ever drive at this speed. 'A noise level that enabled people to talk with normal voice between the front seat and the back seat, even at a fairly high speed', and that allowed an 'acceleration from 100 to 200 km/h without having to touch the volume-button of the car stereo' was requested. The fuel consumption should be low enough to avoid the American gas-guzzler tax. The Cd-value should be lower than the benchmarking models (less than 0.30) and the car should also be 50 kg lighter than the other two. In addition, the car should have a price that was between $5,000 and $10,000 lower than that of its competitors. These targets were set regardless of paradoxical trade-offs. Even though they were preceded by discussions with product engineers, most of the targets were set by Suzuki himself.

Root-cause Problem Solving Penetrated the Supplier Pyramid

In summary, to be able to compete with Mercedes Benz they would have to compete with the Mercedes Benz image, which required a car with superior performance on a number of contradictory measures despite a lower price. Even within Toyota, engineers found the targets ridiculous and unrealistic.

Facing this resistance, Suzuki realized a need to solve the trade-offs by identifying the root cause of the various problems that emerged and then going upstream to the initial source of the problem. This would require not only extraordinary efforts and resources in terms of testing and experimenting, but also a higher level of interaction between many different specialists from a large number of departments engaged in the various stages of the development process. Moreover, it would call for stricter requirements vis-á-vis key suppliers, who carried out large parts of the development work. Suzuki thus made use of this root-cause problem solving slogan[15] in order to persuade the engineers.

Taking noise reduction as an example, a major factor is engine and transmission noise. As for the engine itself, more accuracy, higher precision and better balance were needed to minimize vibrations. It was also to fit into the engine compartment, the shape of which affects noise as well. A light but rigid car body in anti-vibration steel was called for with a design that minimized windnoise and Cd-value. Hence, product design, product development engineers of body, transmission and engine had to co-operate with production engineers and people from engine plants, including their suppliers of both components and steel. Senior engine engineer Hane[16] states that for the development of the Lexus engine,

> we made clear to the suppliers at a very early stage that accuracy requirements on components would be much stricter, with significantly higher levels of quality control. Of course, we had to help them improve through technology transfer and financial support.

Suzuki realized the need for cross functional co-operation as soon as he approached the engine division with his needs, whose ability to help was limited by a lack of accurate machine tools, both within the internal division and within key suppliers. They did not have the money, nor the authority to mobilize necessary resources. Hence, people at a higher level had to be involved, which is why the FQ (Flagship Quality) Committee was created as an interlinking mechanism.

A High-level Steering Committee Secured Immediate Mobilization of Resources

The FQ committee was headed by the highest executives in charge of general product development, project development and factory-level production. It involved both designers, product engineers and production engineers. Coordination committees between product and process engineering were nothing new, but the Lexus project was the first in Toyota's history to achieve such extensive integration across divisions and high-level hierarchies. The core of the FQ committee consisted of executive level managers from the above three functions. Director Jinbo was head of general product development, Suzuki was the Lexus project leader (chief engineer) and Takahashi was a highly experienced and respected director of production engineering and, according to

Suzuki, the most important contributor to the Lexus project.

As Suzuki headed the FQ Committee, he was actually heading his own boss, Jinbo. Suzuki thus crossed both vertical and horizontal borders in a project where both of these influential and respected persons worked as his mentors and sponsors. General meetings were held every three months, but informal meetings were frequent as well. The committee was divided into 11 subcommittees, each of which was headed by a department manager (*buchoo*) and included key suppliers. These subcommittees met every six weeks, but also met with the main committee every three months.

The entire FQ team was characterized by comparative informality in structure and form, which did not diverge from the Toyota way of product development, but instead emphasized some of its main ingredients. In the first half of the project, product engineering people had the initiative. Then in the second half of the project, as process issues became increasingly important, the initiative was gradually passed on to the production engineers, which was not the typical Toyota way.[17]

Another feature of the project was the so called F-room.[18] Whenever conflicts above a certain level occurred, people involved gathered in this room and discussed the problem. In the beginning, the actual design work was made in this room as well, but as the project succeeded and grew, its different tasks had to be done in separate rooms, conceived for the respective purpose. As the F-project eventually came to involve 1,400 people, it would have been impossible to gather them all in this room. Instead, representatives of each of the involved groups could be collocated here.

Thanks to the high-level members, important decisions could be made instantly, which facilitated rapid mobilization and allocation of resources through joint decision-making at the executive level. Hence, a lot of trade-offs could be identified and evidently rapid root-cause problem solving was possible. Taking noise reduction as an example, Jinbo had the authority to mobilize capital, which Takahashi could allocate to investments in high precision machine tools and high accuracy measurement equipment, both within Toyota and within some affiliated subsidiaries and key suppliers. Total project cost was ¥135 billion (approximately $1.2 billion) until start of mass production in 1988, including large spending on technical equipment. As mentioned earlier, 50 billion of this amount was spent within affiliated companies.

Apart from the root-cause philosophy, Suzuki had other slogans that he did his best to spread to the people involved in the project. One was 'not yet', meaning that in order to break the various trade-offs without making compromises, engineers had to say 'not yet' to compromises, until problems were totally eliminated. These slogans were also disseminated across corporate boundaries all the way to part suppliers and material producers.

A Focus on Prototypes Made Possible Immediate Evaluation and Communication of Results

Engine Development

As for the engine, Toyota set high targets based on world top-level performance, and challenged their engineers to meet them. Root-cause problem solving of noise reduction called for high accuracy, well-balanced engine and drive train, preferably in anti-vibration steel. The initial proposal from the product planning department was a V6 3 litre turbo engine, but Jinbo, at the time chief engineer, wanted a V8 3.5 litre engine, for which a prototype was developed in 1985. Referring to the American gas guzzler tax that limited fuel consumption to 22.5 miles on a gallon, Toyota US and other foreign divisions argued that the 'yuppie' target customers would want a compact and intelligent engine that was fuel efficient. This lead to the development of a V8 3.8 litre engine, which however did not meet the speed target of 250 km/h.

In April 1986, only 13 months before line-off, Kanahara, managing director in charge of engines, finally decided on a V8 engine of 4.0 litre. Some engineers were against this idea, but when he said that this was the final word and the only possible solution, everybody obeyed his idea, which was also approved by the product planning committee. Suzuki did not decide in this case, but allowed for a shift of authority to division manager Kanahara.

Styling Design

In May 1985, Calty Design developed a full-scale clay model. The car should be like the 'David statue' – full of wisdom and beauty, and enriching for the owner. A first Japanese full-scale model was made and presented in late 1985, but because it looked too American, designers had to make a large number of changes. The resulting model looked too small and too streamlined. Hence, a more boxy car was designed, but this did not look new. A large number of modifications and presentations followed.

In 1986, the second big presentation was made of a model with Cd 0.30. The product planning committee found that it looked too small. A specialist in aerodynamics developed a model that had a Cd value of 0.28. Though the designers were very negative and called it 'awful', Suzuki encouraged him by saying that it was a good try, and made him work together with the designers. In this way, his ideas were included although his first concept was discarded. This iterative process of model changes and presentations went on for another good year, but after the eighth design review, a final presentation could be held for the product planning committee, i.e., for top management, in late 1987.

Component Design

For a distinctive interior, Toyota wanted high accuracy, and fashionable and visible dashboard instruments. As an example, Nippondenso was requested to make dashboard instruments with an illuminated needle that:

- was bright enough even in daytime;
- had an equal distribution of light with no electrode on the top;
- responded quickly;
- had strong resistance against vibrations; and
- was unaffected by high temperature.

Some Nippondenso engineers were already members of FQ subcommittees, which facilitated a thorough understanding of Toyota's needs. Through intensive trial-and-error activities and the involvement of specialized sub-suppliers, a miniaturized glass tube of 2.4 mm diameter filled with xenon gas was developed that fulfilled the requirements.

Prototype Production

A lot of pre-prototypes were made with the Cresida exterior, mainly for engine testing, the first one being ready in July 1985 with a 3.5 litre engine. This was too heavy, had a Cd of 0.32 and did not clear the fuel-tax limit. In June 1987, a first real prototype was made even though the styling was not yet final. Altogether there were 450 different prototypes made.

Excessive Autobahn-testing Ended the Benchmarking

Extensive testing was run in parallel with prototype production. A test course was built in Hokkaido, more or less tailor-made for Lexus. Final test-driving began in 1986 on the Autobahn in Germany. They now realized that the engine was too small to reach 250 km/h. After completion of the 4.0 litre V8 engine, test driving continued on the Autobahn. A group of ten engineers was driving three cars: one MB 420SE, one BMW 735i and one Lexus, which made possible a comparative evaluation. In three weeks, they drove 10,000 km with each vehicle.

Pilot Study

In 1987, the layout design of the Tahara plant was made, and machine tools were designed. Thanks to financial support and promises of long-term orders, key suppliers could invest in new equipment, necessary for high precision components. Out of Lexus' total cost of ¥130 billion, a large part was spent on new machine tools and ¥50 billion went directly to subsidiaries or suppliers. Normally, two pilot runs are made, but in the case of Lexus there were three.

Total lead-time was close to seven years, as opposed to the usual four years. This, however, included close to three years of marketing research and preconcept generation. The last clay model was made 1.5 years before line-off. The project was highly front-loaded, with a lot of time and resources spent on planning and design, rather than on engineering. The entire project, including production engineering, involved around 1,400 persons and the number of engineering hours was twice that of a normal project.

Lexus Channel

In June 1986, Toyota decided that a second sales channel in the US would be necessary, and a committee called Lexus was formed in August, gathering people from PR, marketing, logistics, service and sales. In July 1988, 1,600 dealers had been selected from 3,000 applicants. Toyota set high evaluation standards based on capital, land, buildings and customer satisfaction.

A sales volume of 3,000 per month was targeted in the US, which was more than any other luxury car sold there. Toyota US suggested a retailer price of $40,000, but HQ in Japan set the price tag at $35,000.[19]

The total development costs of ¥135 billion ($1.1 billion) were as much as four times those of a normal project. Still, Lexus turned out to be profitable, mainly because many more cars were sold than expected. Also, the project had many spin-off effects and caused an intense upgrading activity among nearly all the chief engineers. In Japan, 1,500 LS 400 were sold per month, which was extremely good for a luxury product. By the end of 1993, the Lexus division contributed with one third of the company's total operating profits, while representing only two per cent of the unit volume.[20]

NOTES

1. Note: in addition to sources indicated throughout the case, some of the data can be found in publications by Toyota Motor Corporation, e.g., Annual Report 1992, 1993, Corporate Directory Nov. 1992, Outline of Toyota Nov. 1992, Company Outline Sept. 1992, The Toyota Group Nov. 1992, Outline of Toyota Technical Center Nov. 1992, Profile of Toyota Technical Center Nov. 1992.
2. These researchers are not included in the aforementioned number of 11,500 engineers.
3. This transfer implies a move from Higashi-Fuji, beautifully located close to Mount-Fuji, to Toyota City, which is not very popular (Hane; Tsurusawa, interviews).
4. Some of these engineers may be assigned to several projects at the same time, at least if they are working on basic components like engines or suspension systems that are the same for several models.
5. Similarly, university professors do not communicate much with each other, but their assistants do. (Fujimoto, discussion.)
6. Nor at any other Japanese manufacturer (Fujimoto, discussion).
7. There is no such thing as 'I have the right to spend six months at this stage, even though it would have to be done in three months, because of previous delays' (Fujimoto, discussion).
8. Cf. Cusumano (1989, 60-71, 375-6).
9. Having had the opportunity to assist Professor Fujimoto in the writing of a Harvard Business School case study on Lexus, the author greatly benefited from his rich experience and openness, without which a lot of the information below would never have been discovered.
10. This market research group thus consisted of product development people. Marketing people

were only added later from Toyota US.

11. The study group found this part to be the most difficult one, as it implied working with intangible factors that did not yet exist.
12. Some directors have past experience as chief engineers (perhaps roughly one-fourth).
13. Suzuki had been in charge of body design in many successful projects, including Celica.
14. Through dismantling and identification of the best technological solutions among the two vehicles; reverse engineering; and subsequent incremental improvements, TMC strove to make effective use of its deeply rooted innovation strategy.
15. Called *genryu taisaku* in Japanese.
16. Hane-san has now been transferred to an airplane project in Tokyo.
17. As mentioned in the first part on TMC, product development usually has a predominant position throughout a development project, despite intensive production engineering involvement.
18. A room of this sort, where a task force or team meets, is usually called 'war room' in Japan. (Fujimoto, discussion.)
19. TMC claims that this price still allowed for the highest price margin of all Toyota vehicles sold in the US (Fujimoto, discussion.)
20. Cf. (Stalk and Webber 1993, 97).

7   Cross-case Analysis

Successful product innovation poses especially tough challenges to companies that continue to rely on internal technology development. Technology and markets now change so fast, product life-cycles have become so short, and R&D projects are so complex and costly that if a company focuses too many of its resources on technological inventiveness this can be self-defeating in the marketplace. The case studies illustrated how Canon, Sony, and Toyota have learned to borrow inventiveness from extracorporate sources of technology. In so doing, they enable themselves to focus their internal R&D efforts on what it takes to incorporate technologies into efficient production processes so as to bring new products to market. To achieve this, they use a unique combination of external and internal networking:

- Based on extensive know-*who*, they deploy a highly effective process of external networking – not only with other firms but also with universities, centres of excellence, and similar extracorporate sources of technology – to acquire both tacit and explicit knowledge. This external networking allows global technology gatekeeping, the gathering of market intelligence, and the acquisition of complementary technologies and competencies. It also frees up R&D managers to focus on the requirements and tasks of successful product innovation.

- Recognizing that successful product innovation requires, above all, a close integration of R&D, manufacturing and marketing, Canon, Sony, and Toyota base their corporate T&I activities on sophisticated processes of internal networking. This internal networking accomplishes three critical objectives: it makes technology fusion and corporate synergies in R&D possible by securing effective learning across divisions and business units, it ensures that R&D activities correspond to market needs, and, above all, that the results of R&D reach all the way through to manufacturing. A failure to attune R&D efforts to market needs, and/or to get from R&D to production, is too often characteristic of firms that rely on internal technology development.

In this chapter, the most important external networking linkages as well as the three internal networking objectives will be emphasized and cross-analysed to demonstrate how the effectiveness of extracorporate linkages can make intracorporate innovation more efficient. This chapter is sufficiently detailed to be understood without continually having to go back to the cases.

ACQUIRING INVENTIVENESS FROM EXTRACORPORATE SOURCES OF TECHNOLOGY

Pushing researchers out of the labs after only a few years leaves little room for technological expertise to develop. The most important mechanism in supporting innovation is therefore extensive extracorporate networking. By developing a multitude of mechanisms to interlink extracorporate sources of technology, the case-study companies reduce their need of intracorporate technology-development activities. Quite simply, they focus their internal R&D efforts on the commercialization of technology, while going outside to source specialized technologies and competencies.

Canon, Sony, and Toyota all exploit a variety of external sources of technology through their kinyu keiretsu, through their vertically structured networks of suppliers (kigyo keiretsu), through governmental R&D networks, and through links with various non-corporate centres of excellence. The organization and management of such networks was explained in detail in Chapter 3, as were the five principal benefits that they confer:

1. Through relatively open sharing of resources and results, they make both collective as well as individual development of technologies and competencies faster and more cost efficient.
2. They enable large-scale technology monitoring and acquisition of market intelligence.
3. They enable core firms to deal with complexity more easily and to reduce risk-taking and lead-time in T&I projects.
4. They allow for pooling and fusion of complementary technologies and competencies with group-wide economies of scale.
5. They free R&D managers and staff to focus on innovation instead of technology.

The last point is particularly important as it implies that engineers can develop a broad competence base which makes cross-functional interaction more efficient and purposeful. In other words, external technology networking facilitates the process of internal networking through which innovation is achieved.

R&D Resources Through Keiretsu Networks

As a full member of the Fuyo Group, Canon takes part in the Fuyo-kai and in the Fuyo R&D co-operation council. It is interesting to note that Canon and Hitachi, two Fuyo members, share premises, and that Canon locates its R&D HQ in this building.

Sony is not an official member of a kinyu shudan, but still participates in some of Mitsui's joint R&D projects. Moreover, Sony's main bank relationships seem to be as strong as those of Canon and Toyota.

Toyota takes part in the Nimoku-kai of the Mitsui Group, which provides a tangible mechanism for the coordination of interfirm co-operation as stated in Chapter 3. Ties within the kinyu shudan allowed electronics engineers from Toshiba (member company in the Mitsui-family) to join Toyota's mechanical engineers for the fusion of electronics and mechanics into new components that previously were entirely mechanical. Such a transfer of skills from one company to another would certainly be less seamless in the absence of supportive 'family ties'.

All three companies have strong kigyo keiretsu of vertically affiliated suppliers, organized in kyoryoku-kai. One pattern in common between Canon and Sony is that suppliers that are not members of the kigyo keiretsu are purchased, if they are technologically advanced.

Canon clearly states that design-in is not possible due to problems of confidentiality. Equipment suppliers do join Canon's development teams, but only in the production plant.

Nevertheless, in the FLC R&D project, technologically advanced suppliers were (and are still) of vital importance for the development of manufacturing equipment, as well as for both research and development of the projects' core technologies, i.e., liquid crystal materials, molecular alignment, cell fabrication and interface software.

Intimate contacts were maintained with several suppliers of equivalent equipment or technologies, with the purpose of keeping updated on the latest technologies and increasing the competitive pressure on the suppliers. As equipment was not purchased until it had been confirmed for full-scale manufacturing, Canon had a considerable flexibility advantage of trying different production technologies and types of equipment throughout the project.

The so called 'co-developers' were not necessarily financially affiliated, but in all cases members of Canon's kyoryoku-kai, which clearly constitutes an important interlinking mechanism.

Sony has a much larger number of consolidated subsidiaries than Canon, and Chairman Morita stated that suppliers 'are true partners in our business'. Even though the MiniDisc case did not display any supplier interaction, some parts were obviously manufactured outside of Sony. However, the MiniDiscman was primarily based upon technologies that already existed in-house and all possible semiconductors and new integrated circuits can be manufactured in the Atsugi plant. From a technological point of view, it thus appears to be natural that supplier interaction was more intense in the cases of FLC and of the Lexus.

Toyota displays the strongest pattern of ensuring the top management positions of key suppliers, transferring and receiving engineers, and maintaining very open bilateral communication, but the same pattern can be observed within Canon and Sony as well. For example, the chief engineer of the Lexus, Suzuki, has now assumed the second highest position of a major body supplier to Toyota Motor (cf. Figure 3.8).

Given the complexity of an automobile, it is quite natural that Toyota needs stronger coordination and integration of suppliers in both R&D and production activities (cf. Figure 6.1). Accordingly, the practices of design-in and black-box design have only received attention at Toyota.

The practice of letting several suppliers compete for the design and delivery of a part seems to be vital to Toyota's short development lead-time and provides an example of how competition and co-operation coexist.

In the development of the Lexus, key suppliers were members of the executive committee that coordinated the entire project. Moreover, of the total project cost of ¥130 billion, ¥50 billion was spent within subsidiaries and suppliers, which radically increased design quality and production equipment. Such extensive and rapid investments would most probably not have been possible in the absence of the strong financial and managerial linkages that tie principal subsidiaries and key suppliers to Toyota, as described in Chapter 3 (pp. 79-81).

Governmental R&D Networks for Know-how Sharing and Uncertainty Reduction

Canon seems to pay little attention to MITI. Its rather exceptional involvement in the VLSI project resulted in the development of aligners and steppers, which have become important businesses of Canon. In addition, the key technologies of this high-precision semiconductor manufacturing equipment have spread to other product areas, such as FLC manufacturing technology.

The relative absence of MITI participation may find an explanation in the fact that Canon usually opts for unconventional technological fields, like the FLC or their unique toner technology, in which they strive to be on their own. In such cases, co-operation in governmental projects is not interesting as it would imply open sharing of information with competitors.

To Sony, the relative importance of national projects and MITI interaction seems to be far greater than in the case of Canon. The main advantage that Sony sees in participation is not funding of research, but networking and the possibility of gaining both know-how and know-who through co-operative relationships with researchers in other companies. The participation in MITI's Photo-Reactive Material Project is likely to bring improvements to the next generation MiniDisc products. The participation in MITI's 6-billion-yen consortium to develop multimedia technology may enable Sony and the six other Japanese members to reduce the knowledge-gap with the US in this field.

In Chapter 2, it was argued that more rapid and reliable innovations are possible when the degree of technological uncertainty is low. In this context, Sony makes use of MITI's sophisticated technology forecasting, thus reducing uncertainty regarding future key technologies. Similarly, the participation in co-operation councils above all serves to reduce uncertainty and increases the underlying knowledge on relevant sciences.

Toyota has a tradition of close interaction with MITI and keeps an office with 30 'contact officers', the only purpose of whom is to maintain the links to MITI. Not all of Toyota's MITI links, however, relate to R&D and no direct relation to the Lexus project was displayed in the case study, although they most probably exist.

It actually seems as Toyota uses MITI-linkages in a broader array of fields than Canon and Sony, perhaps as an attempt to find new paths of diversification. Two very concrete examples are mobile communication and new power-generation technology.

This also fits very well with Toyota's 90/10 principle, meaning that all current activities of each employee should be accomplished in 90 per cent of the available work time in order to spend the remaining 10 per cent thinking of and eventually starting a new business.

It would actually not be a surprise to see Toyota as a major player in the jet aviation industry by year 2010.

Additional Technology Linkages For More Innovation

Canon pursues targeted acquisition of specialized skills

Several interviewees clearly stated that overseas R&D labs were established for targeted sourcing of Western creativity, while avoiding the bureaucratic atmosphere of large organizations. Canon maintains close links both with domestic and foreign universities and professors. In Japan, approximately 20 professors are linked to Canon through one-year co-operation contracts, which make possible open discussions with and visits by the professors and transfers of researchers to the university laboratories.

Chapter 3 disclosed how the closing down of a research project caused the researchers involved to join university laboratories instead of accepting Canon's request to assume more production-oriented activities, and that all the equipment related to the project was donated to the university laboratory in which some of the Canon researchers ended up.

The practice of hiring senior researchers from other companies aims at breaking routines in R&D and in the company as a whole, but is also a mechanism to bring in new ideas. The Advanced Technology Division provides additional global technology scanning, working like an intelligence agency.

University interaction played a vital role in Canon's development of FLC displays. First, the initial invention was acquired from Chalmers Institute of Technology and from the University of Colorado. Second, Canon secured the right to send engineers to these scientific institutions. Third, the inventors, Dr Lagerwall and Dr Clark, continually fed scientific progress to Canon through several visits per year. Fourth, for further support in research on liquid crystal materials, Canon also established co-operation with two domestic universities for scientific discussions and also for joint research in the university laboratories.

Moreover, we have seen a concrete example of how a researcher left the Canon Research Centre to acquire a specific competence at Tokyo University, which he then brought back both to the Research Centre and to the next-generation FLC project.

Like most Japanese companies, Canon also has a tradition of sending promising engineers overseas for post-graduate studies in technological fields, but we did not see any example of this related to the FLC project.

Canon's use of foreign scientists in Japan is rather limited. The main-argument is that as soon as they are 'Japanized' in their way of behaving and thinking, they become less useful. Therefore, and also for economic reasons, Canon prefers to expand its overseas R&D facilities, which presently house more than 200 researchers in four different countries.

The R&D centre in Sydney was of particular importance in the development of interface software for the FLCD. Dr Albrecht's (a foreign scientist at Canon in Japan) special competence in Langmuir Blodgett films also appeared to provide rewarding input to the FLC technology. Personal interaction always constitutes the major link between foreign knowledge and intracorporate competence. Three Japanese engineers work continuously with the German solid-state physicist and relate his thin film technology to other research projects, in which they take part concurrently.

Canon's numerous strategic alliances and joint R&D projects with Western partners also offer additional sources of technology. Potentially important links in the FLC-case were the possible technology sourcing from Bell Labs and the intimate contacts with Hoechst and Merck in Europe.

Among the overseas allies, we identified Apple Computer (NeXT), Eastman-Kodak, Energy Conversion Devices, General Electric, Hewlett Packard, Kodak, Live Picture, Microsoft, Olivetti, Plasma Physics Corporation, Siemens, and TI.

No strategic alliances with Japanese companies were identified.

Sony has continuous access to leading thinking in global networks of universities and strategic alliances

Sony stresses the need for interlinking universities, much like Canon does. One important rationale of networking with universities is that Sony's research results have become too advanced to be analyzed within Sony. Instead, more scientific resources are needed. In return, scientists from the academy enjoy access to and stimulation from Sony's sophisticated equipment, while Sony profits from scientific input that is related to practical applications.

A much higher number of engineers are allowed to pursue studies overseas within Sony than within Canon, and the studies do not necessarily have to be technical, as they are supposed to be within Canon.

In the development of the next-generation MiniDisc, we have seen clear examples of networking with both American and British universities. This case also displayed examples of joint research with several Japanese universities.

Sony has several spin-offs that aim at tapping extracorporate competence, mainly within computer software. Sony's Science Art Laboratory provides a good example of this. The majority of all 'experimenters' in the laboratory are invited young computer experts, who get access to a state-of-the-art computer facility. Under the supervision of Sony's own software engineers, these experts are free to do whatever they want. Eventually, their co-operative experimentation may yield new computer programs or product concepts.

Of all three companies, Sony also seems to have the largest network of international university connections when it comes to R&D. Professors' chairs and various research programs are being financed in a large number of scientifically leading countries.

As an additional means of tapping Western 'uniqueness of ideas' (page 91), the sabbatical chair in the Research Centre brings in Western professors on a yearly contract.

Sony may not have as developed a network of overseas R&D operations as Canon has, but has in any case the second highest number of foreign researchers in Japan, with more than 60 scientists engaged in their Research Centre. Interestingly, these scientists are also discouraged from adopting Japanese habits, as in the case of Canon.

Strategic alliances appear to bring in an impressive amount of extracorporate know-how. Clearly, Sony has been most successful among the three in establishing learning alliances with many unchallenged centres of excellence across the globe.

Among the overseas allies, we identified Anelva, AT&T, General Major (subsidiary of Apple), HP, IBM, Intel, Microsoft, Oracle, PC Financial Network, Philips, Samsung Electronics, Seagate, Siemens, Tektronix Inc., TI (giving access to a unique mirror chip technology co-developed with the US Department of Defense), and Verbatim.

In Japan, Sony has created alliances with Fujitsu, Hitachi, Maxell, Mitsubishi, NEC Nintendo, Nissan, NTT, Oki, Olympus, Ricoh, Sharp, Sanyo, Sega Enterprises, and Yamaha.

Based on an old tradition of learning relationships toyota has developed alliances with the best across the world

Toyota has an old tradition of university co-operation and is actively engaged in joint research with leading universities and research organizations when tackling unfamiliar fields. We have seen that researchers, mainly from the Central R&D Laboratories, can do some of their work in the universities and they also have very free communication with a large number of professors.

Toyota is increasingly turning to foreign universities, and between 30 and 60 researchers and engineers per year are offered the possibility of going to one of the 'affiliated' ones, sometimes as degree students and sometimes as visiting researchers.

There is also the Toyota Technological Institute, which aims at attracting seasoned professionals from Japanese industry and engaging them in joint research projects, an idea that resembles Sony's SALA lab.

Other important units of networking are provided by the overseas design centres and, above all, by the technical centres with their 400 engineers who mainly have roles of global technology gatekeeping. Some of these centres are also linked to other Toyota Group members, like Aisin Seiki and Nippondenso. Hence, intensive technology scanning through a global network of technical centres and design centres is possible, thereby cultivating the old tradition of eclectic borrowing and indirect transfer of technology.

In the development of the Lexus, the European centres most certainly played important roles in the dismantling, emulation and improvement of the key technology areas of the targeted Mercedes Benz and BMW models.[1] Just like BMW in the late 1980s and like Mercedes Benz in the early 1990s, Toyota has now also launched a twelve-cylinder engine for the Lexus. The Lexus design was made by California-based Calty Design Research, in co-operation with both Europe-based and Japan-based design centres.

The tradition to identify and learn from experts was also noticed in Toyota's internal 'sempai-system'.

In terms of overseas strategic alliances, we identified Daimler Benz, Delco Motors, Family Mart, Ford, GM, Hamilton Standard, and Shell Oil.

Excluding alliances within the Toyota group and the Mitsui kinyo keiretsu, three allies were identified in Japan: Matsushita, Mitsubishi, and Nippon Oil.

Table 7.1 summarizes the relative strengths of the companies' most important external linkages.

As indicated earlier, it is difficult to obtain exact and comparable data on these issues. At least, we can conclude that all three companies maintain strong links to extracorporate sources of technology. Canon may have the most elaborate network of overseas R&D laboratories, but Sony employs a significantly higher number of foreign scientists in Japan. Both companies discourage their Western scientists from adapting Japanese habits and encourage them instead to keep and spread their Western style of conducting scientific research. It thus seems quite clear that Japanese R&D managers find Western researchers to be more creative, which partly explains their strong focus on Western sources of invention. Toyota does not appear to employ any foreign researchers in Japan, but all three companies clearly strive to increase the number of foreigners in their research activities, with an increasing focus on those located overseas.

In terms of strategic alliances, the numbers indicated above are obviously much lower than the absolute numbers of alliances held by these companies. Given that the same sources and types of data-gathering were used for all three companies, the relative difference should be fairly correct, revealing Sony as the unchallanged master of alliance creation.

Table 7.1   Linkages to Extracorporate Sources of Technology

Linkage/Company:	Canon	Sony	Toyota
Kinyu Shudan	••	(•)	••
Kigyo Keiretsu	••	••	•••
Spin-offs	••	•••	•••
MITI	•	•••	•••
Domestic Universities	••	••	•••
Foreign Universities	••	•••	•••
Foreign R&D Subsidiaries	•••	••	••
Foreign Researchers	•	•••	–
Strategic Alliances	••	•••	••
	12 identified	30 identified	10 identified

•••	strong linkage
••	moderate linkage
•	weak linkage
–	no linkage
()	Indirect

Note: Indications are purely based on the author's own estimates from company interviews, literature reviews and data searches.

CREATING CORPORATE SYNERGIES IN T&I MANAGEMENT

As indicated in Chapter 2, it is only through interlinking the intracorporate activities of technology and product development that an invention can be turned
into an innovation. The following sections will, therefore, analyze the managerial mechanisms and principles that promote this interlinkage. To begin
with, we will examine the mechanisms with which R&D resources can be
shared and fused together within the case-study companies.

Canon: Technology Fusion Through Old-boys' Networks and Corporate Core-technology Coordination

Not long ago, Canon started as a camera manufacturer, diversifying into copiers and other office equipment. This expansive diversification caused people,
who knew each other well from working closely together, to spread throughout
the organization. As a result, communication is said to remain strong between
key persons, which may provide an explanation for the relative absence of organizational interlinking mechanisms between business groups. Technology
fusion at Canon thus seems to be based much on personal relationships, which
may disappear over time as the company grows and key persons move up the

ladder.

Scarcity of engineering manpower is given as the main argument against human resource exchange between business groups, but it also seems that the sense of belonging of the company members is actually linked to their business group more than to the company as a whole. Competition seems to be strong between business groups, each of which works much like an independent company.

The main actors in Canon's intra-organizational interaction are separate HQs, which are not tied up to a specific business group. The Products Technology Development HQ, which ensures coordination of Canon's various core technologies, can also discover and create possibilities for technology fusion.

The fact that many different divisions and operations can be represented in one and the same task force creates the conditions for both vertical and horizontal integration of individual competence, and possibly also of technologies. One example of this is the cartridge technology developed for a personal copier that came to be used in laser beam printers, facsimile machines and micrographic equipment.

Within the development centre of each business group, a matrix organization aims at the integration of its engineers and the different skills they have.

In the Canon Research Centre, relocation of all the researchers every six months aims at extending the number of personal relationships, thus promoting cross-fertilization of ideas and technologies.

The Development of FLCD Required More Fusion of Competencies than of Actual Technologies

In the development of the FLC displays, some technology fusion occurred at an early stage when engineers of a rivalling technology, TFT, joined the FLC project, thus bringing new display technology competence into the project.

There were also synergies within the Component Business Operations HQ, partly between flat panel displays and solar cell panels, and also with semiconductor production technology, all of which require high-precision mounting techniques. Similarly, toner and optical products technologies, developed in the Canon Research Centre, benefited the development of FLC materials. The fusion was in these cases more related to competencies than to actual technologies. The FLC technology was quite new and did not, therefore, require fusion of old technologies. Instead, the fusion of various competencies was important to the advancements of the project.

Sony: Free Flows of People Nurture Corporate Synergies in T&I

Sony, much in contrast to Canon, seems to base its typical technology and innovation process upon interaction between the development divisions of different business groups, which may reflect a greater potential of intra-corporate technology fusion. It was also revealed that Sony has a higher degree of intra-corporate exchange of engineers. The practice of job rotation and transfer of engineers between business groups is more frequent.

Moreover, Sony's shanai koubo system allows open borrowing of engineers across development divisions and business groups. The development engineers themselves can volunteer for a specific development project, regardless of which business group or research unit that initiates the project. This system also increases the chances for a project to be supported by truly motivated members.

Biannual Open-house Meetings gather approximately 1,000 people. Managers of research divisions and their different research group leaders; sales-, development- and production managers of all product groups; patent engineers and patent attorneys all get together to discuss possible future research projects and technologies.

Every three months, Technology Symposia gather between 150 and 200 engineers and scientists. The main purpose is to engage all participants in a large-scale brain-storming process, aiming at solutions to possible research problems. This large-scale networking process also provides ample opportunity for technology fusion.

Networking within Sony's Research Centre seems to be equally intensive. For example, the development of Low-pressure Chemical Vapour Deposition technology called for interaction between different research groups, focusing on, respectively, semiconductor materials, super molecular materials, structure characterization, and thin film semiconductors. Both chemists and physicists were needed. By combining their scientific competencies with fine mechanics and electronics engineers, and by finally moving skilled scientists and competent engineers to the semiconductor plant in Atsugi, Sony's VLSI radically improved. This improvement spread, among other places, to the junctional laser, which constitutes the core technology of products like the CD and the MiniDiscman.

Similarly, in the project on perpendicular magnetic recording, the scientific competencies of several research groups were useful for achieving the super-conductive ultra-thin films composed of single atomic layers, e.g., magneto-optical recording materials, superconducting materials, supermolecular materials, and structure and surface characterization. The result of the project has been incorporated into several Sony products, one of which is the Mini-Discman.

Corporate-wide Technology Fusion was Critical in the Development of the MiniDiscman

The development of the MiniDiscman was highly based upon adoption and fusion of existing technologies. To begin with, there were important synergies between the Car Navigation system and the MD, as very special integrated circuits and semiconductor devices constituted core technologies in both of the products. The integrated circuits were already developed and applied to low-noise amplifiers that Yoshida, the joint chief engineer of the MD and the Car Navigation system, had previously developed. The semiconductor devices were, in turn, the result of fusion between two different technologies (superlattice structure and MOCVD) developed in the Research Centre.

The disc mechanism was based on another existing technology, the Digital Data Storage system, developed jointly with Hewlett Packard.

In order to have a smaller disc format than that of the traditional CD, the sound would have to be compressed before storage on the minidisc and then decompressed before reaching human ears, which called for sophisticated sound-compression technology. By using an existing (ATRAC) technology – designed specifically for high-fidelity audio – adequate sound compression could be achieved. Also, in order to reduce space and complexity, an existing magnetic-field-overwrite technology was further developed and adopted.

Recordable MD uses magnetic field modulation, a technology which originally was developed for the recordable version of the CD. Radical improvements were, however, necessary and the original technology was transferred back to the Research Centre for further research. In the Research Centre, the fusion of physics and chemistry was necessary for achieving higher recording reliability, thereby enabling the final application to the MD.

By fusing a previously developed CD pickup technology with sophisticated magnetic recording technology, magneto-optical recordable MiniDiscs and playback-only MiniDiscs can be played back with the same pickup. Moreover, through a shock-resistant memory, developed by the Semiconductor Group, the MD can endure up to 15 seconds of repeated shocks, without the music being affected.

It follows from the above examples that technology fusion was a prerequisite to the development of the MD and that it also made possible miniaturization of the final product.

Sony Profits More from Intra-corporate Technology Fusion than Canon

The nature of the two companies' products may explain why there is more interaction between business groups at Sony than at Canon. Canon's new products are usually technology driven, and therefore based on entirely new technologies that do not exist in any of the business groups. Consequently, a new R&D project is not likely to draw on technological resources from different business groups within Canon.

Moreover, there are probably fewer parts and technologies in common among products like cameras, copiers, computers and printers, which constitute Canon's core products, than among audio, video and television equipment that dominate Sony's VLSI-based products. It is thus likely that the need for interaction between business groups is greater within Sony than within Canon.

Perhaps more within Sony than within Canon, development engineers can without apparent restrictions be transferred back to a research laboratory for the acquisition of necessary competence, or for further applied research on the product that is being developed in the development division. Apart from that, researchers who have once left the laboratory for more production-oriented R&D activities are usually not allowed back into the research activities, either at Canon or at Sony. The main reason in the case of both companies appears to be that research positions are reserved for attracting the brightest graduates, who are lured into well-equipped laboratories, and then simply requested to follow the mainstream towards manufacturing-oriented 'promotions'.

Toyota Profits From Keiretsu-wide Technology (Dif)fusion

Toyota has organized its most upstream research activities into a matrix structure in order to enhance possibilities of technology fusion within the Central R&D Laboratories. At a higher level, we have seen how ties within the kinyu keiretsu allowed electronics engineers from Toshiba to join Toyota's mechanical engineers for the fusion of electronics and mechanics into new components.

Moreover, the kigyo keiretsu structure enables suppliers with specialized skills to take part in larger development projects. As an example, Nippondenso was requested to make special dashboard instruments with an illuminated needle. Some Nippondenso engineers were already members in FQ subcommittees, which facilitated a thorough understanding of Toyota's needs. Through intensive trial-and-error activities and the involvement of specialized second-tier suppliers, a miniaturized glass tube, filled with xenon gas, was developed.

Hence, the organization of companies into kinyu shudan and of suppliers into kigyo keiretsu definitely facilitates technology fusion between different industries and suppliers and may, in Toyota's case, compensate for the relatively weaker emphasis on intra-organizational technology-fusion. The structure thus offers an extracorporate solution to an intracorporate problem.

Most research activities seem to take place independently with one clear application in mind. Similarly, instead of fusing different technologies in the development of components and systems, most development activities in a vehicle project are made separately. Eventually, the results of these development efforts are fused, or rather, assembled, into a finished product. Interaction between the three different vehicle centres is equally weak. In contrast, the development of the MiniDiscman required technology fusion in the actual development of components, thus calling for interaction between different business groups.

It is, therefore, quite natural that Toyota's organization of R&D emphasizes coordination of independently-performed development activities, rather than technology fusion. A car requires fusion of components and systems, whereas a miniaturized consumer electronics product requires technology fusion into integrated circuits.

The cross-functional task-forces of Canon are replaced by Toyota's cross-functional concept-generation groups. Perhaps as a result of Sony's multiple intra-corporate linkages, cross-functional task-forces for the concept-generation stage do not seem to be similarly used by Sony.

Table 2.2 summarizes the relative strengths of the companies' most important intracorporate linkages that support technology-fusion.

Table 7.2   Linkages for Technology-fusion

Linkage/Company:	Canon	Sony	Toyota
Inter-Business Groups	•	•••	• (Keir.-wide fusion)
Research Centre Bus. Gr.	•	•••	•
Intra-Research Centre	•••	••	••
Cross-Functional Task-Force	•••	••	•••

•••   strong linkage
••   moderate linkage
•   weak linkage

Note: Indications are based on the author's own estimates from company interviews.

Both between business groups, between business groups and the research centre and within the research centre, linkages are strong within Sony. To some extent, Canon and Toyota seem to compensate for their linkages through more forceful cross-functional task-forces. Toyota also enjoys stronger keiretsu-synergies.

A second factor that brings technology- and product-development closer to each other is the interlinkage of market needs. Let us, therefore, look for mechanisms that serve this purpose.[2]

ATTUNING INTRACORPORATE R&D TO GLOBAL MARKET NEEDS

Internal networking and know-*who* management is needed to ensure that R&D activities correspond to market needs. The ways in which Canon, Sony, and Toyota implement mechanisms for this purpose include the following:

1. They require sales experience of those engineers and researchers who are licensed to do R&D.
2. Their R&D people remain in frequent contact with customers and with marketing and sales (M&S).

3. They use prototypes to fill communication gaps between R&D and M&S.
4. They maintain R&D-sponsoring mechanisms that function as internal market forces.
5. They have regular forums for interaction among researchers, design and manufacturing engineers, and product managers.
6. Product planning and other important M&S functions are usually staffed by engineers who remain in frequent contact with R&D.

Canon: Technology-oriented Product Planning

All Canon researchers and development engineers are passed through initial sales training programs with an average of three months of sales in Canon shops. In order to strengthen market linkages of Canon's R&D efforts, R&D members participate along with those of marketing organizations in semi-annual international product strategy meetings and sometimes in rotating meetings at principal sales subsidiaries. Product planning and marketing functions are staffed by engineers who have been transferred from a research, development, or a production plant function, which should increase the likelihood of strong linkages between market needs and R&D functions.

Still, it is claimed by most interviewees that this link not is strong enough, mainly as a result of each business group's evolving into an independent company. Consequently, product planning is largely controlled by the development engineers of each business group, which is very likely to have caused the 'over-development' that, in Canon's own view, has made some products too complicated.

In the FLC case, we saw how several engineers were dispatched from R&D to assume the M&S activities for the new display. Chemical engineer Tanaka who joined Canon in 1986, spent her first two years testing and measuring the results of extensive trial-and-error activities of (FLC) liquid crystal materials. In 1988, she changed field and started to develop software for the display-computer interface. Then in 1990, she was dispatched to the Planning and Marketing HQ to perform market research, i.e. identifying what computer companies and other potential customers need and want. She also observed what competing display companies offered, by using computer manufacturers and classmates in competing companies as sources of information.

Both at Canon and Sony, R&D Projects Are Killed Very Quickly Unless They Attract Business Group-Support

We have seen that the Products Technology Development HQ acts as possible sponsor of promising technologies that cannot find applications and funding within Canon's existing product groups. Apart from this, an R&D project is not likely to be pursued unless one of the business groups agrees to sponsor the project.

Intracorporate sponsoring of R&D was vital to the choice of FLC technology. Both display teams were competing to develop the most convincing prototypes. Having two competing task forces in the D-stage would have required too much money and people. The Camera Development Division was quite interested in TFT technology, but as it concentrated on the development of video cameras, it could not, at that time, afford to sponsor the TFT project, which was therefore discontinued. The sponsorship of a business group thus, to a large extent, dictated which technology eventually was going to win out.

TFT was also discontinued as a result of market considerations. Canon wanted to avoid the price dumping wars in TFT displays. However, when Canon had made significant progress in manufacturing technology, they applied this progress to the previously discontinued TFT equipment and became world-leaders in this field instead.

In the development of the MD, market needs had to be weighed against market rules. For fear of objections from the music industry, Sony did not announce the recordable CD, but decided to develop the MiniDisc technology instead. Both independent companies and a Sony-affiliated market research institute conducted series of market analyses that were linked to the development process of the MD. The choice of the MD-technology was thus based on market considerations, much like Canon's choice of the FLC-technology.

This sponsoring system certainly provides a strong market mechanism to development efforts, as a business group normally only supports a technology for which it has a commercial application in mind.

Sony Ties Customers and Their Feedback More Directly to the Innovation Process

Sony has several mechanisms that serve the purpose of bringing in market needs into the development process. Every Japanese researcher and development engineer who is recruited upon graduation at Sony, passes through an average of three months of sales before doing anything else, which is similar to Canon's system. Continuous interaction with the domestic Sony Showrooms further strengthens the link between the development engineer and the customer.

The showroom staff also writes two different monthly reports: one on the number of visitors, their questions, complaints and positive impressions; and a similar one, relating to telephone contacts. The reports are distributed to all R&D departments, product groups and marketing departments.

In order to get additional customer feedback on certain products, registers are kept on the most fanatic and dedicated Sony customers, who buy almost each new product launched by the company. Sometimes, new products are sent to some of these customers with an invitation to come to Sony after some period of testing. Shortly before launching the new MiniDiscman, Sony Music of

Japan advertized a campaign of lending MDs, addressed to an existing list of highly 'sony-dedicated' customers. An MD was sent to those who were first to notify their interest, with an invitation to come to the Sony HQ building, a few weeks after, for focused group discussions. These discussions bring immediate feedback into the core of the development process for next-generation products.

Organizational mechanisms to interlink customer needs seem to vary with the different nature of Canon's products. Development engineers of office automation equipment are regarded as expert users and do, therefore, not have strong links to market needs. In contrast, the development centres of camera products have focused group discussions with selected users.

Sony makes similar distinctions between the need for market information about different types of products. For example, focused group discussions, which utilize listening expertise, are particularly frequent in the Audio Group.

If You Want Funds For R&D You Had Better Develop Convincing Prototypes Right Away

At least 70 per cent of all R&D expenses in Sony's Research Centre stem from business groups which may, or may not, be willing to support a certain field of research. The practice of technical samples is a concrete managerial mechanism, functioning as a tangible research proposal, that gears research efforts towards market needs. Only if a business group has a commercial application in mind for this sample will the project be pursued. The subsequent engineering and commercial samples serve as further guarantees that the evolution corresponds to the application. If this is not the case, the project will be discontinued. This mechanism – which is quite similar to Canon's R&D sponsoring system – provides a strong link between research activities and market needs. Prototypes also serve as a communication-enhancing tool as most people understand the sometimes tacit ideas behind a tangible prototype better than they understand written, and often quite technical, research proposals.

The Business Development Division supports the development of entirely new businesses that are unable to find a sponsor within the existing business groups.

Sony's frequent Forums of Interaction Foster Cross-functional Learning between R&D, M&S and Production

Sony's Technology Exchange Forums offer an extensive presentation of technological capabilities to all product, marketing and sales managers, who are potential buyers of technologies or sponsors of research projects. The Research Centre's divisions and groups, all peripheral R&D units within Sony Corporation, as well as all development divisions of the different product groups and the research departments of the Corporate Research Laboratories display, are present. Here, they can demonstrate embryos that they want to develop and commercialize by attracting funds from the potential sponsors.

Similarly, the aforementioned biannual Open-House Meetings offer the possibility for researchers to upgrade their knowledge on market needs and requirements from production.

Sony's development divisions have responsibility for their own product planning and development. Accordingly, each development division has a product planning section that dispatches Japanese 'resident product planners' overseas to every important market and lets them rotate every three years. These resident product planners are in daily phone contact with their development divisions, and come to Japan on a monthly basis, thereby ensuring continuous information on competing products, customer feedback and market needs.

Biannual line-up meetings gather product planners from the entire world, who bring back the specific trends and needs of their markets to planners, development engineers and to production control and scheduling engineers.

Compared to Canon, these mechanisms provide Sony with significantly stronger market linkages both to research and to product development.

Canon's approach to these feedback links may be less international than Sony's highly international network approach. There are semiannual line-up meetings, but we have not found an equivalent emphasis on expatriating product planners to all important markets around the globe.

Toyota: A Human Link Secures the Interconnection of Business and Technology

At Toyota, almost all researchers and engineers receive initial training in production and sales. Only the most 'upstream' researchers in the spun-off Central R&D Laboratory are excluded from both sales and production training.

As with Canon and Sony, a sponsoring system gears research activities toward market needs. Beginning upstream in the innovation process, the Toyota Central Research and Development Laboratories work independently for Toyota Motor and also for other group members like Nippondenso. As the budget of each project is provided by the buying unit, the projects necessarily relate to what is demanded within the group.

The largest single buyer of research services, the Higashi-Fuji Technical Centre, in turn only pursues R&D projects that are approved by the board members of Toyota Motor. These projects aim at supporting the Component and System Development Centre or are sometimes directly related to a Vehicle Development Centre. In either case, the research project would have a direct application in a component, system, or directly in a vehicle. The board members themselves are said to interact frequently with distributors and dealers, thereby ensuring a human link between development strategies and market needs.

The 1982-merger of Toyota Motor Corporation and Toyota Motor Sales aimed at a stronger integration of marketing and sales into product development. Both sales, development, and production executives now sit on the same board. The extensive domestic and overseas sales networks are strongly interlinked with product planning of the vehicle development centres through job rotation and frequent meetings.

Chief Engineers Engage in Proactive Gathering of Customer Needs

Perhaps most important of all, the chief engineer of each vehicle actively assesses market needs before conceiving a new model. We have seen that the marketing group is intimately involved in the new product development process (Figure 6.4) and the development of the Lexus exemplifies a strong interlinkage of market needs.

To begin with, the chief engineer headed a large study team that went to America to study the luxury car market. They made visits to dealers of Mercedes Benz, BMW, Volvo, Audi and other up-market cars, arranged cocktail parties and conducted focused group discussions with 21 owners of the previously mentioned cars. Instead of only focusing on success factors of these vehicles, a lot of time and resources was also spent on exploring what the luxury car owners and dealers were *dissatisfied* with and what additional functions and options they would see as valuable improvements.

Hence, Toyota's relatively weak direct linkages between R&D people and market needs are compensated by a strong and direct market interlinkage of the concept-generation process, direct top-management involvement and a mechanism for sponsoring of R&D activities.

Table 7.3   Linkages for R&D-market Interface

Linkage/Company:	Canon	Sony	Toyota
Sales training: Researchers	~3 months	~3 months	–
Ditto: Development engineers	~3 months	~3 months	~3 months
Research Centre – MN	•	•••	•
Business Group – MN	••	•••	••
Prototypes serving as communication tool	••	•••	•••
R&D Sponsoring reflecting Market Needs	•••	•••	••

MN	Market Needs
•••	strong linkage
••	moderate linkage
•	weak linkage
–	no linkage

Note: Indications are based on the author's own estimates from company interviews.

Table 7.3 summarizes the relative strength of major mechanisms and interlinkages that orient R&D activities towards market needs.

Again, Sony has established the strongest market linkages, both to the research centre and to the business groups. The strongest point in common between the three companies is their strict mechanisms for intracorporate sponsoring of R&D activities that bring in market needs at an early stage. They also make intensive use of prototypes.

Now that we have seen how technological resources are fused and by what mechanisms R&D activities respond to market needs, only one factor remains before these activities can result in a product to be commercialized – the interlinkage of and transfer to production.

MANAGING A SEAMLESS TRANSFER FROM RESEARCH TO PRODUCTION

Internal networking also ensures that a greater proportion of the R&D effort results in tangible prototypes that can be mass-produced in manufacturing and, ultimately, commercialized. Canon and Sony have a seamless innovation process that can be described in terms of research followed by D&M, i.e., Design and Manufacturing.[3] In these companies' terminology, research mainly consists of building and trying a product prototype until it works. Design usually implies the designing and development of a manufacturing process that can produce a perfect copy of the prototype. D&M runs and develops the trial manufacturing line until quality, speed and costs are adequate. Five networking mechanisms and principles (some of which are also used by Toyota) support the seamlessness of this process:

1. They provide on-the-job training and strategic rotation that ensures that every member of the innovation process understands both the seeds of the technology and the needs of manufacturing.
2. They transfer researchers to the factory floor to drive technological competence into products. This is – especially for new technologies – the only effective route to commercialization.
3. They collocate design and manufacturing (D&M): instead of attempting to achieve design for manufacturing, they conduct research for D&M.
4. They instil respect for the factory floor as the place where real value creation takes place.
5. They use prototypes as funding mechanisms at extremely early stages of R&D projects, forcing R&D people to consider manufacturability and to collaborate with production upfront.

Canon Has no Other Choice but to Transfer Researchers to the Manufacturing Floor

The basic principle that lays the groundwork for the strong sense of partnership that reigns between research and D&M is that of building multiple skills through training and job rotation.

All researchers and engineers at Canon pass through an initial training program which begins with three months of work on a production line. In recent years, however, Canon has had to keep some trainees off the lines due to declining sales figures.

Regardless of their own desires, it seems that most researchers at Canon are requested to join a development centre after some period of time in research. We have seen that if seven to eight researchers take part in the most upstream stage of an R&D project, an average of five remain at the different production stages.

Canon's quasi-institutionalized transfer of engineers from development to production again reflects their technology-driven R&D projects. If the technology of a product is new, none of the existing engineers in production is likely to have prior experience in the field. Consequently, the transfer of the original researchers becomes imperative.

We have also seen examples of how an engineer of the Planning and Marketing Centre went to the plant manager three times per month to report on customer complaints and on future products. The same plant manager received a whole team of 10 to 20 engineers from the development centre in question, usually as often as three times per month. These numbers do perhaps not represent averages for the company as a whole, but they illustrate the relative intensity of interaction between development engineers and production plants.

In the development of FLC displays, research on liquid crystal materials was initially pursued in the Canon Research Centre by approximately ten researchers. As the project advanced, most of these researchers were dispatched to the site of production. We have also seen that a senior researcher was assigned to the new-generation FLC task force, for which he now works three days a week. At present, he commutes between the Research Centre and the Display Centre, but in the near future, he is likely to be entirely transferred to the Display Centre for more production-oriented activities.

From being a three-man task force ten years ago, the FLC project expanded to a 200-person operation, with 90 per cent of all members located directly at the site of production. Most of these members were mobilized from within the company, mainly from the Research Centre and from some supporting headquarters operations. The project was thus highly dependent upon transfer of researchers and engineers for development and production of the initial invention.

Sony More Frequently Uses Initial Immigration of Production Engineers in Combination with Transfer of Researchers

Sony's initial training program includes on average one month of production for both researchers and development engineers. Corporate Research Laboratories usually assume the practical application of the Research Centre's activities by linking them to the development divisions of the Business Groups. We have seen that not only are research projects moved from the Research Centre to a product group, or directly to production in Atsugi, but also that engineers from the product group in question join the research project long before the actual transfer takes place. The link is thus twofold, supported by initial immigration of production engineers into the R&D project and a subsequent transfer of most of the project members, including upstream researchers, from the research laboratory to the prototype production line.

We have not identified equally extensive patterns of immigration in the case of Canon. This may find an explanation in the fact that Canon is mainly developing new technologies that have not been in production before. Therefore, there are probably less manufacturing experts available in the plants who can be helpful in the R&D project before it reaches the production stage.

Interaction with production is intense in most of Sony's R&D projects. We have seen that the rapid commercialization of the CD player was possible by developing a small production line of junctional lasers (for the pickup) in the actual Research Centre. A larger-scale production line was developed in parallel with commercial production in the Research Centre, which went on for two years. It is hard to imagine a more intimate interplay between research and production.

Representatives of the Production Control Group and the Scheduling Group take part in the aforementioned line-up meetings with expatriated product planners, laying the initial groundwork for new product developments.

In the development of the MiniDiscman, production engineers from the General Audio Group were in constant interaction with the chief engineer's development group from the beginning of the project, supporting the development of a production line. The various production plants of Sony already had the necessary competencies and resources to deal with the key components of the MiniDiscman. No extensive transfer of researchers or development engineers to production was therefore necessary.

At Toyota the Transfer of Researchers and Engineers is Replaced by Early Involvement of Production

Toyota does not, in contrast to common belief, manage the interlinkage of production by transferring a large team from research, via development, to production. Instead, these activities are conducted quite independently and also in different geographical locations.

In the Central Research and Development Laboratories, the 900 researchers and engineers are – in contrast to Canon and Sony – not exposed to the imperatives of job rotation. Instead, they have long-term careers within the centre, which allows for extensive specialization. Projects are not directly linked or transferred to production, but rather to the Higashi-Fuji research centre, where more applied research activities take place. The transfer is facilitated through frequent interaction between the two centres, but no permanent transfer of engineers is considered to be necessary. As most researchers have life-time careers in these centres, strong interlinkages in terms of personal relationships compensate for some of the personnel transfers practised by Canon and Sony.

In addition, as much of the commercial product development is done by parts suppliers and body makers, some projects of the Higashi-Fuji technical centre and sometimes also of the Toyota Central R&D Laboratories are directly transferred to them for production.

Once a project is close to completion and approved by the board members of Toyota Motor Corporation, the entire project is moved to the Component and System Development Centre, or directly to a Development Centre. This time, the technology transfer is slightly dependent on human transfer. Approximately 90 per cent of all researchers in Higashi Fuji stay for their entire careers in the Technical Centre. The remaining ten per cent are transferred with a project. As Toyota plans to increase the share of transfers to 30 per cent of the researchers, it is probably a necessary interlinking mechanism at this stage of the R&D process.

In the vehicle development centres, the main interlinking mechanism is some immigration, and extensive collection of information from downstream to upstream. The interlinkage of production is mainly taken care of by the production engineering group. This group acts as an integral part of the development process by letting some of its engineers participate from concept generation to the design of prototypes, thus supporting design for manufacturing. Collaboration is facilitated through an initial 3-month production training of all development engineers. Collocation in one large site provides room for daily interaction and exchange of information between development and production. The prototype production lines that are developed here are also used in mass production.

At this downstream stage of the R&D process, linkages to suppliers are yet stronger and formalized. They include active participation in development project meetings, and even involvement in design activities within the premises of Toyota.

For example, the development of the Lexus engine required more accuracy, higher precision and better balance to minimize vibrations. It also had to fit into the engine compartment, the shape of which affected noise as well. A light but rigid car body of anti-vibration steel was called for with a design that minimized wind-noise and Cd-value. Hence, product design, product development, and engineers in body, transmission and engine had to co-operate with production engineers and people from engine plants, including their suppliers of both components and steel. A highly experienced and respected director of production engineering and several representatives of key suppliers were involved throughout the development project. The chief engineer even claims that the production manager was the most important contributor to the Lexus project.

Canon and Sony Focus on Prototyping Already in the Research Stage

The research for D&M approach of Canon and Sony also implies that practically no research activity is approved unless the researcher(s) has (have) a commercial application already in mind at the initial stage of the research proposal.

This market-driven research is maintained through the aforementioned practice of internal sponsoring of individual researchers' projects, demonstrated through prototypes. Initially, researchers have some liberty in choosing fields of research, but after a certain period of time, they must find a sponsor for their research. In order to attract sponsoring, they prepare a so called technical sample. Once this is prepared, the researcher must identify and convince a business group to sponsor further research. If this succeeds, the researcher gets the necessary resources to develop his technical sample further into more advanced prototypes which will be demonstrated to the sponsoring business group throughout the innovation process.

Toyota also exploits the power of prototypes as evaluation and communication tools, but at a later stage of the innovation process. As illustrated in the Lexus case, 450 different prototypes were made, tested and evaluated before engine and body designs were frozen for final production.

Most important of all, Canon, Sony and Toyota all instil respect for the factory floor as the place where real value creation takes place. This respect works like mental oil that lubricates the seamless research for D&M process.

Table 7.4 summarizes the relative strength of the companies' most important linkages between research, development and production activities.

Transfer of researchers seems to be more practised in cases where the technology is new and complicated instead of mature and well-established. Researchers from the Canon Research Centre were transferred from their research activities on liquid crystals to assume both marketing and production activities.

Table 7.4   Interlinking R&D and Production

Linkage/Company:	Canon	Sony	Toyota
Prod.-training of researchers	(2 months)	one month	–
Prod.-tr. of development eng.	(2 months)	one month	3 months
Transfer of researchers to development	•••	•••	•
Transfer of development engineers to production	•••	••	•
Immigration of production engineers to R&D	•	••	•••
Focus on prototyping in – Research	•••	•••	•
– Development	•••	•••	•••

()	In recent years this training has been cancelled for some researchers and engineers
•••	strong linkage
••	moderate linkage
•	weak linkage
–	no linkage

Note: Indications are based on the author's own estimates from company interviews.

This kind of horizontal transfer of engineers seems to have been less common at Sony in the development of the MiniDiscman, which was mainly based upon existing technologies that were fused, miniaturized and put into a casing that was designed by a separate division. Cross-departmental interaction could replace most of the transfers that were necessary in the FLCD project. Marketing of the MiniDiscman was headed and planned by a non-engineer, who was quite unrelated to the actual development of the product. In contrast, marketing activities related to the FLC displays were conducted by engineers, who had been transferred from FLC software development in the Canon Research Centre. Apart from the MD case, transfer of researchers seems to be equally frequent within Sony and within Canon. Toyota, in contrast, strongly reduces the need for transfer of engineers through intensive exchange of information between the different stages of the innovation process, coordinated by a strong project manager.

Accordingly, the last part of this cross-case analysis will deal with project creation, project coordination and project managers. It is their capability to lose the traditional focus on internal technological know-how and reorient it towards global know-who through linkages of extracorporate and intracorporate networks that makes the difference.

MANAGING THE PROJECT CREATION PROCESS

The Project Creation Process is Driven by Visions at Canon

The Corporate Strategy and Development HQ has an overall control of all project creation within Canon, as it ensures that task forces at all levels set goals in accordance with top management visions and that managers at lower levels translate the guidelines of the overall visions when they formulate visions with more tangible and specific goals for their own divisions or groups. The fact that evaluation of division managers and project leaders is mainly based upon the extent to which their achieved goals correspond to the visions provides an important mechanism for creating alignment among company members and their activities.

A development project is usually initiated by a task-force that examines possible technologies, through technology scanning, patent mapping and trial-and-error activities.

Canon's trial-and-error activities usually aim at preparing a prototype that can be demonstrated to managers in charge and, eventually, to top management. If these presentations are successful, i.e., convincing in terms of technological possibility and of market prospects, then top management will appoint an adequate chief engineer and allocate resources to the project. The chief engineer will be in charge of setting up his concept of the product and of managing the entire project.

In the case of FLC displays, Canon knew that several competitors were conducting research on flat panel display technology, mainly focusing on the conventional TFT technology. A small task-force of three engineers was, therefore, put together to search for a future key technology within displays. Their guiding vision was 'big and fine' (fine meaning thin). Once the FLC technology had been identified at a foreign university, a lot of trial-and-error activities followed and a small FLC display prototype was eventually presented to the division manager, who encouraged and supported presentations to upper management. The task force was allowed to continue its work, but had to compete with another task force, working on the TFT technology.

At the early stages of the development process, it is very common that Canon has two or three task forces working on different technologies, but targeting the same application and thereby competing with each other.

In the display development project, Canon thus had two task forces working on rivalling key technologies. They both succeeded in reaching the stage of trial manufacturing and could make presentations of prototypes to top management, but larger facilities would be required to go from trial- to real manufacturing. Therefore, one task force had to be discontinued.

By opting for FLC, Canon avoided direct competition in the highly competitive TFT field. Moreover, a business group that had resources to sponsor the project was interested in the technology, and a powerful division manager was interested in assuming the position as a chief engineer. He was assigned the job of chief engineer of what became the FLC project.

Almost Everybody can Start a Project within Sony

At Sony, we have seen that a new R&D project can be proposed by any researcher, but that (s)he usually needs the support of a business group for the pursuit of the project. The aforementioned process of mobilizing resources from a business group is mainly based upon presentation of prototypes to managers of the potentially interested business groups, and eventually also to top management. Through this system, a newly created technology project always finds an application, or else it will be discontinued early on.

The numerous forums of interaction between researchers in the Research Centre and development engineers and marketing people of the business groups also aim at the generation of new product ideas and projects.

Another initiator of a new product development project may be the product planner at a line-up meeting. If he is persuasive enough, he will convince the engineers of a certain business group to develop and produce the product that he believes has a market.

A project may also evolve within a business group, as in the case of the MiniDiscman. Just like in the case of the FLCD, Sony let several competing development groups work on technologies that would replace the old audio-cassette. At most, four different groups were working in parallel. The DAT technology emerged from one of the groups and, by 1987, another group had developed a prototype of a recordable CD player.

Owing to market considerations and the strong resistance that the music software industry caused, Sony finally decided to abandon the recordable CD and instead develop a new music format – the MD – for which President Ohga expressed an enthusiasm that radically reduced lead-time.

At Toyota the Chief Engineers are Champions of Project Creation

Toyota has a different approach to project creation, which is managed by the 20-odd chief engineers, all located in one large product management office. This does not mean that they conceive everything themselves. In contrast, the actual concept-generation process that initiates each new development project involves a large number of actors, such as the research and advanced development planning division from the Higashi-Fuji Technical Centre, the component and system development centre, the product planning division, design divisions and offices, the marketing group and the production engineering group (see also Figure 6.4).

Through an interactive consulting process, a concept that represents a hybridization of the departmental positions can be developed. The result of this interactive process is a proposal for development, which, like Canon and Sony, is presented to top management for approval.

For the concept-generation of the Lexus, the chief engineer headed a study team that went to America to do initial market research. Its assignment was to study the American luxury car market in Los Angeles, New York and San Francisco. As Mercedes Benz and BMW were given the highest scores in terms of prestige and dealer satisfaction, they were designated as target vehicles to emulate and outperform.

When Jinbo presented his product development proposal to the product planning committee, consisting of top managing directors, Chairman Eiji Toyoda summarized the project in a wide, yet goal-oriented vision: 'Making an ultimate luxury car by injecting Toyota's fifty-year experience and skills in automobile development and manufacturing into the project'. The Lexus-project was born.

We have now followed the birth of three projects in parallel. The next step is to clarify when and how the vital actors, activities and resources were interlinked and coordinated, which will also be the terminus of this case analysis.

INTERLINKING AND COORDINATING VITAL ACTORS, ACTIVITIES AND RESOURCES IN THE HOLISTIC T&I PROJECTS

Canon Transferred Critical Multicompetent Engineers to the Factory Floor while Drawing on Global specialized Know-how

As Canon decided to concentrate its resources on the FLC technology, the core of the project's activities were transferred to a production engineering and final production facility where approximately 20 engineers were directly assigned to the FLC project. Many of the 'defeated' TFT researchers joined this project as well.

Research agreements were signed with the inventors in order to provide the necessary scientific know-how in material design and other related research activities. For further support in the development of liquid crystal material, Canon engaged in joint development activities with a supplier and maintained co-operation contracts with three professors at two domestic universities.

After a few years, the FLCD project expanded to a Display Business Operations Centre, consisting of three different sub-projects focusing, respectively, on materials, production technologies and software engineering. Financial resources were still supplied by the same business group, which also provided some additional engineering resources to the Display Business Operations Centre.

Patent engineers were constantly involved in the different sub-projects. Research on liquid crystal materials was pursued in the Canon Research Centre, initially involving approximately ten researchers. As the project advanced, most of these researchers were dispatched to the Display Business Operations Centre, where production-oriented development activities were required.

In a similar pattern, many of the other engineers who were involved in the project initially performed their activities in their home locations, but were transferred to the Display Business Operations Centre as the project approached the production stage. Some engineers from those Headquarters that relate to operations management, i.e., Cost Engineering HQ, Quality Management HQ and Production Management HQ, also joined the centre.

As illustrated in Figure 4.8, an increasing number of quasi-extracorporate actors became involved: suppliers, named co-developers, and R&D subsidiaries in Australia, the US and the UK for software development, to mention a few. These actors did not, however, join the centre, but were in frequent interaction with it.

Most of the interrelated intracorporate actors were, eventually, transferred to the production centre, which finally numbered approximately 200 members.

The Old Boys' Network Mobilized Massive Resources for the FLCD Project

The initial task force, which later evolved into the FLC project, was put together by division manager Takahashi and headed by Dr Kanbe, who was a leading engineer within Takahashi's division. Division manager Takahashi left the task force with three overall visions, indicating what he considered important fields of the future. These visionary directives indirectly encouraged the task force to concentrate on future display technologies.

As top management made the decision to opt for FLC technology, Takahashi himself was assigned as chief engineer, thereby increasing the relative importance of the project. Takahashi's close relationship to R&D manager Endo and to President (and later, vice-chairman) Dr Yamaji – two important members of the board – certainly facilitated his task of mobilizing resources.

As economic conditions became bad for Canon, Takahashi's strong leadership became necessary in the business group that was sponsoring the FLC project. He could thus remain linked to the FLC project, although he was no longer the chief engineer. His successor, Kawashima, was concurrently the assisting senior general manager of the entire development centre. Hence, his position of project leadership was stronger than those of the other chief engineers in the centre, which made for a faster mobilization of resources for the project. However, over time the management structure of the FLC project was based both on very strong project leaders and on direct support from key persons within top management. The strong empowerment certainly contributed to the survival of an otherwise risky project, which for a long time has failed to achieve a sufficient production yield.

The MD Project Would Never Have Succeeded without the Seamless Co-operation Typical of Sony's T&I Management

Sony's MD project initiated a lot of activities throughout the corporation. Several of the aforementioned competing development groups merged with the MD project. At least five business groups, two corporate research laboratories and the Research Centre were directly involved.

There was no time for developing entirely new technologies to the MD. Instead, the disc mechanism was based on the previously developed digital technologies, used in Sony's different CD players and on the Digital Data Storage system, which had resulted from a joint project with Hewlett Packard.

As most of the required technologies were available in development divisions of different business groups, chief engineer Yoshida acquired them both by sending his engineers to the respective development divisions and by borrowing engineers directly from the divisions, who joined the MD group for a certain period of time, but never stayed on a permanent basis.

Some technologies required further research activities in the Research Centre, where approximately 20 researchers were related to the MD project.

Production engineers from the General Audio Group were in constant interaction with the MD group from the beginning of the project, supporting the development of a production line, which was already started when a functioning prototype of the MD was ready.

Patent attorneys were in close interaction with the MD group during the entire innovation process, thus offering protection of emerging intellectual property and, to some extent, supporting licensing negotiations that were run in parallel with competitors like Sharp, Sanyo and Matsushita.

Perhaps the most important activity of all was the aggressive licensing process that was run by the MD Promotion Department immediately after Sony's official announcement of the MD technology in May 1991. Two persons were appointed to establish links with music software producers overseas, one in New York and one in London. Both of them were in daily communication with the MD promotion department in Japan.

A new market research study was prepared in May 1992 by a private market research company in the US. Early customer feedback was interlinked through the establishment of a monitor program, and through focused group discussions with specially selected Sony customers.

For the development of the next-generation MD, a lot of interaction with foreign and domestic universities took place. This extracorporate interaction was mainly with the Research Centre, but a large number of Sony's business groups were involved in miniaturization activities, related to the MD.

Although the MD project involved altogether some 300 engineers, there was hardly any permanent transfer of engineers. All technologies were assembled in the MD Group, which never exceeded 30 engineers. The project strategy thus differs totally from that of the FLC project, which was largely based upon permanent transfer of all internal engineers and researchers involved.

The Corporate Project Status of the MD Further Supported Mobilization and Coordination of Resources

Sony's development of the MiniDiscman was quite different from Canon's FLCD-development. The actual MiniDisc project team never exceeded 30 members. Hence, most activities were performed by researchers and engineers who were not members of the actual project team. These supporting engineers were not transferred to a growing project team, but remained instead in their original locations. The chief engineer and his deputy coordinated the entire process by continually meeting with the managers of the different interrelated divisions, centres and business groups.

The management structure of the project appeared to be yet more powerful than that of the FLC project. Because of the strict deadline set by President Ohga and also his own strong belief in the MD, the development project received the status of 'corporate project', thereby enabling a more effective mobilization of resources. This had only happened to three other projects during Sony's history: the Betamax, the 8mm video camera and the CD player.

Consequently, a highly empowered steering committee was formed, including the development centre manager and overall chief engineer Tsurushima, the Senior General Managers of the most involved Business Groups, and President Ohga, who headed the committee. Tsurushima was eventually promoted to director, which may reflect the importance attached to project-leaders.

With the backing of this committee, it became easier to encourage the large number of interrelated engineers to co-operate, and monetary resources were mobilized more easily. At some points, the project involved close to 300 engineers and 20 researchers of the Research Centre.

When the 20 key persons from the related units gathered on a monthly basis to discuss the advancement of the project's interrelated parts with Tsurushima and his deputy, President Ohga usually participated as well. A stronger top-management involvement is hard to imagine.

By creating and launching the MD format, Sony follows the Schumpeterian pattern of creative destruction, as this format could reduce, or perhaps even destroy the market for both audio cassettes and digital audio cassettes (DAT), but at the same time open a new market for the new MD technology. This may partly explain the need for such strong top-management support. For understandable reasons, divisions and business groups with rival technologies could possibly have refused to co-operate otherwise.

A High-level Steering Committee Enabled Immediate Mobilization of Massive Resources for the Lexus Project

In the Lexus project, a tremendous amount of time and resources was spent on the early concept/project generation phase. As it eventually became clear to Toyota that they were going to compete with Mercedes Benz and BMW a high-level steering committee was assigned, which instantly mobilized a large number of actors. The total number of people involved at any single time reached 1,400 on some occasions.

As a consequence of the market research activities, the chief engineer set extremely demanding targets for the Lexus regarding speed, fuel-consumption, noise-level, weight and Cd-value. Even inside Toyota, engineers found the target of outperforming Mercedes Benz and BMW on these criteria – not to mention at a lower price – to be ridiculous and unrealistic. The project required not only extraordinary efforts and resources in terms of testing and experimenting, but also a higher level of interaction between many different specialists from a large number of departments engaged in the various stages of the development process. Moreover, harder requirements vis-á-vis key suppliers were necessary, as they assumed large parts of the development work.

It goes without saying that 1,400 engineers could not gather at the same place. As in the MD-case, most activities were performed in separate locations and divisions to be integrated in the prototype production later on.

The Lexus Coordinator was Actually the Head of All Chief Engineers

The Lexus project received just as much top management support as did the FLCD and the MD projects. As in the case of the FLC, the chief engineer was exchanged. Instead of selecting one of the existing chief engineers, the manager of all chief engineers was put in charge of the Lexus project. It was, therefore, quite natural that he had more authority than any other chief engineer within Toyota. This highly empowered chief engineer headed and participated actively in all activities: concept generation, development of components, internal structure, external design, production and marketing of the new vehicle. In order to mobilize necessary resources, particularly in terms of production equipment, he gathered a steering committee that was quite similar in structure to that of the MD project.

The steering (FQ) committee was headed by the highest executives in charge of general product development, project development and factory-level production. Director Jinbo was head of general product development, Suzuki was the Lexus project leader and Takahashi was director of production engineering. It also involved designers, product engineers and production engineers. This coordination committee was the first in Toyota's history to achieve such extensive integration across divisions and high-level hierarchies.

The actual development of the Lexus was managed much in line with Sony's

MD project. The chief engineer and his numerous deputies coordinated and integrated the results of the different units' efforts. No large Lexus team was formed and no permanent transfer of engineers was required.

Table 7.5 summarizes the relative strength of linkages and mechanisms used in the three T&I projects.

Table 7.5   Strength of Linkages and Mechanisms in T&I Projects

Linkage/Company:	Canon	Sony	Toyota
Fusing competing task-forces	••	••	Supplier competition
Direct top-management involvement	••	•••	•••
Presentation of prototypes	•••	•••	•••
Steering committee	not observed	•••	•••
Coordinating visions	••	not observed	••

•••	strong linkage
••	moderate linkage
•	weak linkage
–	no linkage

Note: Indications are based on the author's own estimates from company interviews.

SUMMARIZING SIMILARITIES AND DIFFERENCES ACROSS THE CASES

At the Extracorporate Level

All three companies maintain strong links to extracorporate sources of technology. Canon and Toyota enjoy stronger linkages to corporate groups than Sony. For natural reasons, Toyota has the most extensive kigyo keiretsu network.[4] Spin-off laboratories are important actors in the research activities, in particular within Sony and Toyota. Their main advantage is to offer a less bureaucratic environment in smaller units. A point in common are the strong links both to domestic and to foreign universities. Canon's stand-alone strategy – with a focus on unique technologies – makes MITI-interaction and certain strategic alliances less interesting. In contrast, Canon seems to have the most elaborate network of overseas R&D laboratories, but Sony employs a significantly higher number of foreign scientists in Japan. Toyota does not appear to employ any foreign researchers in Japan, but all three companies clearly strive to increase the number of foreigners in their research activities, with an increasing focus on those located overseas.

At the Intracorporate Level

Sony demonstrates the strongest linkages, both between different business groups and between the research centre and the business groups. Perhaps as a result of its multiple intra-corporate linkages of seamless co-operation, Sony has neither demonstrated any equivalent of Canon's cross-functional task-forces for the concept-generation stage, nor of Toyota's concept-generation groups.

For the R&D-market interface, again, Sony has established the strongest linkages, both to the research centre and to the business groups. The strongest point in common of the three companies is their high degree of market-linked sponsoring of R&D activities. Toyota's relatively weak direct linkages between R&D people and market needs are compensated by a strong and direct market interlinkage of the concept-generation process, and direct top-management involvement and sponsoring of R&D activities.

The interlinkage of production through transfer of researchers seems to be more practised in cases where the technology is new and complicated instead of mature and well established. Consequently, researchers from the Canon Research Centre were transferred from their research activities on liquid crystals to assume both marketing and production activities. In contrast, the development of the MiniDiscman was mainly based upon existing technologies that were fused, miniaturized and put into a casing that was designed by a separate division. Cross-departmental interaction could, therefore, replace most of the transfers that were necessary in the FLCD project. Apart from the MD case, transfer of researchers seems to be practised equally often within Sony and within Canon. Toyota, in contrast, strongly reduces the need for transfer of engineers through intensive exchange of information between the different stages of the innovation process.

At the Project Level

Both Canon and Sony had several internally-competing task forces that were fused into the FLC and the MD projects. This mechanism was not observed in the Lexus case, where intensive supplier competition for one and the same component certainly replaced some of this intracorporate competition.

Direct top-management involvement was strong (or moderate) in all three cases. Presentation of R&D proposals and prototypes were frequently used across the cases as a primary link to top management and as a means to mobilize resources, but other coordinating mechanisms demonstrated important differences that may reflect the different nature of the products.

A car is a typical architectural innovation, in which the actual components do not change much, but the systems or ways of combining them and putting them together do. Compared to Canon and Sony in the consumer electronics and office automation equipment industries, Toyota has the characteristics of longer product life-cycles with greater continuity in terms of technological advancements, i.e., less invention-based product renewals, significantly lower numbers of products, but a higher number of optional product variations. The typical innovation process of Toyota involves a significantly higher number of divisions, functions and engineers.

The complexity of a car calls for larger projects with more extensive coordination, especially between external design and internal layout. In contrast, a consumer electronics product does not require an equally strong coordination between design and internal structure other than fitting the size. VLSI has made possible extensive miniaturization and reduction of the number of parts, which can more easily be dominated by a specific external design. A car still contains approximately 25,000 parts on average, most of which are mechanical.[5] Therefore, design has a less predominant role that has to be carefully coordinated with body and mechanical parts, as demonstrated by the noise-reduction activities in the Lexus case.

This is why the Lexus steering committee consisted of executive level managers of design, product engineering and production engineering.

The MD project was also coordinated by a powerful steering committee, but this did not include design, which instead was performed by Sony's separate design office. The purpose of the MD steering committee was rapid mobilization of resources, i.e., empowerment, whereas the Lexus committee, in addition to empowerment, served the purpose of strictest possible cross-functional coordination between design, product engineering and production.

In the case of the FLC project, the emphasis rapidly shifted from applied research towards production technology, which called for a massive transfer of researchers and engineers to the production floor. Design was not an important issue, nor was coordination across different centres and business groups. Hence, a steering committee was not equally important as in the two other cases. Moreover, the smaller size of Canon probably reduces the need for formal steering committees.

A natural consequence of product complexity is an increased need for concurrent engineering, which, in turn, calls for stronger coordinating mechanisms between the larger number of interdependent activities. This provides another explanation to the highly empowered cross-functional steering committee of the Lexus project and the possible absence of such a committee in the case of FLCD.

Visions penetrate and guide the development processes both at Canon and at Toyota, but we have not observed any equivalent mechanism at Sony. These visions align corporate activities with top-management's strategic directions. In the case of Sony, the fact that top management is so closely involved in the major R&D projects of the company may reduce the need for propagating strategic visions. A large part of Sony's R&D activities are managed directly by the Research Planning and Coordination Group, which mainly consists of research directors and top management.

The decision-making process was not entirely dominated by one project leader in any of the projects, but involved top management and other key persons as well. Moreover, both the FLC project and the Lexus project had their project leaders replaced, one or several times.

A final difference worth mentioning in the context of project management is that Canon and Sony do not seem to have professional chief engineers, but instead assign any suitable senior engineer, researcher, or general manager to the task of managing an R&D project. Toyota, in contrast, has full-time chief engineers who always work with the management of vehicle projects. Once they have finished a project, they are charged with a new one.

All three companies attach a lot of importance to the function of project management. One third of Toyota's current directors have past experience as project managers.

NOTES

1. According to Professor Fujimoto, Toyota designers themselves admit that the Lexus ended up looking too much like a Mercedes Benz.
2. This interlinkage was also described in a separate article (Harryson, 1996).
3. This approach to innovation was also described in separate articles (Harryson, 1995b; 1997).
4. The effects on T&I of keiretsu interlinkages were summarized in Chapter 3.
5. Fujimoto (1993, 26).

8   Moving from Know-how to Know-who

Everybody is aware that networking is good for business results. Still, it only happens to an adequate degree in very few companies. Why? Because many companies still take an excessive pride in defending their technological leadership, which brings most of their attention to internal specialization.

Instead of a researcher's focusing on one single task, the frequent circulation between different research divisions as practised by Canon, or also between BUs as within Sony, promotes the synergistic knowledge-creation process through cross-fertilization of ideas and fields of experience. The importance of building, nurturing and leveraging learning relationships is clear to all members of the seamless innovation processes that characterize these world-class innovators.

This open sharing of resources is further promoted through holistic performance measurement systems that most companies should find compelling. For firms that wish to emulate the T&I management practices of the Japanese innovators, it is important to understand not only their processes of external and internal networking but also the organizational outlook, structures, and principles that underpin them. While many Western companies continue to encourage a high degree of technical and functional specialization, and to maintain a strong business unit focus with individual P&L (profit and loss) accountability, Canon, Sony, and Toyota exhibit a more holistic approach to managing organizational activities and resources. This holistic approach not only enhances the processes of external and internal networking but creates and exploits powerful synergies between them.

In addition, these different organizational structures and principles completely change the name of the game for CTOs and heavyweight project leaders. By acting like intelligent know-who webs in dual know-how, they can circumvent the dilemmas of innovation that have prevented many Western companies from commercializing their bright inventions.

The holistic approach characteristic of the three companies studied here results in the creation of borderless organizations that reward collective action rather than individual performance. This chapter will include a couple of recent examples from Western companies to make the point that many CEOs have been too focused on optimising isolated functions and on implementing controlling tools to track the progress of their efforts. The examples highlight the contrast to the holistic network approach:

A. While many Western companies still have a high degree of technical and functional specialization, Canon, Sony, and Toyota see to it through a variety of formal means (described throughout the book) that researchers and engineers acquire a broad competence base, and that key personnel at all points of the process of developing new products have a comprehensive understanding of this overall process.

B. Whereas most Western firms maintain a strong business unit focus with individual P&L accountability, Canon, Sony, and Toyota encourage corporate-wide co-operation and sharing of resources in the interests of forceful innovation. They do this by a number of means, including holistic performance parameters, strong project leaders, and open recruiting for project members across business units.

C. Companies that strive to achieve similar synergies in their T&I Management also need a corporate infrastructure that resonates with the systemic mechanisms and principles outlined above. Though not intuitively obvious, it is certainly true that a broader and more holistic approach is needed to attain deeper understanding of how to improve the performance of T&I management. Ultimately, global know-*who* becomes more important to corporate success than specialized know-*how.*

The purpose of this study was to identify the managerial mechanisms that have enabled Japanese companies, in the relatively successful industries of office automation equipment, consumer electronics and automobiles, to enjoy shorter development lead-time and higher R&D productivity than their Western competitors.

Detailed empirical data on the case-study companies have been presented in Chapters 3, 4, 5 and 6, and have been analysed in accordance with the theoretical framework that was developed in Chapter 2. The analysis has offered a detailed presentation of the most important interlinking mechanisms at both the extra- and the intra-corporate levels of the companies. The resulting linkages, as used in three specific R&D projects, could then be analysed more purposefully. The identification and analysis of these linkages, together with the managerial mechanisms that establish them, constitute the most important contribution of this study, but some additional contributions still need to be presented before the move from know-how to know-who can be made.

CONCLUDING REMARKS ON CANON, SONY AND TOYOTA

The practical contribution of this study is a deeper penetration of how T&I is managed in three relatively successful Japanese companies, proposing concrete interlinking mechanisms which serve the purpose of increasing R&D efficiency and shortening development lead-time. In addition, more nuance has been added to what previously has been described rather simplistically as 'Japanese'. Canon, Sony and Toyota all emphasize the linkages that are vital to circumventing the dilemmas of innovation, but the ways in which they are managed displayed considerable differences.

Canon: World Champion in Commercialization of Unique Technologies

Canon is highly technology-oriented, focusing strongly on the development of a few – and possibly unconventional – technologies that are brought to production through extensive transfer of researchers and development engineers to production. Learning linkages to extracorporate sources of technology are numerous, but focus on a reduced number of technologies.

Links to market needs are not considered to be equally important as within Sony and Toyota. The focus is less on new products than on alternative technologies for existing products.

It is common knowledge that Japanese companies produce very high numbers of patents, but it had not been observed how all these patents are achieved. Perhaps more within Canon than any other large company in the world, researchers and development engineers alike are requested to submit a certain number of patent applications to the national Patent Office, thus disclosing their ideas, but also preventing other companies from making applications in the same field.

Weekly brain-storming meetings use both awarded patents and patent applications – foreign and Japanese – to generate ideas of how to make similar products without violating existing patent rights.

The requirement of generating new applications appears to be the most frequently used mechanism in Japanese companies for 'enforcing' creativity, or rather, perhaps productivity. This requirement is so strong within Canon that it has caused researchers to leave.

Sony: World Champion in Product Innovation through Corporate Synergies

Sony is, above all, innovation-oriented, fostering a cross-fertilizing environment that yields a multitude of highly innovative product concepts. In order to provide all new concepts with the necessary technologies, Sony needs a multitude of linkages to many different extracorporate sources of technology. As opposed to Canon, the uniqueness of Sony's products is rarely based upon single, new technologies, but rather upon the fusion and miniaturization of established technologies that usually yield trend-setting products. The focus is thus not so much on new technologies as it is on new products.

Market links are very strong, to remind engineers about the necessity of satisfying customers, but also to educate the customer about new products.

While Sony strives to become or remain number one in a highly competitive field of multiple products, Canon is the only one in a highly specialized field of one, or a few, technologies.

While Sony competes, Canon attempts to avoid competition through unique technologies and excessive patenting, which builds a protecting wall around each technology.

Toyota: World Champion in Management of Complexity and Heavyweight Projects

Toyota is efficiency-oriented, but in combination with high technology and high quality. Extracorporate linkages seem mostly to aim at design input for the generation of new concepts, in addition to actual technology development.

That Toyota's supplier structure is more extensive and rigid than that of Canon and Sony finds an explanation in the complexity of a car. Moreover, there is a higher degree of company-specific standards in the automobile industry, whereas office automation equipment and consumer electronics products are more based upon interchangeable VLSI.

Toyota's state-of-the-art R&D productivity is mainly based upon interlinkage and coordination of extensive supplier networks that provide a tremendous support in the management of complexity. Clearly, these networks will be hard to emulate in absence of an environment that promotes long-term relationships.

Another key-lesson is that, for large projects, it is not by putting an enormous cross-functional team together that we will arrive at Toyota's short development lead-time. Rather, it is the art of coordinating interdependent – but not collocated or continuously interacting – actors towards clearly defined goals, and at the same time having links and the power to mobilize all necessary resources in a timely manner, that make the difference. This calls for sophisticated network organizations and powerful project management, which also provide effective means of circumventing the dilemmas of innovation.

CIRCUMVENTING THE DILEMMAS OF INNOVATION: EXPLAINING THE PERFORMANCE GAP

Chapter 2 revealed that an undiscovered, but critical rationale for outsourcing specialized R&D is that two fundamental dilemmas of innovation limit seriously the efficacy of internal technological development:

- The dilemma of technological leadership is that successful pursuit of technological leadership tends to focus firms on intracorporate activities. This decreases their sensitivity and responsiveness to external technological and market factors that ought to guide product development. Moreover, the rigidity of typical technology problem-solving processes impedes cross-

departmental collaboration and technology fusion, which are vital enablers for radical innovation.
*   The organizational dilemma of innovation is that the creative development of inventive technologies appears to require a small and organic organizational structure, whereas rapid innovation, in contrast, calls for large and stable organizations. Companies trying to achieve both creative invention and rapid innovation in one and the same organization are most likely to be caught in this dilemma.

Both of these dilemmas cause the vital interlinkages of R&D projects – those between external sources of technology, corporate technology development and product development, as displayed in the figure below – to become weaker.

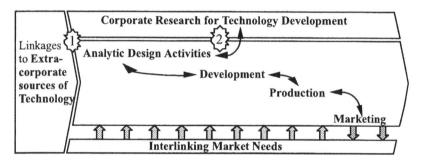

Source: Adopted from Chapter 2.

Figure 8.1   Vital Interlinkages of T&I Projects

In this study, the dilemmas have been confronted with detailed, multi-level empirical observations and can now be proposed as rationales of the specific interlinking mechanisms in Japanese T&I management. Accordingly, the purposeful circumvention of these two dilemmas is hereby offered as theoretical explanation to the short lead-times and the high R&D efficiency of the case-study companies.

Intracorporate Benefits of Interlinking Extracorporate Sources of Invention

Instead of concentrating all resources on internal corporate research for technology development, our case-study companies strive to interlink extracorporate technological resources. By encouraging all researchers to assume a gate-keeping role and by letting many of them interact with extracorporate fields of action – such as foreign R&D subsidiaries, universities and national projects – new trends and scientific discoveries are not neglected, which is otherwise a risk of technological leadership.

Through the interlinkage of extracorporate scientific skills, it is possible – instead of developing them internally – to avoid excessive specialization of engineers who, quite in contrast, profit from a multi-skilled knowledge-base that promotes the interlinkage of technology-development and product-development processes in several ways.

To begin with, researchers who devote some time to sales training and to interaction with sales people are more likely to consider market needs and understand the requirements that are imposed by the sponsoring business groups. Hence, instead of becoming self-driven and insensitive to external influence, their technology development activities are oriented towards market needs.

Intracorporate development of technological leadership is likely to call for lifetime careers in research, which also may keep the possible results in the research laboratory. By profiting from ample extracorporate technological resources, the case-study companies can reduce the time in research of most researchers to the necessary minimum for acquiring the knowledge that is linked to the laboratory. Instead of keeping this knowledge within the laboratory during a life-time career, most researchers can secure the transfer to development and production by actually going there themselves.

As most of these multi-skilled engineers and researchers have already received some production training before starting their research activities in a laboratory, they are more likely to consider manufacturing aspects from the beginning and more able to maintain open communication with production engineers, thereby linking technology development to product development.

Linking an R&D project to production as early as possible, instead of waiting for a technological breakthrough, also has the advantage of enabling earlier market feedback through experimental commercialization. Market needs are thus linked to the R&D process at an earlier stage, when changes can be made more easily. This increases the flexibility of the process and has a clear advantage over an excessive pursuit of internal technology development, where changing the direction of the process becomes increasingly difficult the greater the amount of accumulated technological knowledge.

Instead of a researcher's focusing on one single task, the frequent circulation of researchers within the research laboratory, as demonstrated by Canon, further promotes the knowledge-creation process, because different fields of experience are exposed to each other and forced to co-operate towards a common goal. Similarly, Sony's open recruiting system for project staffing and the numerous forums of interaction between researchers, development engineers and sales people lay the groundwork for cross-fertilization and of ideas and technologies. Hence, the prospects of analytic design activities for technology fusion are better with cross-trained – as opposed to specialized – researchers and engineers.

Using specialized Actors and Resources in the Surrounding R&D Networks Provides the Most Important Defence Against the Dilemmas of Innovation

Thanks in great part to the cross-industrial keiretsu structure of horizontal and vertical interlinkages that we have seen in Chapter 3, a more effective mobilization of corporate energies is possible through the seamless exchange of information, technologies and competencies. Moreover, resources for large-scale operations can be mobilized more easily and enjoy protection from the pressure of capital markets.

Another important key to innovation lies in the flexible shift between individual concentration and focused integration, the management of which sometimes tends to split up the components of a technology and concentrate on their individual improvement, while at other times it is necessary to bring the components together and focus on their integration (cf. Figure 2.7). This sort of flexibility is something that a kigyo keiretsu structure of interlinked suppliers and spin-offs seems ideally adapted to provide, since it contains both centralized and decentralized means of fusing and diffusing technology and the results of research and development. Linkages to overseas R&D subsidiaries can provide similar mechanisms.

We have seen many examples of how technology development is avoided by extracorporate sourcing of technology. Still, there are examples in which internal technology development has been necessary, thus calling for specialized activities. In order to reduce the potentially negative organizational impacts of internal specialized technology development, these activities are spun off from the large case-study companies. Thus, inventive specialists find an outlet in the structure of otherwise intensive rigidity, where the compulsory stream of continuous job rotation produces only generalists. By separating specialized research from product development in this way, and maintaining a strong linkage between the two, the organizational dilemma of innovation (Figure 2.9) can be overbridged.

In all three cases, we have noticed a high degree of spun-off units, aiming at more specialized inventional activities than those remaining within the corporate walls. The perhaps most obvious examples are the Sony Kihara Research Centre and the Sony Computer Science Laboratory, which openly aim at a freer spirit in research by breaking with traditional bureaucracy and hierarchies.

Similarly, Canon has opted to spin off some of its more specialized activities, but these seem to be more related to production technology than to actual research activities. Chapter 3 also mentioned that the overseas R&D laboratories partly aim at avoiding the increasing bureaucratization of R&D at Canon in Japan and, instead, profit from the very informal and non-hierarchical atmosphere that these labs were said to offer.

Toyota's most upstream R&D activities are spun off to Toyota's macrocosm of principal subsidiaries, among which Toyota's Central R&D Laboratory exemplifies little hierarchy and small research groups. In addition, lifetime careers in research facilitate specialization, and the laboratory has ample linkages to extracorporate actors of science and technology. This separate unit thus fits well into the creative field of Figure 2.9. The primary mechanism of linking its activities to product development processes is financial. Toyota will obviously only sponsor projects that can be related to the needs of product development. Chapter 3 also provided an example of how researchers of the Toyota Central R&D Laboratory, along with R&D staff of Nippondenso, were linked to the Technical Centre at Toyota's HQ through a joint R&D project on a three-way catalyst.

Foreign researchers seem to be preferred for upstream research activities both at Canon and at Sony. Canon's highest R&D executive clearly stated that the availability of entrepreneurial spirit and experienced researchers is greater overseas than in Japan and it was also emphasized that the overseas labs offer a 'very informal and non-hierarchical atmosphere' (cf. page 88). Sony's senior executive research adviser stated that Western researchers' uniqueness of ideas is lacking in Japan and that hierarchy is lower in overseas R&D units. Similarly, Toyota sources foreign design expertise through its design centres in California and in Brussels and through a multitude of university interaction.

Both Canon and Sony view Japan-acclimatization of their Western researchers as a problem and state clearly that they want them to remain Western in their ways of thinking and conducting research. For this very reason, Canon prefers to keep Western researchers overseas, instead of placing them in the Canon Research Centre in Japan.

Hence, the surrounding R&D networks offer several possibilities, not only to circumvent the dilemma of technological leadership, but also to overbridge the organizational dilemma of innovation, by interlinking inventiveness and innovativeness.

By Organizing Internal R&D into Interconnected Microcosmic Networks the Dilemmas are Further Reduced

At the intracorporate level, the organization of T&I into 'microcosmic' networks of interconnected activities also provides an organizational mechanism that reduces the dilemmas of innovation. The best example is provided by Toyota, where – apart from the spun-off Central R&D Laboratory – 11,500 R&D-related engineers are divided into three separate centres, as displayed in Figure 6.1. The largest of these centres is in turn split into three vehicle-development centres, one component and system development centre, and a large number of supporting and administrative functions (Figure 6.2). The component and system development centre is technology-oriented, performing advanced engineering of components and large vehicle systems, which are to be integrated in entire vehicles by the three vehicle centres.

This tripartite R&D system allows for the different time perspectives and organizational needs of research, advanced development and commercial development to coexist. A certain degree of specialization is possible without reducing the prospects for co-operation and integration of results. From the upstream Higashi-Fuji laboratory to the development centres in Figure 6.1, the focus shifts from technology development, via system development, to project management. Interlinked suppliers and spun-off body makers assume specialized parts of the T&I activities. Hence, different organizational needs of these interrelated activities can coexist, thanks in part to strong coordinative efforts of the project leader, to whom we turn below.

By Finally Managing T&I Projects as Holistic Networks the Dilemmas are Completely Defeated

The preceding sections have proposed that, whether at the extra-, or at the intra-corporate level, networking is a main theme within all three companies. The project leaders circumvent the dilemmas of innovation by being main co-ordinators of R&D projects managed as networks of interlinked extra- and intra-corporate actors, resources and activities as displayed in the figure below:

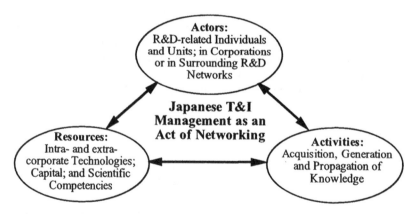

Source: Adopted from Chapter 1.

Figure 8.2   Japanese T&I Management as an Act of Networking

This system includes both competition and complementarity. R&D projects are in competition with each other for resources. The primary means of competition is to develop prototypes that please top management. Competing task forces are eventually fused, and a variety of supporting headquarters (Canon), business groups (Sony), and engineering divisions (Toyota) are called upon by the project leader and his deputies.

Complementarity can be enjoyed by dispatching multi-skilled engineers, with practical problems in mind, to the source of required scientific knowledge (for example, in-house research facilities, corporate R&D satellite labs, university-labs, MITI projects, suppliers or foreign partners). Thus, the required scientific knowledge is acquired and brought to the final destination, i.e., the project involving a product, or a production process and the incorporation of the knowledge into a product is secured. This incorporation depends not only on transfer of researchers to development and production, but often also on initial immigration of development and production engineers to inventional activities. Similarly, extracorporate professors, researchers and engineers may be interlinked (and sometimes imported) from the same sort of sources to the project.

Strong leadership and challenging target-setting by the project leaders serve to reduce the hierarchical layers that normally would separate them from many of the engineers involved. Instead of taking the routes of formal hierarchies, communication flows directly to them through a new, informal hierarchy, imposed by the project leaders themselves. This is where the flat multinetworked organizations appear. Creative and participative thinking can be combined with rigid structures for rapid processing of information and high pace of innovation.

It is thus through the extensive use of networking at several interrelated levels that the case-study companies and their project leaders arrive at circumventing the dilemmas of innovation. Flexible specialization and the creativity of small separate groups can be linked to efficient, large-scale production sites. The necessary resources can be mobilized on short notice thanks to the highly-empowered project leader with close links to top management, in addition to dedicated support from assistants and subordinates throughout the organization and its flexible borders. Powerful visions support the alignment of all activities in their collective efforts. Flexible, informal project organizations can exist rather independently in the formal and rigid organization, thereby enabling explaining the coexistence of heterarchy and hierarchy, which overbridges the organizational dilemma of innovation.

As witnessed in the next section, current literature gives quite a different picture of Japanese organizations.[1]

PERSONAL OBSERVATIONS VERSUS CURRENT LITERATURE

The frequent descriptions of Japanese organizations as simple and flat (cf. page 42) do not correspond to any of the case observations. In contrast, the overall impression is that Canon, Sony and Toyota – as well as the other Japanese companies observed by this author – have complex and rather hierarchical organizations, although to varying degrees. The relative strength of project leaders simplifies the line of communication by imposing a new informal hierarchy that directs all relevant communication directly to his group, without delaying deviations on the way. This is the only, but highly effective, 'flatness' identified at the companies studied in this book.

It is thus through strong and sometimes informal project leadership that a flat project can exist as an overlay-structure in an otherwise hierarchical organization. Many decisions are made by the formal project leader, but some are made by his deputies, equals, or by top management. Some decisions are based on consensus, others on individual conviction. This interchange of formal and informal leadership permits hierarchy and heterarchy to coexist in the Japanese T&I process, thus exploiting the benefits of both productivity and creativity (cf. Figure 2.9). It also suggests that project management is not ensured by one single leader. Most projects are managed by strong leaders, but they also have strong supporters, who sometimes assume a leadership role which is then supported by the formal leader.[2]

Most of the relevant literature stresses the use of continually-interacting cross-functional teams. The case studies have, however, demonstrated that although R&D projects involve a large number of engineers, only a very limited number of them are gathered in a team. Instead, the main task of the project manager is to coordinate an extensive network of separately performed activities. His important role certainly merits a lot of the attention received in current literature, but the strong support that he receives from top management, steering committees and from his assistants has, for some reason, been less apparent in previous studies.

In contrast to Aoki's (1988, 237) finding that corporate R&D is divided into two levels – central R&D and divisional R&D in the manufacturing division – the empirical findings of this study suggest that both Toshiba and the three case-study companies divide their corporate R&D into three different levels. The intermediate level appears to serve as an appropriate host and sponsor of development activities for research projects that cannot find funds directly from a business group or division.

Both Canon and Sony were described by Prahalad and Hamel (1990, 87) as companies in which people can be rapidly moved from one business unit to another, but we have seen that interaction between different business groups is actually as frequent in Sony as it is rare in Canon.

Most of the networking practices also have a strong historical background which merit some attention as well.

HISTORICAL RATIONALES OF NETWORKING IN JAPANESE T&I MANAGEMENT

One factor worth mentioning in respect of external networking is that these companies, like most other Japanese companies, have had no other alternative but to exploit extracorporate sources of technology. As pointed out in the beginning of Chapter 3, the whole networking principle in the Japanese management of technology emerged as a result of an acute urge to catch up with the West. The propensity for technology-scanning and pooling of resources has continued ever since the Meiji era in, e.g., zaibatsu, kinyu shudan, kigyo keiretsu, MITI projects and also within companies' task forces and project teams. The urge to catch up through a follower strategy has left little room for the dilemmas of innovation to develop. By continually imposing new, quasi-impossible goals to reach and by stressing all possible competitive threats, Japanese project leaders, top managers and MITI officials prevent the feeling of complacency from arising, as does the extraordinarily high degree of domestic competition.

All cases have emphasized the importance of strong project leadership, the origins of which take us back to the World War II. According to Mayuzumi-san, who is an ex-Mitsubishi engineer, the first project manager to become 'heavyweight' was chief engineer Horikoshi at Mitsubishi Heavy Industries. As the war began, he was ordered by the Ministry of Commerce and Industry (which came to be called MITI after the war) to develop and produce a large number of fighter planes – the Zero Fighters. Owing to the time pressure and the scarce resources of the country, the strong backing of this ministry was required to help him mobilize all the necessary resources. Six years later, the development and production of jet engines took place through an equivalent ministry-empowerment of a chief engineer.

As the war ended and the war industry was divested, some of these powerful chief engineers joined the automobile industry,[3] thereby introducing the 'heavyweight' project management style, from which most competitors around the world are trying to learn.

Stepping Back to a Future Outlook

Japan's historical follower strategy presupposes the existence of technological leaders to follow and of scientific centres of excellence to network with. These conditions may no longer exist for companies that, themselves, have achieved technological leadership in certain fields. The relative prosperity and important technological achievements of successful Japanese companies may also cause the not-invented-here syndrome to emerge, which so far seems to have been mainly a Western plague. In addition, some Western centres of excellence may close their doors. The possibility of locating R&D overseas, however, remains and is likely to be increasingly exploited in the future, as are strategic alliances and joint research projects with Western partners.

Hence, even though a future paradigm may bring changes in the types of linkages, it is most unlikely that the Japanese propensity for networking will decrease. If it does, this will certainly also cause dilemmas of innovation in Japan.

So What can We Learn from All This?

All results presented in this book indicate that the registered performance gap in terms of development lead-time and R&D productivity is primarily related to a unique effectiveness in the management of linkages in T&I networks. Only when similar networks have been developed with the appropriate inter-linking mechanisms will Japanese-style heavyweight project management provide a useful object of emulation for those who strive to close the gap. Essentially, there are six critical principles which need to be in place before this can happen:

SIX CRITICAL PRINCIPLES LACKING IN MANY WESTERN COMPANIES

The importance of building, nurturing and leveraging learning relationships within and beyond the corporate borders is clear to all members of the seamless innovation processes that characterize world-class innovators. In addition to the critical focus on extracorporate sources of invention, five managerial principles are necessary for implementing the network mechanisms that Canon, Sony and Toyota have in common. Unfortunately, these principles are still weak, if existing at all, in many Western companies.

Open Sharing of Know-how

First, the corporate infrastructure needs to resonate with the open sharing of ideas, technologies and human resources both within and between business units. Not only job rotation practices, but also Sony's mistake-sharing-related promotion criteria provide compelling ideas on how to make this happen. We have also seen how the open-recruiting system enables project leaders to draw on resourses across Sony's all Business Groups, and how development engineers are free to volunteer for R&D projects regardless of which Business Group or research unit initiates the project.

Many European companies are not even close to fulfilling this principle: The R&D manager, responsible for one of the four Business Areas of a notorious European company stated:

> I would rather throw all my R&D results out through the window than share them with my colleagues in the other Business Areas. I would not allow them to borrow any of my people either.

The Director of Technology Management of another Business Area confirmed that:

> Sometimes, good engineers get transferred between projects within our Business Area to

spread their know-how, but we never lend our people to other Business Areas . . . Actually, we don't know much about the know-how and technologies that are available within the company as a whole.

An equally worrying statement was made by the CTO of the same company:

The only thing that is faster than it should be at this company is the speed at which we manage to hide mistakes. We neither recognize nor communicate any mistakes committed. This lack of honest communication is particularly strong between Business Areas and towards top management.

In spite of these deficiencies, at least some Business Areas of this European company are successful. In fact, the biggest deficiency is the way in which this success is measured. As most managers in this company are measured on the performance of their *individual* Business Area, Business Unit, or project, it is quite natural that they do not help colleagues in other BAs, BUs or projects. If the R&D manager had shared his R&D results with a rivalling BA, the performance of the receiving BA would be likely to increase as would the promotion possibilities of that BA's R&D manager. This is why most Japanese companies pay much less attention to individual performance, in accordance with the second principle.

Holistic Performance Measurement

The incentive and performance measurement systems must consider holistic results and reward co-operation and collective achievements instead of individual performance. Only then will the corporate-wide forums of interaction that are applied at Canon and Sony bring the intended benefits: individual know-how will be continually enriched and applied throughout the company instead of remaining isolated in competing Business Units or divisions.

The Canon case described how the Corporate Strategy and Development HQ formulated corporate visions and ensured that Business Groups and divisions at all levels set goals in accordance with these visions. This HQ also plays a key role in the evaluation of Business Group leaders, division managers and project leaders. The key performance criteria is the extent to which their achieved goals correspond to the visions, not their individual P&L results.

The overall responsible for Canon's FLCD project provides another example: As the financial outcome of this specific project was very negative, most Western organizations would probably have fired Takahashi-san, or 'punished' him with a lateral move. At Canon, he was promoted to CTO after completion of this project. Why? Because of the holistic results. Although the FLCD-project investments may never be recovered through pure sales of FLC displays, the unique production technologies and skills that were acquired and created throughout the project have already been shared freely across the company. As a consequence, Canon is today the worldwide leader in TFT display manufacturing equipment, i.e., of a product that is a direct competitor of

FLCD, which illustrates another important principle as well.

The Courage to Perform Creative Destruction

Developing an entirely new product that outcompetes other products offered by the same company is a difficult task that usually meets a lot of internal resistance, especially if the holistic performance measurement is lacking. A surprisingly high number of interviewees in Western companies complain about the absence of managerial courage to take risks and to try new things:

> We need more entrepreneurial bosses who dare to take risks and expand the horizon. (Senior Project manager in a Western IT company)

Both Sony's MD and Canon's TFT provide examples of product developments that not only compete with other internal products, but actually make entire product families obsolete. The audio cassette and the DAT are no longer necessary if you have the MD. A company is unlikely to buy both TFT and FLC display manufacturing equipment, but will rather make the choice between the two.

This kind of Schumpeterian creative destruction needs to be fully accepted and promoted within companies that want to accomplish breakthrough innovation. Schumpeter (1951) also argued that such creative destruction causes a 'dynamic disequilibrium', which promotes creativity for further innovation.

Only those entrepreneurs who have the courage to lose sight of the shore will catch the waves of dynamic disequilibrium and discover new oceans.

Multi-competency and Meta-knowledge for Accelerated Cross-functional Learning

As the primacy of the whole suggests that learning through relationships is more important than internal specialization, engineers should also have a broader systemic competence profile that facilitates cross-functional learning within and across corporate borders.

This author has noticed how excessive employee specialization and corporate fragmentation prevents both cross-functional learning and technology transfer from taking place in a large number of Western companies. The lack of knowledge of where to find the relevant knowledge and technologies is a frequent cause of long lead-times and expensive projects. A division manager of a European telecommunications company stated that:

> There is some good know-how around in our company, but very few people know where to get it. Our engineers only see their own limited parts without considering the whole.

The most important barrier to implementing multi-competency and meta knowledge is that a bilateral transfer from one function to another often is percieved as a punishment and clear sign of individual failure in many companies.

A senior manager of engineering in a large European company stated that:

> We had a problem with an engineer who was not bright enough. We gave him extensive training, but it didn't help. Instead of firing him we sent him to production where he could take care of some practical tasks.

The case-study companies show a different picture: Although Dr Kanbe joined Canon with a Ph.D in solid state physics, his two first job experiences at Canon were in production. He gained direct production experience first working on a calculator production line and then working on the inspection line in a camera production plant. When he finally arrived at his desired destination – the Research Centre – he had both respect and understanding for production. He still had the necessary scientific roots to spot the Applied Physics Letter that reported on the FLC technology, and to establish learning relationships between Canon and the two scientists behind the invention. While drawing on this learning, he had a lot of samples of the new FLC liquid formula prepared by engineers in the Central Research Laboratory, evaluated through techniques acquired in parallel from domestic universities. More important still, it was through his production experience and the close involvement of former colleagues in production that critical glass plate prototypes for FLC technology could be successfully prepared.

The Power of Alliances and Human Know-how Shuttles For Effective Technology Transfers

Many Western companies are still quite reluctant to rely on external sources of technology, as stated by the R&D manager of a large engineering-intensive company:

> We develop all our technologies ourselves. If we do this with external partners we cannot be sure to get full access to the results.

For those cases in which Western companies do create R&D alliances, a frequent weakness is that little or no transfer of R&D staff takes place between the allies. This isolation of know-how prevents a lot of potential learning from taking place. Again, the FLCD-case provides an impressive counter-example, as rotation of researchers was employed to secure an effective know-how transfer from the external labs to the Display Business Operations Centre. Japanese engineers were acting as human know-how shuttles between Japan and the different overseas R&D labs. By going there and taking part in the different overseas teams they could both align external research activities with the application-oriented needs of the display centre, as well as learning from the overseas expertise and bringing the results directly back to the team in Japan.

It is clear that Canon's vital transfer of both explicit and tacit knowledge from inventive concept ideas to innovative production processes could take place through the immigration of engineers from specialized and sometimes external units to a rather organic project team with a clear application focus. Then by transferring 90 per cent of this team directly to the manufacturing floor, Canon secured that all necessary competencies were effectively integrated into a production process instead of remaining isolated in upstream research labs. Such a transfer was possible because most of these internal researchers and engineers already had prior experience from personal connections within and respect for production. Through the frequent changes a sense of belonging towards the company as a whole, rather than to a specific function or location, had emerged. Hence, the transfer was not resented, but instead seen as a necessity to make innovation happen. This is why Canon succeed in commercializing a technology that was invented, but never produced in the West.

This approach to technology transfer strongly supports Allen's (1977, 43) statement that 'the best way to transfer technical information is to move a human carrier'. In an interview, Dr Kikuchi of Sony actually stated that 'the transfer of researchers is like breathing: both necessary and natural', and that those who do not have the necessary flexibility to move into manufacturing should stay in the universities.

The Primacy of Manufacturability and Customer Needs Also in R&D

One serious problem in many Western companies is the way in which people in R&D look at production. The following quote from an R&D section leader of a very large European company expresses an attitude that this author has encountered many times:

> One of our researchers was doing such a poor job that we actually transferred him to production.

The case-study companies' high degree of rotation and transfer of researchers and engineers is achieved not so much through individual motivation as through the corporate-wide implementation of a uniform rotational training program. The importance of adding value to the company is also made clear to all researchers, who understand this is best achieved by sharing their R&D achievements openly and by bringing them directly to the manufacturing floor – a place of true value creation that is known and respected by everybody. This respect is enhanced by the fact that most researchers and engineers either have come from R&D to production or knows that (s)he will end up in production at some point. Co-operation thus comes naturally to both functions.

The perhaps most well-known weakness in many companies is the lacking market-orientation of R&D. Here is an example from a European company, where the section leader from marketing wanted information about what his colleagues in R&D were doing. As he met with the head of new product offerings, he also tried to bring some market-feedback to his attention, but was faced with a total lack of interest:

> We don't need those market-observations! Our new product will have the best technology in the world. You'll just have to wait and see. In one year when it is ready you will understand . . . We'll just have to convince the customers that this is exactly what they need.

It turned out that this R&D section had developed a technology that was already available on the market. Nevertheless, the project went on and took a lot of resources away from important product development projects which all suffered from massive delays. As the new technology finally was ready, no business unit wanted it.

Such a technology-orientation is less common within the case-study companies. As hardly any researchers or engineers are allowed into a lab before they have completed an initial sales training – in addition to the production training – their research activities will be far more attuned to market needs than those of a researcher who did not want – or was never given a chance – to discover these needs.

A stronger market-orientation of the internal R&D activities is also achieved through the application-driven research for D&M approach, which only sponsors R&D projects that correspond to what the market, or at least the SBU managers, really need.

Ultimately, the knowledge-creating T&I process is no longer limited to internal know-how but draws instead on know-who and global sources of invention that continually nurture corporate learning. This is why Canon, Sony and Toyota can focus on tangible applications with clear market needs so as to d(e)rive product innovation from technological invention.

As indicated in Chapter 1, several non-Japanese companies have already begun to adopt some of these principles as well. In order to accelerate this learning process, a list of managerial recommendations will be outlined as a reminder of the key points in Japanese T&I management. This list will be the terminus of this book.

PRACTICAL IMPLICATIONS FOR T&I MANAGEMENT

Although this study has only covered three Japanese companies in depth, their relative success in terms of commercialized innovations and of short development lead-time suggests that the following points can be convincingly made about the field of T&I management:

- Linkages to extracorporate sources of technology are not only vital to technological followers, but also of major importance to technological leaders. The stronger these linkages, the more a firm can focus its internal efforts on forceful innovation.

- An early and extensive involvement of strategic partners and suppliers in the T&I process will in most cases enhance and accelerate the collective results.

- No level of technological leadership authorizes a company to neglect the link to market needs. In contrast, this link should be given an increasing degree of attention, the more a company progresses towards technological leadership, which on its own does not guarantee market success.

- Internal development or external sourcing of technology is not only a make-or-buy decision, but also one that has important organizational implications. An organization certainly increases its knowledge-base through internal technology development, but may, *ipso facto,* cause organizational barriers that impede the incorporation of the technology into a product. Only if these barriers are circumvented will internal technology development efforts result in innovation.

- An invention will only bring revenues if it can be manufactured at an affordable price. Most R&D functions would, therefore, profit from an early interlinkage with production. The contribution of both researchers and development engineers will in many cases increase radically if they follow their inventions to production.

- The more time a researcher spends on scientific technology-development activities, the more reluctant (s)he may become to be transferred to production. In contrast, the more multi-functional the background of a researcher, the smoother his communication with and transfer to production.

- A lack of scientific expertise in a multi-skilled researcher can be compensated for through linkages to extracorporate sources of science and technology, especially if these linkages focus on learning and understanding, rather than on mere transfer of technology. In contrast, the lack of cross-functional experience and strong intraorganizational relationships is difficult and very time-consuming to compensate for.

- By giving all researchers and engineers a chance to start a project as long as they can find business groups to sponsor them, the degree of entrepreneurship and new product generation will increase.

- The richer the sales and marketing experience of these researchers and engineers, the more likely they are to come up with inventions that respond to market needs.

- By letting R&D personnel volunteer for the different project activities that take place in a company, their personal motivation, creativity and productivity will increase.

- Even though knowledge is the most valuable corporate asset it should not be managed as a monetary resource. In contrast, the more it is used, shared and cross-fertilized, the more it will grow and enrich the company as a whole.

• The open sharing of resources (like Sony's open recruiting system) may cause problems in individual (raided) projects, but it will bring tremendous benefits to the company as a whole in terms of diffusion of technologies and skills.

• Unless R&D managers and CTOs are integrated at the top management level, corporate R&D strategy-formulation is unlikely to consider the overall corporate strategy, and *vice versa*.

• The presentation of prototypes to top management provides an interlinking mechanism to align R&D efforts and corporate strategy and to ensure that resources flow to the most relevant R&D projects.

• As the size of a team is less important than its number and quality of cooperative linkages within and beyond the corporate borders, the T&I impact of the project leader and his/her assistants is mainly defined by their ability to develop and coordinate these linkages.

As once stated by Albert Einstein: 'the significant problems we face cannot be solved with the same level of thinking we were at when we created them'. This is why it not only makes sense, but is an absolute necessity to reach out across the globe for additional knowledge and expertise. Accordingly, the high-performers in the technology and innovation race are those who shift their focus from individual know-how to global know-who.

NOTES

1. The only exception being Nonaka's (1994, 32-5) definition of the hypertext organization.
2. See, for examples of sharing and shifting authority, the three T&I projects described at Canon, Sony and Toyota.
3. Toyota's first chief engineer, Hasegawa, who managed the initial Corolla project, was an ex-aircraft engineer (Hane; Tsurusawa, interviews; cf. Fujimoto 1994a, 16).

References

Abegglen, J. and Stalk, G. (1985) *Kaisha: the Japanese Corporation*, Tokyo, Tuttle Company.

Ackenhusen, M. and Ghoshal, S. (1992) 'Canon: Competing on Capabilities', INSEAD Case Study 05/92-223.

Ackoff, R. (1981) *Creating the Corporate Future*, New York, Wiley and Sons.

Adler, N. (1991) *International Dimensions of Organizational Behaviour*, 2nd edition, Boston: PWS-Kent Publishing Company.

Adler, P., Riggs, H. and Wheelwright, S. (1989) 'Product Development Know-How: Trading Tactics for Strategy', *Sloan Management Review*, Fall 1989, pp.7-17.

Adler, P., McDonald, D. and MacDonald, F. (1992) 'Strategic Management of Technical Functions', *Sloan Management Review*, Winter 1992, pp.19-35.

Allen, T. (1970) 'Communication Networks in R&D laboratories', *R&D Management*, No. 1, pp.14-21.

Allen, T. (1977) *Managing the Flow of Technology*, Cambridge, MA: MIT Press.

Anchordoguy, M. (1990) 'A Brief History of Japan's Keiretsu', *Harvard Business Review*, July-August 1990, pp.58-9.

Aoki, M. (1988) *Information, Incentives, and Bargaining in the Japanese Economy*, New York, Cambridge University Press.

Arthur, C. (1993) 'Small is Powerful', *New Scientist* (special issue on Japan), 2 October, pp.44-7.

Badaracco, J. (1991) *The Knowledge Link: How Firms Compete Through Strategic Alliances*, Boston, MA, Harvard Business School Press.

Ballon, R. (1992) *Foreign competition in Japan: human resource strategies*, London, Routledge.

Bartlett, C. and Ghoshal, S. (1989) *Managing Across Borders: The Transnational Solution*, US, Harvard Business School Press.

Beer, S. (1985) *Diagnosing the System for Organizations*, Oxford: University Press (John Wiley and Sons).

Betz, F. (1987) *Managing Technology: Competing through new Ventures, Innovation, and Corporate Research*, New Jersey, Prentice-Hall.

Bleeke, J. and Ernst, D. (1993) *Collaborating to Compete: Using Strategic Alliances and Acquisitions in the Global Marketplace*, US, John Wiley and Sons.

Bonora, E. and Revang, Ø. (1993) 'A Framework for Analysing the Storage and Protection of Knowledge in Organizations', in: Lorange, P. (ed.) *Implementing Strategic Proceses: Change, Learning – a co-operation*, Oxford, Blackwell, pp.190-213.

Brauchlin, E. (1988) 'Technology Initiatives and Corporate Policy', Discussion to Session 2 of the 5th St. Galler Forschungsgespräche on Technology and Public Policy, August 27-29, 1987, in: *Aussenwirtschaft*, 43 Jahrgang – Heft I/II – Juni 1988, pp.201-5.

Brauchlin, E. and Wehrli, H. (1991) *Strategisches Management: Lehrbuch mit Fallstudien*, München, Oldenbourg Verlag GmbH.

Brockhoff, K. (1990) *Management von Forschung, Entwicklung und Innovation*, Stuttgart, Metzlersche Verlagsbuchhandlung und Carl Ernst Poeschel Verlag GmbH.

Buckley, P. and Casson, M. (1988) 'The Theory of co-operation in International Business', in: Contractor, F. and Lorange, P. (eds.) *co-operative Strategies in International Business*, Massachusetts, Lexington Books, pp.31-53.

Burns T. and Stalker, G. (1961) *The Management of Innovation*, London, Tavistock.

Burrell, G. and Morgan, G. (1979) *Sociological Paradigms and Organizational Analysis*, London, Heinemann.

Canon (1987) *The Canon Handbook*, Corporate Communications Centre, Canon Incorporated, Nakamura Seiko Printing Co. Ltd., Tokyo.

Canon (1991) Press Release on the Development of the Ferroelectric Liquid Crystal Display, October.

Canon (1992) *Canon Fact Book 1992/93*, Corporate Communications Centre, Canon Incorporated.

Canon Chronicle (1993), No. 172, 173.

Charan, R. (1991) 'How Networks Reshape Organizations - For Results', *Harvard Business Review*, September-October, pp.104-5.

Clark, K. and Fujimoto, T. (1988) 'The European Model of Product Development: Challenges and Opportunity', unpublished paper presented at the International Motor Vehicle Program, Harvard University, Graduate School of Business Administration.

Clark, K. and Fujimoto, T. (1989) 'Reducing the Time to Market: the Case of the World Auto Industry', *Design Management Journal*, 1 (1), 1989, pp 49-57.

Clark, K. and Fujimoto, T. (1990) 'The Power of Product Integrity', *Harvard Business Review*, November-December, pp.107-18.

Clark, K. and Fujimoto, T. (1991) *Product Development Performance: Strategy, Organization and Management in the World Auto Industry*, US, Harvard Business School Press.

Clark, K. and Fujimoto, T. (1992) 'Product Development and Competitiveness', *Journal of the Japanese and International Economies*, No. 6, pp.101-43.

Collinson, S. (1993) 'Managing Product Innovations at Sony: The Development of the Data Discman', *Technology Analysis and Strategic Management*, vol. 5, no. 3, pp.285-306.

Contractor, F. and Lorange, P. (1988) 'Why should Firms co-operate?: The Strategy and Economics Basis for co-operative Ventures', in: Contractor, F. and Lorange, P. (eds.) *co-operative Strategies in International Business*, Massachusetts, Lexington Books, pp.3-28.

Cooper, R. and Kleinschmidt, E. (1991) 'New Products: What Separates Winners from Losers?', in: Henry, J. and Walker, D. (eds.), *Managing Innovation*, London, Sage Publications Ltd., pp.127-40.

Cusumano, M. (1989) *The Japanese Automobile Industry: Technology and Management at Nissan and Toyota*, Cambridge, US, Harvard University Press.

Cutts, R. (1992) 'Capitalism in Japan: Cartels and Keiretsu', *Harvard Business Review*, July-August, pp.48-55.

De Meyer, A. (1991) 'Tech Talk: How Managers are Stimulating Global R&D Communication', *Sloan Management Review*, Spring 1991, pp.49-58.

De Meyer, A. (1992) 'Management of International R&D Operations', in: *Technology Management and International Business*, Granstrand, Håkanson and Sjölander, S. (eds.) UK, John Wiley and Sons, pp.163-79.

De Woot, P. (1990) *High Technology Europe: Strategic Issues for Global Competitiveness*, Oxford, Basil Blackwell.

Deschamps, J. and Nayak, P. (1992) 'Competing Through Products: Lessons from the Winners', *The Columbia Journal of World Business*, Summer, pp.38-54.

Deschamps, J.-P. and Nayak, P. R. (1995) *Product Juggernauts*, Harvard Business School Press

Dodwell Marketing Consultants (1990) *Industrial Groupings in Japan: the anatomy of the keiretsu*, 9th ed., Tokyo, Dodwell Marketing Consultants.

Dodwell Marketing Consultants (1992/93) *Industrial Groupings in Japan: the anatomy of the keiretsu*, 10th ed., Tokyo, Dodwell Marketing Consultants.

Dore, R. (1983) *A Case Study of Technology Forecasting in Japan*, London, The Technical Change Centre.

Doz, Y. and Prahalad, C. (1989) 'Collaborate with your Competitor – and Win', *Harvard Business Review*, January-February, pp.113-139.

Drucker, P. (1985) *Innovation and Entrepreneurship: Practice and Principles*, US, Harper and Row, Publishers.

Drucker, P. (1991) 'The Discipline of Innovation', in: Henry, J. and Walker, D. (eds.), *Managing Innovation*, London, Sage Publications Ltd., pp.9-17.

Ealey, L. and Soderberg, L. (1990) 'How Honda Cures Design Amnesia', *The McKinsey Quarterly*, Spring, pp 3-14.

Easton, G. (1992) 'Industrial Networks: a Review', in Axelsson and Easton, in: *Industrial Networks. A New View of Reality*, London, Routledge, pp.3-27.

Eisenhardt, K. (1989) 'Building Theories from Case Study Research', *The Academy of Management Review*, vol. 14, no. 4, October, pp.532-50.

Erickson, T., Magee, J., Roussel, P. and Saad, K. (1990) 'Managing Technology as a Business Strategy', *Sloan Management Review*, Spring, pp.73-9.

Evan, W. and Olk, P. (1990) 'R&D Consortia: A New US Organizational Form, *Sloan Management Review*, Spring, pp.37-45.

Ferguson, C., H. (1990) 'Computers Keiretsu and the Coming of the US', *Harvard Business Review*, July-August, pp.55-70.

Florida, R. and Kenney, M. (1991) 'Transplanted Organizations: The Transfer of Japanese Industrial Organizations to the US', *American Sociological Review*, Vol. 56,, pp.381-98.

Ford, D., Håkansson, H. and Johanson, J. (1986) 'How do Companies Interact?', *Industrial Marketing and Purchasing*, No. 1, pp.26-41.

Frankel, J. (1991) 'The Japanese Cost of Finance: a Survey', *Financial Management*, Spring, pp.95-127.

Fransman, M. (1990) *The Market and Beyond: co-operation and Competition in Information Technology Development in the Japanese System*, US, Cambridge University Press.

Freeman, C. (1982) *The Economics of Industrial Innovation*, London, Frances Printer.

Freudenberg, T. (1988) *Aufbau und Management internationaler Forschungs- und Entwicklungssysteme*, Ph.D thesis, Hochschule St. Gallen.

Friedland, J. (1994) 'Un-Japanese Risk Taking Pays Off: Cover Story on Canon', *Far Eastern Economic Review*, February 24, pp.72-8.

Fruin, M. (1991) 'Good Fences Make Good Neighbors: in Product Development as in most everything else, in Japan as most everywhere else', unpublished workshop paper presented at the Euro-Asia Centre, INSEAD, 27-29 June.

Fruin, M. (1992) *The Japanese Enterprise System*, Oxford, Oxford University Press.

Fujigane, Y. (1991) 'Financial Keiretsu Strengthen Solidarity', *Tokyo Business Today*, February, pp.26-30.

Fujikura, K. (1992) 'Changing Values and the Legal Culture in Japan', in: *Japanstudien: Jahrbuch des Deutschen Institutes*, München, Iudicum Verlag, pp.209-18.

Fujimoto, T. (1989) *Organizations For Effective Product Development: The Case of the Global Automobile Industry*, unpublished DBA Diss., Harvard Business School.

Fujimoto, T. (1991) 'Product Integrity and the Role of Designer as Integrator', *Design Management Journal*, Spring, pp.29-34.

Fujimoto, T. (1993) 'Comparing Performance and Organization of Product Development across Firms, Regions and Industries: The Applicability of the Automobile Case', Discussion Paper 93-F-3, Faculty of Economics, University of Tokyo.

Fujimoto, T. (1994a) 'The Dynamic Aspect of Product Development Capabilities: An International Comparison in the Automobile Industry', Discussion Paper 94-F-29, Faculty of Economics, University of Tokyo.

Fujimoto, T. (1994b) 'The Origin and Evolution of the 'Black Box Parts' Practice in the Japanese Auto Industry', Discussion Paper 94-F-1, Faculty of Economics, University of Tokyo.

Fujimoto, T., Iansiti, M. and Clark, K. (1991) *External Integration in Product Development*, Discussion Paper, Faculty of Economics, University of Tokyo.

Gerlach, M. (1992a) *The Keiretsu: A Primer*, The Japan Society, New York.

Gerlach, M. (1992b) 'Twilight of the Keiretsu? A Critical Assessment', *Journal of Japanese Studies*, Vol. 18, No. 1, pp.79-118.

Gerlach, M. (1992c) *Alliance Capitalism: The Social Organization of Japanese Business*, Berkeley, University of California Press.

Gerybadze, A. (1993) 'Management technologischer Verbundprojekte. Vergleich von Strategien und Organizationsmodellen – Deutschland, EG, Japan', in: Zahn, E. (HRSG.) *Technologie-Management und Technologien für das Management*, Schäffer-Poeschel, pp.133-51.

Gerybadze, A. (1994) 'Technology Forecasting as a Process of Organizational Intelligence', *R&D Management*, Vol. 24, No. 2, pp.131-40.

Giersch, H. (1992) 'Japan's Schwächen', *Wirtschafts Woche*, No. 19, pp. 56-8.

Glaser, B. and Strauss, A. (1967) *The Discovery of Grounded Theory: Strategies for Qualitative Research*, Chicago, Aldine, ch. 1-2.

Goto, A. (1982) 'Business Groups in a Market Economy', *European Economic Review*, No. 19, pp.53-70.

Goto, A. (1992) 'Search For Success: Corporate Society R&D', *Look Japan*, May, pp.18-19.

Gregory, G. (1985a) *Japanese Electronics Technology: Enterprise and Innovation*, Tokyo, The Japan Times Ltd.

Gregory, G. (1985b) 'The Logic of Japanese Enterprise', Sophia University, Institute of Comparative Culture, Business Series No. 92.

Gregory, G. (1988) *The Canon Production System: Getting the Bottom Line Right*, Sophia University, Institute of Comparative Culture, Business Series No. 119.

Hagedoorn, J. and Schakenraad, J. (1990) 'Inter-firm Partnerships and Co-operative Strategies in Core Technologies', in: Freeman, C. and Soete, L. (eds.) *New Explorations in the Economics of Technical Change*, London, Pinter Publishers, pp.3-37.

Hagedoorn, J. and Schakenraad, J. (1994) 'The Effects of Strategic Technology Alliances on Corporate Performance', *Strategic Management Journal*, Vol. 15, No. 4, pp. 291-310.

Håkansson, H. ed. (1987) *Industrial Technological Development: a Network Approach*, Beckenham, UK, Croom Helm Ltd.

Håkansson, H. (1989) *Corporate Technological Behaviour: Co-operation and Networks*, London, Routledge.

Håkansson, H. (1990) 'Technological Collaboration in Industrial Networks', *European Management Journal*, Vol. 8, No. 3, September, pp.371-79.

Håkansson, H. (1992) 'Evolution Processes in Industrial Networks', in: Axelsson, B. and Easton, G. (eds) (1992) *Industrial Networks. A New View of Reality*, London, Routledge, pp.129-43.

Håkansson, H. and Henders, B. (1992) 'International Co-operative Relationships in Technological Development', in Forsgren, M. and Johanson, J. (eds) *Managing Networks in International Business*, Philadelphia, Gordon & Breach, pp.32-46.

Håkansson H. and Snehota, I. (1989) 'No Business is an Island: The Network Concept of Business Strategy', *Scandinavian Journal of Management*, Vol. 5, No. 3, pp.187-200.

Hamel, G. (1991) 'Competition for Competence and Inter-Partner Learning within International Strategic Alliances', *Strategic Management Journal*, Vol. 12, pp. 83-103.

Hamel, G. and Prahalad, C.K. (1994) *Competing for the Future*, Boston, Harvard Business School Press.

Hammer, M. and Champy, J. (1993) *Reengineering the Corporation: a manifesto for business revolution*, New York, HarperCollins Publishers.

Harryson, S. (1992) *Japanese R&D Management: Innovation through Intracorporate Communication and Intercorporate co-operation*, unpublished Literature Digest prepared for Professors E. Brauchlin and H. Schütte respectively at Hochschule St. Gallen and INSEAD.

Harryson, S. (1994) *Japanese Corporate Networks and R&D*, unpublished course material for: International Business and Multinational Enterprises; and International Marketing and Management in East Asia, at the School of Economics and Management, Lund University.

Harryson, S. (1995a) *Japanese R&D Management: A Holistic Network Approach*, Ph.D thesis submitted at the University of St. Gallen in Switzerland, Research Institute of International Management.

Harryson, S. (1995b) 'The Japanese Approach to Innovation – Research for D&M', *PRISM*, First Quarter.

Harryson, S. (1996) 'Improving R&D Performance through Networking – Lessons from Canon and Sony, *PRISM*, Fourth Quarter.

Harryson, S. (1997) 'From Experience: How Canon and Sony Drive Product Innovation Through Networking and Application-Focused R&D', *Journal of Product Innovation Management*, July Vol. 14, No. 4.

Hatvany, N. and Pucik, V. (1982) 'Japanese Management: Practices and Productivity', in: Tushman, M. and Moore, W. (eds) *Readings in the Management of Innovation*, London, Pitman Books Ltd., pp. 520-34.

Hayes, R. and Schmenner, R. (1982) 'How should you Organize Manufacturing?', in: Tushman, M. and Moore, W. (eds) *Readings in the Management of Innovation*, London, Pitman Books Ltd., pp.448-63.

Hedlund, G. (1986) 'The Hypermodern MNC – A Heterarchy?', *Human Resource Management*, Spring, Vol. 25, No. 1, pp. 9-35.

Hedlund, G. and Nonaka, I. (1991) *Models of Knowledge Management in the West and Japan*, Research Paper: RP 91/9, Stockholm School of Economics.

Hollomon, H. (1982) 'Government and the Innovation Process', in: Tushman, M. and Moore, W. (eds) *Readings in the Management of Innovation*, London, Pitman Books Ltd., pp. 612-25.

Howard, R. (1990) 'Can Small Business Help Countries Compete?', *Harvard Business Review*, November-December, pp.88-103.

Imai, M. (1986) *Kaizen: the Key to Japan's Competitive Success*, Singapore, McGraw-Hill Book Co.

Imai, K. (1989a) 'Evolution of Japan's Corporate and Industrial Networks', in: Carlsson, B. (ed.) *Industrial Dynamics. Technological, Organizational and Structural Changes in Industries and Firms*, Boston, Kluwer Academic Publishers, pp.123-55.

Imai, K. (1989b) *The Japanese Pattern of Innovation and its Evolution*, Tokyo, Hitotsubashi University, Institute of Business Research, Discussion Paper No. 136.

Imai, K. (1990) 'The Legitimacy of Japan's Corporate Groups', *Economic Eye*, Autumn, pp.16-20.

Imai, K. and Baba, Y. (1991) 'Systemic Innovation and Cross-Border Networks: Transcending markets and hierarchies to create a new techno-economic system', in: OECD (ed.) *Technology and Productivity*, Paris, pp. 389-406.

Imai, K., Nonaka, I. and Takeuchi, H. (1985) 'Managing the New Product Development Process: How Japanese Companies Learn and Unlearn', in: Clark, K., Hayes, R. and

Lorenz, C. (eds) (1985) *The Uneasy Alliance: Managing the Productivity-Technology Dilemma*, Boston, Harvard Business School Press, pp.533-61.

Irimajiri, S. (1992) 'Highlighting the Contrasts in Japanese and American Business', *Economic Eye*, Autumn, Vol. 13, No. 3, pp.22-5.

Itami, H. (1987) *Mobilizing Invisible Assets*, Cambridge, MA, Harvard University Press.

IVA (1993) *Profit From Innovation: a Comparison of Swedish and Japanese Intellectual Property Management*, published by the Royal Swedish Academy of Engineering Sciences in Stockholm.

Jansson, H., Saquib, M. and Sharma, D. (1990) 'A Methodology for the Study of Trans-Organizational Networks', Lund University Working Paper Series.

Japan Almanac (1993), Tokyo, Asahi Shimbun Publishing Company.

Japan's Fair Trade Commission (1992) *The Outline of the Report on the Actual Conditions of the Six Major Corporate Groups*, Executive Office, February.

Japan Foreign Trade Council (1992) *The Sogo Shosha*, Japan Foreign Trade Council, Japan.

Japan-US Business Council (1992) *Japanese Keiretsu*, Japanese Staff Members, Tokyo, January.

Johnson, C. (1990) 'Keiretsu: an outsider's view', *International Economic Insights*, Vol. 1, pp.15-17.

Johnstone, B. (1994) 'Canon, Lone Wolf', *Wired*, October, pp. 97-9 + 147-9.

Jones, D. (1990) 'Beyond the Toyota Production System: The Era of Lean Production', Paper for the 5th International Operations Management Association Conference on Manufacturing Strategy Warwick, 26-27 June.

Karlsson, C. (1989) 'High Rates of Innovation: The Japanese Culture Shock to Europe', *European Management Journal,* Vol. 7, No 1, pp. 31-9.

Kennard, R. (1991) 'From Experience: Japanese Product Development Process', *Journal of Product Innovation Management*, Vol. 8, pp 184-8.

Kenney, M. and Florida, R. (1993) *Beyond Mass Production: The Japanese System and its Transfer to the US*, New York, Oxford University Press.

Kenward, M. (1992) 'Bottom of the League', *International Management*, September, pp. 66-9.

Kester, C. (1991) *Japanese Takeovers: the global contest for corporate control*, Boston, Harvard Business School Press.

Kikuchi, M. (1983) *Japanese Electronics*, Tokyo, The Simul Press.

Kindel, S. (1994) 'Sweet Chariots', *Financial World*, 18 January.

Kline, J., Edge, G. and Kass, T. (1991) 'Skill-Based Competition', *Journal of General Management*, Vol. 16, No. 4, pp.1-15.

Kline, S. and Rosenberg, N. (1986) 'An Overview of Innovation', in: Landau, R. and Rosenberg, N. (eds): *The Positive Sum Strategy: Harnessing Technology for Economic Growth*, Washington DC, National Academy Press, pp. 275-305.

Kobayashi, H. (1990) 'Organization Development Efforts by "Self-Confirming" Task Groups: A Japanese Case', in: Massarik, F. (ed.) *Advances in Organization Development*, US, Ablex Publishing Corporation.

Kodama, F. (1986) *Technological Diversification of Japanese Industry, Science*, Vol. 233, July, pp. 291-6.

Kodama, F. (1991) *Analyzing Japanese High Technologies: The Techno Paradigm Shift*, London, Printer Publishers.

Kodama, F. (1992a) 'Technology Fusion and the New R&D', *Harvard Business Review*, July-August, pp.70-78.

Kodama, F. (1992b) 'Keiretsu Transfers Technology Efficiently', *The Nikkei Weekly*, 25 April.

Kojima, K. (1992) 'The Long-Term Relationship in the Japanese Distribution System', *Kobe*

Economic and Business Review, 37th Annual Report, Research Institute for Economics and Business Administration, Kobe University, pp. 55-9.

Krackhardt, D. and Hanson, J. (1993) 'Informal Networks: The Company Behind the Chart', *Harvard Business Review,* July-August, pp.104-11.

Kusunoki, T. (1992) 'The Dilemma of Technological Leadership: a Conceptual Framework', *Hitotsubashi Journal of Commerce and Management,* Vol. 27, No. 1, November, pp. 63-79.

Kusunoki, K. and Numagami, T. (1993) 'Intra-firm Transfer of Engineers in Japan', Unpublished Research Paper, Hitotsubashi University.

Laage-Hellman, J. (1989) *Technological Development in Industrial Networks,* Doctoral Dissertation, Uppsala University, Reprocentralen.

Laage-Hellman, J. (1993) 'organizerande av FoU-baserad företagsutveckling', in: Håkansson, H., Laage-Hellman, J., Lundgren, A. and Waluszewski, A. (eds) *Teknikutveckling i Företaget: Ett Nätverkperspektiv,* Lund, Studentlitteratur, pp. 301-43.

Laage-Hellman, J. (1997) *Business Networks in Japan: Supplier-customer interaction in product development,* London, Routledge.

Laage-Hellman, J. and Nonaka, I. (1994) *Supplier-Customer Interaction in Product Development: a Network Study of two Japanese Material Innovations,* Dpt. of Business Studies, Uppsala University and Institute of Business Research, Hitotsubashi University.

Lamming, R. (1993) *Beyond Partnership: Strategies for Innovation and Lean Supply,* UK, Prentice Hall International Ltd.

Larsson, R. (1990) *Coordination of Action in Mergers and Acquisitions,* DBA Diss., Sweden, Lund University Press.

Lawrence, R. (1991) 'Efficient or Exclusionist? The Import Behaviour of Japanese Corporate Groups', Brookings Papers on Economic Activity, 1, pp. 311-41.

Lee, T., Fischer, J. and Yau, T. (1986) 'Is Your R&D on Track?', *Harvard Business Review,* January-February 1986, pp 34-44.

Leonard-Barton, D. (1992) 'Core Capabilities and Core Rigidities: A Paradox in Managing New Product Development', *Strategic Management Journal,* Vol. 13, pp.111-25.

Leontiades, M. (1991) 'The Japanese Art of Managing Diversity', *The Journal of Buiness Strategy,* March/April, pp. 31-6).

Lewis, J. (1990) *Partnership for Profit: Structuring and Managing Strategic Alliances,* New York, The Free Press.

Lieberman Research East (1992) 'MiniDisc Concept Test among Music Buyers', unpublished study by Lieberman Research East, New York, prepared for Sony Software Corporation in May.

Lincoln, E. (1992) 'Japan's Keiretsu System: a prepared statement', in 'Hearing before the Committee on Finance, 16 October, 1991, United States Senate', printed for the use of the Committee on Finance, Washington, US Government Printing Office.

Lindsay, B. (1994) 'Stamping the Neon', *Automotive Industries,* August.

Lu, D. (1987) *Inside Corporate Japan: The Art of Fumble-free Management,* Tokyo, Charles E. Tuttle Company, pp. 27-54.

Makino, N. (1992) 'The Advantages of Japan's Management Strategy', *Economic Eye,* Autumn, Vol. 13, No. 3, pp.18-21.

Malnight, T. and Yoshino, M. (1990) 'Sony Corporation: Globalization', Harvard Business School Case Study no. 9-391-071, Rev. 2/14/91.

Mansfield, E. (1968) *Industrial Research and Technological Innovation: An Econometric Analysis,* New York, W.W. Norton and Company.

Mansfield, E. (1971) *The Economics of Technological Change,* New York, W.W. Norton and Company.

Mansfield, E. (1988) 'The Speed and Cost of Industrial Innovation in Japan and the United

States: External vs. Internal Technology', *Management Science,* Vol. 34, No. 10, October, pp.1157-68.

Mansfield, E., Rapoport, J., Romeo, A., Villani, E., Wagner, S. and Husic, F. (1977) *The Production and Application of New Industrial Technology,* New York, W.W. Norton and Company.

MAP (1991) *Keiretsu, US: a tale of Japanese power,* unpublished study by the Mid-America Project.

McKelvey, M. (1993) 'Japanese Institutions Supporting Innovation', in: Sjöstrand, S. (ed.) *Institutional Change: Theory and Empirical Findings,* New York, M.E. Sharpe Inc, pp.199-225.

Meyer, M. and Utterback, J. (1993) 'The Product Family and the Dynamics of Core Capability', *Sloan Management Review,* Spring, pp. 29-47.

MITI (1992a), Research Institute of International Trade and Industry, Discussion Paper # 92-DOJ-38, pp. 44-6.

MITI (1992b), Research Institute of International Trade and Industry, Discussion Paper # 92-DOJ-39.

Mitsubishi Research Institute (1987) 'The Relationship between Japanese Auto and Auto Parts Makers', Paper written for the Japanese Automobile Manufacturers Association, Tokyo.

Miyazaki, K. (1994) 'Competence Building in Japanese and European Firms: the Case of Opto-Electronics', in Schütte, H. (ed.) *The Global Competitiveness of the Asian Firm,* New York, St. Martin's Press, pp. 289-303.

Morita, A. (1988) *Made in Japan,* London, Fontana.

Murakami, T. and Nishiwaki, T. (1991) *Strategy for Creation,* England, Woodhead Publishing Ltd.

Nakamura, H. (1987) 'Japan's Venture Business: its Problems and Prospects', *Géstion 2000,* No. 4, pp.19-31.

Nakatani, I. (1984) 'The Economic Role of Financial Corporate Groupings', in: Aoki (ed.) *The Economic Analysis of the Japanese Firm,* Holland, Elsevier Science Publishers.

Nakatani, I. (1990) 'Effectiveness in Technological Innovation: Keiretsu Versus Conglomerates', in: Heiduk, G. and Yamamura, K. (eds): *Technological Competition and Interdependence,* US, University of Washington Press, pp. 151-62.

Nakatani, I. (1992) 'Offering a Challenge to the Theory of Capitalism', *Economic Eye,* Autumn, Vol. 13, No. 3 pp. 26-7.

Nester, W. (1990) *The Foundation of Japanese Power: Continuities, Changes, Challenges,* London, The Macmillan Press, pp. 290-93.

Nevens, M., Summe, G. and Uttal, B. (1990) 'Commercializing Technology: What the Best Companies Do', *The McKinsey Quarterly,* No. 4, pp. 3-22.

Nichiguchi, T. (1994) *Strategic Industrial Sourcing,* Oxford University Press.

Niederkofler, M. (1989) *External Corporate Venturing: Strategic Partnerships for Competitive Advantage,* St. Gallen, Forschungsstelle Für Internationales Management.

Nonaka, I. (1988a) 'Toward Middle-Up-Down Management: Accelerating Information Creation', *Sloan Management Review,* pp. 9-18.

Nonaka, I. (1988b) 'Creating Organizational Order Out Of Chaos: Self Renewal in Japanese Firms', *California Management Review,* No. 3, pp. 57-3.

Nonaka, I. (1990) 'Redundant, Overlapping Organization: A Japanese Approach to Managing the Innovation Process', *California Management Review,* Spring, pp. 27-38.

Nonaka, I. (1991) 'The Knowledge-Creating Company', *Harvard Business Review,* November-December, pp. 96-104.

Nonaka, I. (1993) 'A Dynamic Theory of Organizational Knowledge Creation', Paper prepared for the International Workshop on 'Interdisciplinary Approaches to Innovation

Based on the Creation, Diffusion and Exploitation of Organizational Knowledge', organized by NISTEP, March.

Nonaka, I. (1994) 'A Dynamic Theory of Organizational Knowledge Creation', *Organization Science*, Vol. 5, No. 1, February, pp.14-37. (Quite different from the 1993 version)

Nonaka, I. and Kenney, M. (1991) 'Towards a New Theory of Innovation Management: A Case Study Comparing Canon and Apple Computer', *Journal of Engineering and Technology Management*, No. 8, pp. 67-83.

Nonaka, I. and Yamanouchi, T. (1989) 'Managing Innovation as a Self-Renewing Process', *Journal of Business Venturing*, No. 4, pp. 299-315.

Ohbora, T., Parsons, A. and Riesenbeck, H. (1992) 'Alternate Routes to Global Marketing', *The McKinsey Quarterly*, No. 3, pp. 52-74.

Ohmae, K. (1985) *Triad Power: The Coming Shape of Global Competition*, New York, The Free Press.

Okumura, H. (1991) 'Enterprise Groups in Japan', JCR Financial Digest, April, Tokyo, article translated and published by Japan Credit Rating Agency, Ltd.

Orru, M. (1993) 'Institutional co-operation in Japanese and German Capitalism', in: Sjöstrand, S. (ed.) *Institutional Change: Theory and Empirical Findings*, New York, M.E. Sharpe, Inc, pp.171-98.

Parsons, A. (1991) 'Building Innovativeness in Large US Corporations', *The Journal of Services Marketing*, Vol. 8, No. 1, Winter, pp. 5-20.

Pearson, A. (1991) 'Managing Innovation: an Uncertainty Reduction Process', in: Henry, J. and Walker, D. (eds), *Managing Innovation*, London, Sage Publications Ltd., pp.18-27.

Peck, M. (1990) 'The Benefits and Burdens of the Technological Leaders', in: Heiduk, G. and Yamamura, K. (eds) *Technological Competition and Interdependence: the Search for Policy in the United States, West Germany and Japan*, US, University of Washington Press, pp. 235-48.

Peck, M. and Goto, A. (1982) 'Technology and Economic Growth: The Case of Japan', in: Tushman, M. and Moore, W. (eds) *Readings in the Management of Innovation*, London, Pitman Books Ltd., pp. 626-41.

Perrow, C. (1993) 'Small Firm Networks', in: Sjöstrand, S. (ed.) *Institutional Change: Theory and Empirical Findings*, New York, M.E. Sharpe, Inc, pp.111-38.

Peters, T. (1991) 'Thriving on Chaos: Facing up to the Need for Revolution', in: Henry, J. and Walker, D. (eds), *Managing Innovation*, London, Sage Publications Ltd., pp. 306-12.

Pilditch, J. (1991) 'What Makes A Winning Company?', in: Henry, J., and Walker, D. (eds), *Managing Innovation*, London, Sage Publications Ltd., pp. 313-22.

Pisano, G. (1991) 'The Governance of Innovation: Vertical Intergration and Collaborative Arrangements in the Biotechnology Industry', *Research Policy* Vol. 20, June, pp. 237-249.

PLAN (1994) *Intelligence Economique et Stratégie des Entreprises*, Commisariat Général du Plan, La Documentation Française, Paris.

Polyani, M. (1948) *Personal Knowledge: Towards a Post-Critical Philosophy*, Chicago, University of Chicago Press.

Porter, M. (1990) 'The Competitive Advantage of Nations', *Harvard Business Review*, March-April, pp. 73-93.

Powell, B. (1991) 'All in the Family: Japan's keiretsu system . . . ', *Newsweek*, 3 June, pp. 38-40.

Prahalad, C. and Hamel, G. (1990) 'The Core Competence of the Corporation', *Harvard Busines Review*, May-June, pp.79-91.

Quinn, J. (1985) 'Managing Innovation: Controlled Chaos', *Harvard Business Review*, May-June, pp.73-84.

Quinn, J. (1992) *Intelligent Enterprise*, New York, The Free Press.

Quinn, J. and Mueller, J. (1982) 'Transferring Research Results to Operations', in: Tushman,

M. and Moore, W. (eds) *Readings in the Management of Innovation*, London, Pitman Books Ltd., pp. 60-83.

Radnor, M. (1991) 'Technology Acquisition Strategies and Processes: A Reconsideration of the "Make Versus Buy" Decision', *International Journal of Technology Management (ITN)*, 1991, pp. 113-35.

Rappa, M. and Debackere, K. (1989) *The Emergence of a New Technology: The Case of Neural Networks*, MIT Sloan School of Management, WP# 3031-89-BPS.

Rosenberg, N. (1982) *Inside the Black Box: Technology and Economics*, MA: Cambridge University Press.

Rosenbloom, R. (1978) 'Technological Innovation in Firms and Industries: An Assessment of the State of the Art', in: Kelly, P. and Kranzberg, M. (eds) *Technological Innovation*, San Fransisco, San Fransisco Press.

Rosenfeld, R. and Servo, J. (1991) 'Facilitating Innovations in Large Organizations', in: Henry, J. and Walker, D. (eds), *Managing Innovation*, London, Sage Publications Ltd., pp. 28-39.

Roussel, P., Saad, K. and Erickson, T. (1991) *Third Generation R&D: Managing the Link to Corporate Strategy*, Boston, Harvard Business School Press.

Saha, A. (1992) 'Zen and Industrial Management in Japan', *Journal of Managerial Psychology*, Vol. 7, No. 3, pp.3-9.

Sakai, K. (1990) 'The Feudal World of Japanese Manufacturing', *Harvard Business Review*, November-December, pp. 38-50.

Samuels, R. (1994) 'Pathways of Technological Diffusion in Japan', *Sloan Management Review*, Spring, pp. 21-34

Schlender, B. (1992) 'How Sony Keeps the Magic Going', *Fortune*, 24 February, pp. 22-7.

Schneiderman, H. (1991) 'Managing R&D: A Perspective from the Top', *Sloan Management Review*, Summer, pp. 53-8.

Schön, D. (1982) *The Reflective Practitioner*, New York, Basic Books.

Schumpeter, J. A. (1951) *The Theory of Economic Development*, Cambridge, MA: Harvard University Press.

Schütte, H. (1989) 'Euro-Japanese co-operation in Information Techology, INSEAD Working Paper No. 89/55.

Schütte, H. (1991) 'Strategische Allianzen mit Japanischen Firmen', in: Schneidewind, D. and Töpfer, A. (Hrsg.) *Der Asiatisch-pazifische Raum*, Lech, Schweitz, Verlag Moderne Industrie AG and Co., pp. 251-75.

Senge, P. (1990) 'Catalyzing Systems Thinking within Organizations', in: Massarik, F. (ed.) *Advances in Organization Development*, US, Ablex Publishing Corporation, pp.197-246.

Sheard, P. (1992a) *Keiretsu and Closedness of the Japanese Market: an economic appraisal*, ISER Discussion Paper No. 273, Osaka University.

Sheard, P. (1992b) *The Economics of Japanese Corporate Organization and the 'Sructural Impediments' Debate: a critical review*, Pacific Economic Papers No. 205, 1992.

Sheard, P. (1992c) *Long-Term Horizons and the Japanese Firm*, ISER Discussion Paper No. 283, Osaka University.

Sheard, P. (1992d) *Stable Shareholdings, Corporate Governance, and the Japanese Firm*, ISER Discussion Paper No. 281, Osaka University.

Shibata, Y. (1984) 'Toward a Policy Guidance System for Complex Innovation', in: Eto, H. and Matsui, K. (eds) *R&D Management Systems in Japanese Industry*, Amsterdam, North-Holland, pp. 29-58.

Sigurdson, J. (1986) *Industry and State Partnership in Japan: The Very Large Scale Integrated Circuits Project*, Discussion Paper No. 168, Research Policy Institute, Lund University.

Sigurdson, J. and Anderson A. (1991) *Science and Technology in Japan*, London, Longman.

Skully, M. (1981) *Japanese Corporate Structure: some factors in its development*, Sydney, Dryden Press.

Smitka, M. (1991) *Competitive Ties: Subcontracting in the Japanese Automotive Industry*, New York, Columbia University Press.

Smothers, N. (1990) 'Patterns of Japanese Strategy: Strategic Combinations of Strategies' in *Strategic Management Journal*, Vol 11, 1990, pp 521-33.

Song, M. and Parry, M. (1992) 'The R&D-Marketing Interface in Japanese High-Technology Firms', *Journal of Product Innovation Management*, No. 9, pp. 91-112.

Sony (undated) 'Sony Research Center'.

Sony (undated) 'Sony Computer Science Laboratory Inc'.

Sony (1989) 'Sony's Way: R&D Strategy', *Sony's Innovation in Management Series*, Vol 3, April.

Sony (1992a) *Sony Research Center*, published by the Sony Research Center in co-operation with the Research Planning and Coordination Group. Main author: Kaneko, K.

Sony (1992b) Internal News and Information Letter on Financial Results, released 19 November.

Sony (1992c) Annual Report.

Sony (1994) Internal News and Information Letter on Corporate Restructuring, released 21 January.

Speir, R. (1989), 'Make or Buy: A Winner's Guide', *Purchasing World (PCW)* Vol. 33, No. 2, February, pp. 32-33.

Spero, D. (1990) 'Patent Protection or Piracy – A CEO views Japan', *Harvard Business Review*, September-October, pp. 58-67.

Stalk, G., Evans, P. and Shulman, L. (1992) 'Competing on Capabilities: The New Rules of Corporate Strategy', *Harvard Business Review*, March-April, pp. 57-69.

Stalk, G. and Hout, T. (1990) *Competing Against Time: How Time-based Competition is reshaping Global Markets*, New York, The Free Press.

Stalk, G. and Webber, A. (1993) 'Japan's Dark Side of Time', *Harvard Business Review*, July-August, pp. 93-102.

Takahashi, T. (1994) 'Intellectual Property Rights and Corporate Strategies', Paper presented at a workshop of the European Institute of Japanese Studies on: 'Corporate Technology Strategies in Japan', 17-19 August.

Takeuchi, H. and Nonaka, I. (1986) 'The new New Product Development Game', *Harvard Business Review*, January-February, pp. 137-46.

Tatsuno, S. (1990) *Created in Japan: From Imitators to World-Class Innovators*, US, HarperBusiness.

Teramoto, Y. (1987) 'Japanese Experiences in Technology Management and Innovation', *Géstion 2000*, No. 4, pp. 153-68.

Teramoto, Y., Iwasaki, N. and Takai, T. (1993) 'Creating Corporate Group Management', Paper presented at the Euro-Asia Management Studies Association, November.

Thoburn, J. and Takashima, M. (1992) *Industrial Subcontracting in the UK and Japan*, UK, Avebury Publishing Ltd.

Timlon, J. (1994) *Defining Core Competence from a Network Perspective*, Unpublished Master Thesis of Uppsala University.

Timlon, J. (1997) *Collective Learning in Business Relationships*, Unpublished Licentiate Thesis of Gothenburg University.

Toda, M. and Sugiyama, K. (1984) 'Needs-Oriented Structural Analysis for Fifth Generation Computer Systems', in: Eto, H. and Matsui, K. (eds) *R&D Management Systems in Japanese Industry*, Amsterdam, North-Holland, pp.1-28.

Toyota (1988) *Toyota: a History of the First 50 Years*, Toyota City, Toyota Motor Corporation.

Tselichtchev, I. (1994) 'Rethinking Inter-firm Ties in Japan as a Factor of Competitiveness', in Schütte, H. (ed.) *The Global Competitiveness of the Asian Firm*, New York, St. Martin's Press, pp. 49-70.

Turnbull, P., Oliver, N. and Wilkinson, B. (1992) 'Buyer-Supplier Relations in the UK Automotive Industry: Strategic Implications of the Japanese Manufacturing Model', *Strategic Management Journal*, Vol. 13, pp. 159-68.

Turner, M. J. (1992) 'The Make/Buy Decision: Getting It Right', *Network World* Vol. 9, No.. 17, April.

Tushman, M. (1982) 'Managing Communication Networks in R&D Laboratories', in: Tushman, M. and Moore, W. (eds) *Readings in the Management of Innovation*, London, Pitman Books Ltd., pp. 349-62.

Tyrni, I. (1994) 'The Japanese Management Structure as a Competitive Strategy: The Importance of a Nexus of Long-term Treaties' in SCHÜTTE, H. (ed.) *The Global Competitiveness of the Asian Firm*, New York, St. Martin's Press, pp. 35-48.

US Committee on Finance (1992) *Japan's Keiretsu System*, Hearing before the Committee on Finance, United States Senate, first session, 16 October 1991, US Government Printing Office, Washington.

Van Dierdonck, Debackers and Rappa (1991) 'An Assessment of Science Parks: Towards a Better Understanding of their Role in the Diffusion of Technological Knowledge', *R&D Management*, Vol. 21, No. 2, pp. 109-23.

Van Wolferen, K. (1989) *The Enigma of Japanese Power*, New York, Alfred A. Knopf.

Vogel, E. (1979) *Japan as No. 1: Lessons for America*, Tokyo, Charles E. Tuttle Company.

Von Hippel, E. (1982) 'Appropriability of Innovation Benefit as a Predictor of the Source of Innovation', *Research Policy*, Vol. 11, No. 2, pp. 95-115.

Von Hippel, E. (1988) *The Sources of Innovation*, New York, Oxford University Press.

Waldenberger, F. (1992) 'Die Heutigen Keiretsu: Review of Kiyonari (1992) '*Gendai no Keiretsu*', in: *Japanstudien: Jahrbuch des Deutschen Institutes*, München, Iudicum Verlag, pp. 272-78.

Walker, D. (1991) 'Creative Empowerment at Rover', in: Henry, J. and Walker, D. (eds), *Managing Innovation*, London, Sage Publications Ltd., pp. 277-86.

Welch, J. and Nayak, R. (1992) 'Strategic Sourcing: A Progressive Approach to the Make-or-Buy Decision', *The Executive*, Vol. 6, No. 1, pp. 23-31.

Watanabe, C., Santoso, I. and Widayanti, T. (1991) *The Inducing Power of Japanese Technological Innovation*, London, Pinter Publishers.

Westney, E. (1990) 'Internal and External Linkages in the MNC: The Case of R&D Subsidiaries in Japan', in: Bartlett, C., Doz, Y., Hedlund, G. (eds.) *Managing The Global Firm*, London, Routledge, pp. 279-300.

Westney, E. (1992) *Cross-Pacific Internationalization of R&D by US and Japanese Firms*, Paper prepared for conference on 'Managing R&D Internationally' at the Manchester Business School, 6-8 July.

Wheelwright, S. and Clark, K. (1992) 'Creating Project Plans to Focus Product Development', *Harvard Business Review*, March-April, pp. 70-82.

Whitley, R. (1990) 'Eastern Asian Enterprise Structures and the Comparative Analysis of Forms of Business Organization', *Organization Studies*, 11/1, pp. 47-74.

Whitley, R. (1992) *Business Systems in East Asia: Firms, Markets and Societies*, London, Sage Publications.

Wilkinson, E. (1990) *Japan Versus the West: Image and Reality*, London, Penguin Books.

Womack, J., Jones, D. and Roos, D. (1990) *The Machine that Changed the World*, New York, Macmillan Publishing Company.

Yamanouchi, T., (1987) 'Research and Development Systems and Corporate Culture of Canon Inc., *Géstion 2000*, No. 4, pp. 137-50.

Yamanouchi, T., (1989) 'Breakthrough: The Development of the Canon Personal Copier', *Long Range Planning*, Vol. 22, No. 5, pp.11-21.

Yin, R. (1984) *Case Study Research: Design and Methods*, Applied Social Research Methods Series, Vol. 5 Beverly Hills, CA: Sage Publications.

Yoshino, C and Rangan, U. (1995) *Strategic Alliances: an Entrepreneurial Approach to Globalization*, Boston, MA: Harvard Business School Press.

Interviewees

QUOTED, OR REFERRED TO

Ando, T., Representative Director, Inventure KK, (18.06.93); 05.10.94.

Arnfalk, P., STA Research Fellow, AIST, MITI, National Institute of Materials and Chemical Research, 22.04.93, 07.07.93.

Bayrleithner, R., Visiting Researcher, Mechanical Engineering Laboratory, Robotics Department, AIST, MITI, 22.06.93.

Bergman, S., Science and Technology Counsellor, Embassy of Sweden in Tokyo, 07.06.93.

Bergquist, J. Senior Researcher at Canon Research Centre, 03.02.93, 09.02.93, (16.02.93), (18.02.93), (24.02.93), (19.07.94), 28.09.94, 06.10.94.

Brunsell, P. (Dr), Visiting Scientist, Electro Technical Laboratory, Tsukuba Science City, 22.04.93.

Doeden, C., Corporate Communications, Sony Corporation, 18.05.93.

Eda, N., Assistant, Corporate Communications Office, Sony Corporation, 04.02.93.

Emura, Y., Executive Director of Production, Canon Inc., Toride Plant, 17.05.93.

Fuji, M., Service Staff, Sony Showroom, Sony Ginza House, 13.09.92, 03.07.93, 21.07.93.

Gérard, G., Manager, Corporate Communications, Sony Corporation, 04.02.93, 01.07.93.

Gibson, D., Canon Chronicle, Corporate Communications HQ, Canon Inc., 19.02.93.

Guy, P., Vice President, The Boston Consulting Group, Tokyo, 26.11.92.

Hane, Y., Manager, Aero-Business Dept., Business Development Division, Toyota Motor Corporation, 05.10.94.

Hatakeyama, N., Vice Minister for International Affairs, Ministry of International Trade and Industry, 25.05.93 and 18.06.93.

Hayashi, K., Assistant Manager, Sony Research Institute of Wisdom, 03.07.93.

Heard, D., (Dr), Functional Device Laboratories, Corporate Research and Development Group, Sharp Corporation, 22.06.93.

Hiraishi, K., General Manager of Production Division 1, Toride Plant, Canon Inc., 17.05.93.

House, A., Assistant, Corporate Communications, Sony Corporation, (02.04.93), 18.05.93, 01.07.93, 07.10.94.

Irie, H. (Dr), Head of 5th Laboratory, National Research Institute for Metals, 18.06.93.

Ishiyawa, K., Toshiba Corporation, Senior Manager, Purchase Management., 16.06.93.

Isobe, N., Manager, HDTV Special Project, NHK, 09.12.92, (07.04.93).

Kageyama, T., Associate Director, Deputy General Manager, Public Communications, Toyota Motor Corporation, 04.10.94.

Kamoshita, R., Manager, Corporate Communications Division, Mitsui and Co., Ltd., 13.01.93, (12.05.93), 03.06.93.

Kanbe, J., Deputy Senior General Manager, Device Development Centre, Canon Inc., 29.09.94.

Kawakami, D. Manager, MD Promotion Dept., Audio Development Group, Sony Corporation, 01.07.93.

Kawashima, H., Senior General Manager, Display Business Operations Centre, Component Business Operations Headquarters, Canon Inc., 25.11.92.

Kikuchi, M. (Dr), Executive Technical Adviser, Sony Corporation and Professor, Tokai University, Dept. of Electronics, 20.11.92, 25.02.93, 08.07.93, 27.09.94.

Kjellgren, P., Visiting Researcher, Tokyo University, Dept. of Quantum Engineering and Systems Science, 22.04.93.

Kozato, Y., Manager of Overseas R&D Promotion Department, Canon Inc., (03.10.94).

Le Bellégo, Y. (Dr), Senior Researcher, Sony Corporation Research Centre, (17.02.93), 24.02.93, 03.07.93.

Lewis, R. (Dr), International and Technical Affairs Manager, Tsukuba Research Consortium, 07.07.93.

Maeda, Toshiba Corporation, Senior Manager, System Computer Development Dept., 16.06.93.

Mayuzumi, H., Director, Siar Bossard K.K., Tokyo, 14.05.93, (14.06.93), 21.06.93, 20.07.93, 28.09.94.

Miyamoto, T., Director, Research Institute of International Trade and Industry, 18.06.93.

Miyata, H., Researcher, Canon Research Centre, Molecular Devices Division, Research Dept. 41, Canon Inc., 19.02.93; (07.10.94).

Mohri, Y., Project General Manager, Technical Administration Division, Toyota Motor Corporation, 30.06.93.

Mori, T. (Dr), Manager, R&D Planning Dept, Technical Development Group, Kobe Steel, Ltd., various discussions at a workshop of the European Institute of Japanese Studies on: 'Corporate Technology Strategies in Japan', 17-19 August 1994.

Morita, A., Chairman of the Board, Sony Corporation, 19.07.93.

Mozjetckov, M., Visiting Scientist, Department of Nuclear Engineering, Tokyo University, 12.06.93; 21.06.93.

Nakada, Y., Director, AT&T Bell Laboratories Japan Ltd., (26.11.92), 07.12.92, 09.07.93.

Nakajima, K., Assistant Manager, Public Communications, Toyota Motor Corporation, 04.10.94.

Nanao, S. (Dr), Professor at the Institute of Industrial Science, Tokyo University, 24.06.93, (06.07.93).

Nannichi, Y. Professor, Vice President, University of Tsukuba, 07.07.93.

Nishisawa, T., Director of Research and Development, Science and Technical Research Laboratories, NHK (Japan Broadcasting Corporation), (07.04.93), 09.04.93.

Nishisawa, J., Professor, President of Tohuku University, 05.07.93.

Noda, A., Assistant Manager, Business Environment Research Departement, Toyota Motor Corporation, 25.06.93.

Nonaka, I., Professor, Institute of Business Research, Hitotsubashi University, 09.05.93, 05.06.93, 29.09.94.

Nosu, K., Senior Research Engineer, Coherent Transmission Research Group, NTT Transmission System Laboratories, 03.07.93.

Ohtani, Y., Toyota Motor Corporation, 29.06.93.

Oka, T., Toshiba Corporation, Senior Manager, Engineering Administration and Factory Information Systems Dept., 16.06.93.

Rubber, R. (Dr), Visiting Scientist, National Laboratory for High Energy Physics, 22.04.93.

Sakakibara, T., General Manager, Tahara Plant (Lexus Production), Toyota Motor Corporation, 29.06.93.

Shill, W., Consultant, McKinsey and Company, Japan, 19.11.92.

Sugiyama, T., Assistant General Manager, Corporate Communications, Sony Corporation, 04.02.93, (05.04.93).

Sunaga, A., Attaché at Science and Technology Office, Embassy of Sweden, 19.02.93, 27.02.93, 14.05.93, 15.07.93.

Takahashi, Takuma, Chief Policy Analyst, Nomura Research Institute, Ltd., various discussions at a workshop of the European Institute of Japanese Studies on: 'Corporate Technology Strategies in Japan', 17-19 August 1994.

Takahashi, T., Director, Senior General Manager of Products Technology Development Headquarters, Canon Inc., 10.11.92.

Takayanagi, S. (Dr) Chief Technology Officer and Senior Vice Executive of Toshiba Corporation, various discussions at a workshop of the European Institute of Japanese Studies on: 'Corporate Technology Strategies in Japan', 17-19 August 1994.

Tanaka, A., Marketing and Management Dpt., Display Business Operations Centre, Canon Inc., 25.11.92, (09.07.93), 23.07.93.

Tanaka, K., Manager, R&D Headquarters, Canon Inc., (07.10.94).

Toyosaki, I., Manager of Public Information, Corporate Communications Headquarters, Canon Inc., (28.10.92), 10.11.92, (16.11.92), 19.11.92, 24.11.92., 25.11.92, (30.11.92), 02.12.92, 03.12.92, 11.12.92, 25.11.92, (22.02.93), (07.04.93), 12.04.93, 17.05.93, 26.09.94.

Tsurushima, K., Director and Member of the Board, Sony Corporation, Executive Vice President, Consumer A&V Products Company, 07.10.94.

Tsuruswa, T., Manager, International Public Affairs Division, Toyota Motor Corporation, 05.10.94.

Yamashita, M., Manager of Vehicle Design Department No. 3, Product Planning and Development Division, Nissan Motor Co., Ltd, 14.07.93.

Yasokawa, Ms., Assisting Director, Products Technology Development Headquarters, Canon Inc., 10.11.92, 21.07.93.

Yoshida, T., General Manager, Div. 1, Audio Development Group, Sony Corporation, 18.05.93.

INTERVIEWEES, NOT QUOTED OR REFERRED TO IN THE STUDY

Arnquist, J., Open Systems Marketing Section, International Computer Systems Group, Fujitsu Limited, 22.04.93.

Chiba, E., Staff Researcher, Marketing Planning Dept., Mitsubishi Research Institute Inc., 16.07.93.

Franceschi, O., Visiting Researcher, Science and Technical Research Laboratories, NHK (Japan Broadcasting Corporation), 09.04.93, 14.05.93.

Grad, O. (Dr), Visiting Scientist, University of Tokyo, RCAST Karube Laboratory, 05.05.93, 13.05.93, 21.06.93.

Hirasawa, Professor, Tokyo University, 22.06.93.

Hoek, M. (Dr), Visiting Researcher, Japan Atomic Energy Research Institute, Naka Fusion Research Establishment, 22.04.93.

Ishioka, S., Head of R&D Administration Office and International Relations, Corporate R&D Promotion Div., Hitachi Central Research Laboratory, 14.07.93.

Kageyama, T., Overseas Procurement Centre, Mitsubishi Heavy Industries Ltd., 12.06.93.

Kampfhenkel, I., Cartography Engineer, Zenrin Ltd., interviews 19.11.92 and 04.12.92.

Kato, M., Development Centre Section No. 1, Photographics Products, Manufacturing HQ, Konica Corporation, 03.07.93.

Kullman, L., Visiting Researcher at the Canon Research Centre from Chalmers Institute of Technology in Sweden, 22.04.93, (10.06.93).

Kurata, M. (Dr), Senior Manager, Educational Systems Department, NEC Corporation, 17.05.93.

Matsuda, S. (Dr), Chief Engineer, Overseas R&D Operation, Hitachi Ltd., 08.07.93.

Matsushita, S., Assistant General Manager, C&C Systems Market Development Division, NEC Corporation, 17.05.93.

Nakano, M., Senior Staff Researcher, Management Consulting Dept., Mitsubishi Research Institute Inc., 16.07.93.

Nakashima, O., Deputy Business News Editor (observing Japanese consumer electronics companies), Nihon Keizai Shimbun, 06.10.94.

Niihara, T. (Dr), Manager International Relations Section, R&D Administration Office, Hitachi Ltd., Central Research Laboratory, 14.07.93.

Nishibe, K., Deputy Director, International Research and Development co-operation Division, Agency of Industrial Science and Technology, MITI, 25.06.93.

Nishimura, H., Manager, International Administration Dept., Bridgestone Corporation, 03.07.93.

Nobutono, H., Senior Research Associate, Management Consulting Dept., Mitsubishi Research Institute Inc., 16.07.93.

Ohbora, T., Principal, McKinsey and Co., 02.07.93.

Ohno, M., Export Operations Dept. 1, Export Operations Division, Canon Inc., 11.06.93.

Oya, K., Vice President, Onex Corporation (first-tier supplier of Nissan and Honda), (06.06.93), 15.06.93.

Parbrook P. (Dr), Research Laboratory III, Toshiba Corporation, Research and Development Center, Kawasaki, 93.05.13, 93.06.22.

Powell, R., First Secretary, Science and Technology, British Embassy in Tokyo, 13.05.93.

Seawright, S. (Dr), Products Development Dept. TDK Corporation, 16.07.93.

Suzuki, K., Manager of R&D, Onex Corporation (first-tier supplier of Nissan and Honda), 15.06.93.

Teramoto, Y., Professor, Graduate School of Systems Management, Tsukuba University, 03.07.93.

Tomiura, A., (Dr), Managing Director of Research, Development and Engineering, Technology Development Bureau, Nippon Steel, 06.07.93.

Yasawa, T., General Manager, Production Administration Dept., Keihin Works, NKK Corporation, 23.06.93.

Yoda, N., (Dr), (Royal Nobel Prize Committee Member), Executive Adviser to the Board in charge of R&D, Toray Corporate Business Research Inc., 09.07.93.

Wright, O., (Dr), Senior Researcher, Applied Electronics Lab, Technical Development Bureau, Nippon Steel, 22.06.93, (04.07.93).

Appendix A

Sigvald Harryson	Private address	Home address
Sophia University	3-23-25 Daisawa	Dufourstraße 80
4 Yonban-cho	Setagaya-ku	CH 9000 St. Gallen
Chiyoda-ku, Tokyo 102	Tokyo 155	
Phone (03) 3238-4026	Phone (03) 3411-4325	Phone 071 23 65 95
Fax (03) 3238-4076		Fax 071 30 25 13

Fax-letter to Mr. A. NODA, External Affairs, Toyota Motor.

Tokyo, 11.06.93

Dear Noda-san,

Thank you for your helpful attitude on the phone yesterday. I would be very grateful if you could help me with one, or a few interviews focusing on the general R&D management of Toyota Motor.

My area of research is management of research and new product development. In September 1991, I was enrolled at the doctoral program of international management at Hochschule St. Gallen. I spent one year taking courses there before I came to Japan, due to an invitation to Sophia University as a visiting researcher. (please see enclosed recommendation)

Directors of thesis are Professors E. Brauchlin at Hochschule St. Gallen in Switzerland and Hellmut Schütte at INSEAD in France and at Harvard University.

Here in Japan, where I will stay for only eight more weeks, I am in close interaction with Professor Gregory at Sophia University, but I also interact and discuss my research with other academics. The name of Mr. Soyama was given to me by Professor Fujimoto at Tokyo University, to whom I refer should further information be necessary.

The planned thesis will to a large extent be based on theories on R&D, but I also wish to include case studies of highly successful and innovative Japanese companies. It would therefore be natural to include Toyota Motor, as you are by far the most successful automobile manufacturer in Japan, and probably also worldwide. So far, I have done case studies at Canon and at Sony through interviews, many of which at Senior General Manager level. It would be an honour and a pleasure to add Toyota Motor, which with your permission perhaps also could be used at my academic institutions.

Looking forward to what I hope will be a future meeting,

Yours sincerely

Sigvald Harryson

Appendix B

Fax to Mr. Takahashi, President and Senior General Manager of Products Technology Development Headquarters at Canon Inc.

INTRODUCTION

The overall goal of my thesis is to describe the New Product Development Process at Japan's most successful companies. Hopefully this will increase the understanding of Japanese management practices and culture among Westerners, thus enabling a stable ground for future co-operation in mutual understanding and respect, instead of today's mistrust and envy coming from the Western side. Many Western countries have not yet realized that Japanese methods of management lead to improved global welfare, rather than threatening it.

I am aware of the fact that general descriptions are difficult and that the New Product Development Process is too complex to be entirely described in a short interview. Therefore I would like to give priority to the **teamwork approach** during this first interview.

THE NEW PRODUCT DEVELOPMENT PROCESS

What were the most important issues to speed up the entire process of commercialization (from idea or concept to finished product put at the market), when developing one of your successful products? **Please feel free to exemplify with a specific product, if this facilitates an answer.**

To which extent did different development phases overlap?

What distinction would you make between R&D activities and new product development activities?

PRODUCT DEVELOPMENT TEAMS

What is a typical configuration of a development team? (How is it put together?) Does it include only engineers or are people from other functional units, i.e. marketing, sales, research, production, etc. included?

Who were the players in your team, when developing a specific product and what were the roles of these players?

What were the incentives of these roles / what motivated the players to work hard and well?

How was the direction of the team organized? Did it have one permanent leader or did the leader position circulate?

Was the entire development process guided and planned in advance, or was the team sometimes working in an atmosphere similar to chaos or ambiguity?

Were team members permanently in one team on a full time basis, or could one person be involved in several teams at the same time.

Where was the team usually located? Were all members together in one single room, or were several smaller groups in different rooms?

How did you improve the performance of the team? Did you have any system of team performance evaluation?

What were the team-member's main incitement? (team-performance, Honorary prizes, longer vacations, higher salary, promotion, a journey abroad, others)

When developing a new product, how many teams did you usually have developing different approaches to the same project/product. For how long time, or until which stage in the development process did you keep several teams competing with each other? How did this in-house competition affect communication between the competing teams?

EXTERNAL COMMUNICATION, CO-OPERATION AND INFORMATION

Did every employee within the team feel responsible of gathering information from the marketplace and from competitors, or did you have special gatekeepers, charged with this mission?

How did your team members coordinate activities with your foreign R&D units?

Did your teams also co-operate with customers and/or suppliers? (Joint development, field-testing etc.) If yes:

On which basis did you select a supplier to co-operate with? (reliability, previous co-operation, member of the same industrial grouping, technical skills and reputation, others)

Did supplier-co-operation and coordination play an important role as far as development lead-time was concerned?

INTERNAL COMMUNICATION AND TRANSFER

What enabled Canon Inc. to spread core technologies so successfully from one product to another? An example of such a spread, or transfer, would be when miniaturized motors, developed for photolithography equipment, were applied in cameras and then incorporated in mini copiers. How did the spread of knowledge between units, teams, divisions and individuals occur?

Did development engineers from different sections or core technologies meet in an organized way? To which extent were staff members rotated between these functions? Between which functions did job rotation occur most frequently?

Did you move individual team-members across business-unit/product-area borders?

Design for manufacturability is one important factor which requires good internal communication. How were the functions Marketing, R&D, Development, Design and Manufacturing linked to each other, so as to communicate, interact and co-operate in an effective and efficient way?

If there were disagreement between two functional units, (e.g. Marketing and Design disagreeing on the ideal shape of a copier) who would decide or settle the dispute? (the product development team manager, the functional unit managers of marketing and design or the product manager?)

How did Management of Canon Inc. communicate a clear vision of corporate objectives to the company team members?

Who assured Total Quality Control?

The development of bubble jet printing technology was helped by accident (when a hot iron was put to a syringe filled with ink). Do you have any other examples of fortunate discovery? Does your organization of new product development increase this possibility of making such fortunate discoveries?

Thank you for taking the time to read all my questions. I am very grateful for your co-operation!

Yours sincerely

Appendix C

Fax-letter to Mr. YOSHIDA c/o Mr. GERARD, Corporate Communications, SONY Corporation.

Dear Mr. Yoshida,

First of all, I would like to thank you for granting me some of your valuable time tomorrow. I am very impressed by Sony Corporation's successful record of achievements and look forward to take part in the development of the MiniDiscman.

In order to facilitate tomorrow's interview, I would like to indicate some questions beforehand.

When did the concept, or the idea of making a MiniDiscman come up? Who was the man, or who were the men, behind the idea? Was it difficult to win support for the idea?

Was the basic technology developed jointly with Philips, or did you develop it on your own? I read that you agreed to jointly license the MD system (Annual Rep. 92, p. 13).

Technical-, Engineering- and Commercial sample: what were their time schedules/deadlines, how big were the teams that were responsible of these different samples, did team members come from different departments or functions? Average age of team members and the team leader?

Production Phase: was anybody from the project team transferred to help establishing trial manufacturing?

Was there any marketing experience added to the team, did you have any discussion with potential customers about the MiniDiscman?

At what stage were component suppliers involved? Was any Sony supplier invited to the team?

Product Launch: was this made by team members, or by an independent marketing/sales section?

Does the team still exist, or are you working on a new product already?

What are the most important tasks of an R&D manager, a team leader, a team member?

What do you think was most important in order to develop and produce the MD quickly?

Thank you for reading all the questions. I hope that we will have a mutually rewarding discussion tomorrow and that I can provide some publicity to your product.

Yours sincerely

Index

Printed and bound by CPI Group (UK) Ltd, Croydon, CR0 4YY

23/04/2025

14661001-0005